Animals, Animality and Controversy in Modern Welsh Literature and Culture

WRITING WALES IN ENGLISH

CREW series of Critical and Scholarly Studies
General Editors: Kirsti Bohata and Daniel G. Williams (*CREW*, Swansea University)

This *CREW* series is dedicated to Emyr Humphreys, a major figure in the literary culture of modern Wales, a founding patron of the *Centre for Research into the English Literature and Language of Wales*. Grateful thanks are due to the late Richard Dynevor for making this series possible.

Other titles in the series
Stephen Knight, *A Hundred Years of Fiction* (978-0-7083-1846-1)
Barbara Prys-Williams, *Twentieth-Century Autobiography* (978-0-7083-1891-1)
Kirsti Bohata, *Postcolonialism Revisited* (978-0-7083-1892-8)
Chris Wigginton, *Modernism from the Margins* (978-0-7083-1927-7)
Linden Peach, *Contemporary Irish and Welsh Women's Fiction* (978-0-7083-1998-7)
Sarah Prescott, *Eighteenth-Century Writing from Wales: Bards and Britons* (978-0-7083-2053-2)
Hywel Dix, *After Raymond Williams: Cultural Materialism and the Break-Up of Britain* (978-0-7083-2153-9)
Matthew Jarvis, *Welsh Environments in Contemporary Welsh Poetry* (978-0-7083-2152-2)
Harri Garrod Roberts, *Embodying Identity: Representations of the Body in Welsh Literature* (978-0-7083-2169-0)
Diane Green, *Emyr Humphreys: A Postcolonial Novelist* (978-0-7083-2217-8)
M. Wynn Thomas, *In the Shadow of the Pulpit: Literature and Nonconformist Wales* (978-0-7083-2225-3)
Linden Peach, *The Fiction of Emyr Humphreys: Contemporary Critical Perspectives* (978-0-7083-2216-1)
Daniel Westover, *R. S. Thomas: A Stylistic Biography* (978-0-7083-2413-4)
Jasmine Donahaye, *Whose People? Wales, Israel, Palestine* (978-0-7083-2483-7)
Judy Kendall, *Edward Thomas: The Origins of His Poetry* (978-0-7083-2403-5)
Damian Walford Davies, *Cartographies of Culture: New Geographies of Welsh Writing in English* (978-0-7083-2476-9)
Daniel G. Williams, *Black Skin, Blue Books: African Americans and Wales 1845–1945* (978-0-7083-1987-1)
Andrew Webb, *Edward Thomas and World Literary Studies: Wales, Anglocentrism and English Literature* (978-0-7083-2622-0)
Alyce von Rothkirch, *J. O. Francis, realist drama and ethics: Culture, place and nation* (978-1-7831-6070-9)
Rhian Barfoot, *Liberating Dylan Thomas: Rescuing a Poet from Psycho-Sexual Servitude* (978-1-7831-6184-3)
Daniel G. Williams, *Wales Unchained: Literature, Politics and Identity in the American Century* (978-1-7831-6212-3)
M. Wynn Thomas, *The Nations of Wales 1890–1914* (978-1-78316-837-8)
Richard McLauchlan, *Saturday's Silence: R. S. Thomas and Paschal Reading* (978-1-7831-6920-7)
Bethan M. Jenkins, *Between Wales and England: Anglophone Welsh Writing of the Eighteenth Century* (978-1-7868-3029-6)
M. Wynn Thomas, *All that is Wales: The Collected Essays of M. Wynn Thomas* (978-1-7868-3088-3)
Laura Wainwright, *New Territories in Modernism: Anglophone Welsh Writing*, 1930–1949 (978-1-7868-3217-7)
Siriol McAvoy, *Locating Lynette Roberts: 'Always Observant and Slightly Obscure'* (978-1-7868-3382-2)
Linden Peach, *Pacifism, Peace and Modern Welsh Writing* (978-1-7868-3402-7)
Kieron Smith, *John Ormond's Organic Mosaic* (978-1-7868-3488-1)
Georgia Burdett and Sarah Morse (eds), *Fight and Flight: Essays on Ron Berry* (978-1-7868-3528-4)
M. Wynn Thomas, *Eutopia: Studies in Cultural Euro-Welshness, 1850–1980* (978-1-78683-614-3)

Animals, Animality and Controversy in Modern Welsh Literature and Culture

WRITING WALES IN ENGLISH

Linden Peach

UNIVERSITY OF WALES PRESS
2022

© Linden Peach, 2022

All rights reserved. No part of this book may be reproduced in any material form (including photocopying or storing it in any medium by electronic means and whether or not transiently or incidentally to some other use of this publication) without the written permission of the copyright owner. Applications for the copyright owner's written permission to reproduce any part of this publication should be addressed to the University of Wales Press, University Registry, King Edward VII Avenue, Cardiff CF10 3NS.

www.uwp.co.uk

British Library CIP Data
A catalogue record for this book is available from the British Library.

ISBN: 978-1-78683-937-4
e-ISBN: 978-1-78683-938-1

The right of Linden Peach to be identified as author of this work has been asserted in accordance with sections 77 and 79 of the Copyright, Designs and Patents Act 1988.

THE ASSOCIATION FOR
WELSH WRITING IN ENGLISH
CYMDEITHAS LLÊN SAESNEG CYMRU

Typeset by Marie Doherty
Printed by CPI Antony Rowe, Melksham

Contents

Series Editors' Preface		vii
Acknowledgements		xi
Overview		xiii
1	Animals and Animality in a Relational Universe	1
2	Rethinking Animal Contexts: Rural and Industrial Wales	23
3	Emerging Animalities in the Victorian and Edwardian Welsh Press	57
4	Exotic Pets and Spectacular Entertainments	69
5	Brief Encounters	91
6	Birds over Wales	105
7	Domestication and 'Domesecration'	131
8	The Children's Book Pet	153
9	Conflicting Cosmologies: Three Stories by Gwyn Jones	167

10	Entangled Empathies: Gillian Clarke and Keith Bowen	179

Afterword 189
Notes 193
Select Bibliography 221
Index 231

Series Editors' Preface

The aim of this series, since its founding in 2004 by Professor M. Wynn Thomas, is to publish scholarly and critical work by established specialists and younger scholars that reflects the richness and variety of the English-language literature of modern Wales. The studies published so far have amply demonstrated that concepts, models and discourses current in the best contemporary studies can illuminate aspects of Welsh culture, and have also foregrounded the potential of the Welsh example to draw attention to themes that are often neglected or marginalised in anglophone cultural studies. The series defines and explores that which distinguishes Wales's anglophone literature, challenges critics to develop methods and approaches adequate to the task of interpreting Welsh culture, and invites its readers to locate the process of writing Wales in English within comparative and transnational contexts.

Professor Kirsti Bohata and Professor Daniel G. Williams
Founding Editor: Professor M. Wynn Thomas (2004–15)
CREW (Centre for Research into the English
Literature and Language of Wales)
Swansea University

i Angela, Kate and Matthew

Bee

A dark, velvet chocolate,
unmoving. In changing light,
becoming the colour of coffee.
Tiny, fragile wings, like rice paper,
lifting slowly from its body,
legs extended, turning its weight
toward my naked finger, my spoon
which is not vulnerable,
before rising, like a helicopter,
into its disappearance.

Acknowledgements

Like all books by teachers in higher education, especially those that chart new territory, this work has benefited from discussions with students and colleagues and participation in conferences and research seminars in the UK and across the world. I am grateful to all at the Prince's School of Traditional Arts, especially my Doctoral students, who have contributed to the development of my thoughts and arguments in ways in which some of them may not even be fully aware.

I have been inspired by colleagues and scholars who have argued for, and have demonstrated in their own works, an interdisciplinary approach to the literature, history and geography of Wales and especially by those who have pursued relationships between Welsh- and English-language writings. Above all, I am indebted to the works, cited in this book, that have opened up for us the interconnections between animal studies and the relational cosmology revealed by the natural and physical sciences.

I am grateful for the encouragement and support of the University of Wales Press, especially Dr Llion Wigley (commissioning editor, Welsh Language and Topics) and his colleagues in the production and marketing divisions.

Many authors are indebted to the patience and support of their families who are up to their necks in their own projects, and, once again, I am pleased to gratefully acknowledge my wife, Angela, and Kate and Matthew to whom this book is dedicated.

Overview

Given that human–animal encounters permeate Welsh- and English-language Welsh writing, it is disappointing that they have received so little critical attention. This book is intended to introduce readers to a broad range of ideas and themes in animal studies and provide frameworks within which to discuss modern Welsh writing about animals and animality.

Chapter 1 introduces some of the more significant scholars, important texts and key themes in contemporary animal studies, including the animal and human divide; human exceptionalism; the concept of animality and how animals have been defined and hidden by cultural taxonomies; animal intelligence, cognition and emotional capacity; animal rights; the diverse and complex communication systems of animals; animal history; the domestication and captivity of animals; post-humanism and the ecological approach to animal studies. It argues that contemporary animal studies reflects, and engages with, the cosmology of a 'relational' universe in which all living things are interconnected as has been revealed in the natural and physical sciences and brought to the fore by contemporary physicists, such as Lee Smolin and Carlo Rovelli, and social scientists such as Roberto Mangabeira Unger and, more recently, Milja Kurki.

Drawing, as do subsequent chapters, on the insights and themes introduced in Chapter 1, Chapter 2 suggests how animal contexts in rural and industrial Wales might be rethought from an animal's perspective and agenda. Drawing on animal theory, literary texts and other cultural and educational publications, it examines the impact on animals (in modern Welsh history and contemporary society) of, for example, the Welsh landscape (with reference to the Welsh countryside memoir) and, in the context of the controversies which they generate, different types of farming and agro-ecology, the slaughter of animals (with reference to texts by Frances Williams, Cynan Jones, Emyr Humphreys and Gillian Clarke), agricultural and industrial work (with a particular focus on colliery horses) and of sporting and leisure pursuits such as hunting, pigeon keeping and greyhound racing.

The book follows a trajectory from a focus on a human-centric cosmology to an emphasis upon the relational universe of contemporary science and how this is reflected in key Welsh texts. Chapter 3 examines the extent to which perceptions of animals and animality, and emergent ideas concerning the emotive and cognitive capacities of animals, began to appear in the Victorian and Edwardian press through its coverage of animal cruelty and animals as sentient beings. By contrast, Chapter 4 discusses Western cultural legacies regarding the domestication, confinement and public display of animals to satisfy human needs for entertainment, to celebrate the success of the imperialist project, to express what was perceived as lying at the limits of so-called Western civilisation and to disclose the subjugation of the 'Other' hidden deep in the human psyche. Assessing how far inherited attitudes toward animals reflect particular cosmologies, it examines the extent to which they have been supplanted by new ways of thinking about the interconnectivity among animals and between human and animals.

Chapters 5 and 6 examine Welsh writing, particularly poetry, about brief encounters with animals and how they may be read in relation to contemporary animal studies, especially the extent to which they call into question the human and animal divide, human exceptionalism, and concepts such as intelligence and emotion that have been generally defined only in human-centric terms. In Chapter 5, texts by R. Williams Parry, Gwynn ap Gwilym, Gillian Clarke and Hilary Llewellyn-Williams, alongside key animal theorists, are seen as engaging, for example, with the ways in which animals have been hidden or distorted by cultural taxonomies and how writers' encounters with animals revise their thinking about them. A particular focus is on the ways in which we think animals perceive the world and the extent to which their sensory and cognitive capacities have been developed by, and in relation to, their environments. Within this context, the chapters examine how far the selected texts depict a shift from a view of animality determined by a hierarchical cosmology, in which animals are perceived as objects and as inferior to humans, to one which is based on interconnections between a diverse range of living beings.

Chapter 6 is devoted to birds, a species which humans encounter most often and which frequent creative and nature writing of all kinds. Through a discussion of work by poets, diarists and prose writers as diverse as Euros Bowen, Gillian Clarke, Jeremy Hooker, R. S. Thomas, Neil Ansell, Leslie Norris and Hilda Murrell, the chapter is focused on how our understanding of the intelligence, sensibilities and emotional lives of birds has changed in recent decades; how our better understanding of them is reflected in and developed in writing about them; and how our fresh knowledge of them is changing our views of animality and our appreciation of the profound interconnections among them and with us.

Chapters 7 and 8 discuss one of the most controversial subjects in animal studies, the domestication or, as one scholar suggests, the 'domesecration', of animals. Drawing on a broad range of animal theory, including psychoanalytic approaches to animality, and primary texts by Mari Jones, Gwyn Jones, Glyn Jones and Leslie Norris – and examples of children's literature, in Chapter 8 – these chapters examine different approaches to the subject of domestication in different contexts as well as affiliated themes, such as domination, affection, play and power relations, and the extent to which the literature suggests the possibilities of alternative animal–human relations.

Chapter 9 discusses the contrasting approaches to animality and their link to different cosmologies in short stories by Gwyn Jones, a Welsh writer whose work reflects his sustained interest in animals. Its focus is on the creative challenge of producing literature in which animals are analogous to human-centred issues and concerns without losing sight of them *per se*; in which animal cognitive and emotional capacities are depicted honestly; and which recognises the importance of achieving empathy with them.

Chapter 10 is rooted in the relational cosmology to which the trajectory of the book has been moving. Through a critical discussion of a poem sequence by Gillian Clarke about a year on a hill farm on Yr Wyddfa, in comparison with the book of photographs and drawings that seems to have inspired it, the chapter provides further analysis of the key themes in contemporary animal studies identified in Chapter 1. These include empathy among animals and between humans and animals, types of knowledge and the sensibilities which animals develop to live, and thrive, within their environment and how far these animal traits and characteristics reflect the cosmological thinking of contemporary biopsychology and of the natural and physical sciences.

In each chapter, the engagement with theoretical approaches to animals and animality is designed to help us think carefully about what it means to be 'animal' or 'human'. The texts discussed have been selected for the light they cast on arguments and debates in animal studies and for how their conceptions of animals and humans stand more fully revealed in that context, providing fresh insights into the way animality and humanity are depicted in Welsh literature and culture.

Any book of this type cannot be exhaustive in its scope and will afford more attention to some areas and themes than others. But, through its textual discussions, it is intended to open up new ways of thinking about relationships between animals and between humans and animals; about different types of intelligence, sensibilities and knowledge; and about the planet and networks that we all share.

1

ANIMALS AND ANIMALITY IN A RELATIONAL UNIVERSE

In a profound sense, contemporary animal studies is based on the cosmology of a relational universe, a concept which emerged from the late-twentieth-century natural and physical sciences and has largely been developed by physicists Lee Smolin and Carlo Rovelli in conjunction with social theorists such as Roberto Mangabeira Unger.[1] There are many introductions to animal studies currently available,[2] but this book recognises the importance to animal theory of cosmology as defined by Audra Mitchell as the 'images of the universe which shape the beliefs of a particular group of people' and 'which designates the place of all beings in the universe and their "proper" relations to another'.[3] It is indebted throughout to key perspectives and arguments in animal studies that reflect, resonate with or anticipate the new ideas about the nature of the universe emerging in contemporary science.

Milja Kurki, a professor of international relations, explains: 'At the core of relational cosmology, is an extension, if you will, of what it means to think relationally ... understanding the universe as bound together, through networks of relations which bring it into being, and through which it unfolds.'[4] This model of the universe encourages us to think about humans as part of the category 'animals' in ways that challenge notions that humans have risen above animality because of, for example, reason, the capacity for end-oriented action and entry into culture which in turn reduces animality – the character and nature of animals – to some kind of base level of humanity. How far the concept of a universe in which all beings are bound together has become important to animal studies is emphasised by animal theorists Marc Bekoff and Jessica Pierce: 'What research into animal cognition and emotion continues to demonstrate is just how intertwined we are, evolutionarily. Human exceptionalism, the idea that we are of a different sort altogether, and thus (in our own self-serving logic) have a right to do as we please, is scientifically unsupportable.'[5] In effect, it is this recognition of our world's dynamic relations which, as literary scholars Bruce Boehrer and Molly Hand have said, makes animal studies 'an act of protest and defiance' that seeks 'to understand what we lose when we cut ourselves off from the fellowship of other living creatures'.[6]

As Kurki argues, how we think and act is 'fundamentally tied up with our cosmological visions of the universe and our understandings of our role in it'.[7] Thus, she points out: 'What is intriguing about relational cosmology is that it results in a "radical" rethinking of not only science but also of views of ourselves, history, and our processing in the world.'[8] Central to this radical new thinking is a rejection of the hierarchical divide between humans and animals based on Cartesian concepts of thought and reason in favour of an agenda around 'fullness', 'embodiedness' and the 'sensation of being'.[9]

How we conceive of animality, respond to animals and accept our own animality in accordance with sharing a relational cosmology has become a particularly important strand in animal studies concerned with animal intelligence, cognition and emotions and with how animals perceive the world initiated, for example, by Jakob von Uexküll, Giorgio Agamben and Brett Buchanan. As the animal theorist Derek Ryan says, their work argues that the world does not have a fixed reality independent of the life within it, that different beings see the same environment differently and that all animals have a world-making capacity.[10] The important point that they introduced as far as the concept of a relational cosmos is concerned is that living beings do not simply share the world but have an ability to construct their relationship to their environments. This argument has been criticised for not being sufficiently nuanced or for not allowing that humans have the ability to transcend their environments.[11] However, accepting animal cognition and emotion, rather than seeing animals only as governed by their genes, in context with a universe in which they make their worlds, has led to some important advances in animal theory.[12]

Of the aspects of the new sciences identified by Lee Smolin that have had an impact on animal theory, two are especially important: that the new cosmology 'has no need of reference to fixed, external frameworks outside of the dynamic system of the world within which life has a natural and comprehensible place' and that 'the process of self-organisation ... takes place in real time in the real world' rather than as 'the manifestation of some fundamental and absolute law'.[13] The new cosmological science and contemporary animal studies can be seen as sharing the view that a true perspective on the world comes from within and not outside nature and that the current crisis in cosmology is rooted in the falsehood that it can only be understood from outside it.[14]

CHANGING CONCEPTS OF 'ANIMAL'

Developing perspectives which look at the world from within, animal studies has acquired an edge of the kind which can be found in other interdisciplinary fields, such as Black and gender studies, in which the harsh realities of social interactions are analysed with a view to restoring rights and dignities to those who have been deprived of them. There is no denying, as the anthropologist and animal behaviourist Paul Waldau says, that animal and human relations has stories of 'breathtaking beauty and eloquent testimony to the breadth and depth of our human spirit', but there are also narratives that 'suggest that the ugly and baffling can also populate the human-nonhuman intersection'.[15] Ryan points out that in animal studies: 'We are forced to confront uncomfortable truths about the way that our culture, our language and our thoughts have become distanced from animal being and from our own animality.'[16]

In European philosophy, the term 'animality' has been used to homogenise animals and keep them separate from, and inferior to, humans.[17] But in contemporary animal studies traditional associations of the word have been challenged, subverted and supplanted as concepts of the relationship between animals and humans have changed. The late French philosopher Jacques Derrida insisted: 'Among nonhumans and separate from nonhumans, there is an immense multiplicity of other living things that cannot in anyway be homogenized, except by means of violence and wilful ignorance, within the category of animal or animality in general.'[18] With typical aplomb, he went on to argue:

> The confusion of all nonhuman living creatures within the general and common category of the animal is not simply a sin against rigorous

thinking, vigilance, lucidity, or empirical authority, it is also a crime. Not a crime against animality, precisely, but a crime of the first order against the animals, against animals.[19]

Animal studies seeks to provide the rigorous thinking about animal–human relations for which Derrida argued and, like Derrida, begins with the word 'animal' itself. As Derrida suggested, that word is 'always seeking to draw the limit, the unique and indivisible limit held to separate human from animal'.[20] Animal theorists are seeking not just a new vocabulary in which to talk about animals, and ourselves as animals, but a reorientation to the subject of 'animal' which allows for new ethical and political commitments to emerge. In thinking, like Derrida, outside the word 'animal', animal studies allows what Derrida calls an 'autobiographical animal' to come to the fore which has 'a spontaneity that is capable of movement, of organizing itself and affecting itself, marking, tracing and affecting itself with traces of its self'.[21]

The anthrozoologist Margo DeMello points out that even though scientists in the eighteenth century began thinking naturalistically, their concept of animality was still based on the Greek and Judaeo-Christian notion of a hierarchical universe with humans constituting the pinnacle.[22] And for animal studies generally, human 'exceptionalism', the way in which we have perceived ourselves different from and superior to animals, has long been the barrier to more fulfilling animal–human relationships.[23] Zoologist and broadcaster John Downer maintains: humans have thought of themselves 'as the most highly evolved form of life on earth' and have built up 'a composite and highly complex picture of the world around [them]'.[24] But contemporary animal studies, reflecting the ways in which physical, social and cultural sciences have been thinking through the implications of the 'relational' nature of the universe, has begun dismantling the ideologically loaded concept of animality which human exceptionalism has created. In doing so, it has sought to redefine the nature and characteristics of animals not through the lens of human exceptionalism but from the perspective of a universe in which all beings are bound together through networks of relations.

Not all animal theorists have derived their understanding of a relational universe directly from the new natural and physical sciences. For example, Donna Haraway, who specialises in relations between humans and companionable animals, came to her views of relationality, as Ryan points out, through the influence of the French sociologist and anthropologist Bruno Latour's arguments that nature and society are not distinct, polar opposites.[25] But many of these theorists, including Haraway herself, have come to speak through, and engage with, the language of the new science. Thus, in a discourse that reflects Smolin rather than Latour, Haraway talks of 'the mortal entanglements of human beings and other organisms'.[26]

Kurki points out that Haraway came to reject thinking in terms of relationships as between things, preferring, in a discourse much more appropriate to contemporary cosmology, to envisage relationships 'in terms of multiplicities of relationalities'.[27] The extent to which the new science, and the unveiling of a relational cosmology, opened up new possibilities for human and animal relations is evident throughout much contemporary theory but especially the work of Bekoff and Pierce who argue: 'Enhancing the freedom and well-being of individual animals, and championing the peaceful coexistence and harmony of animals and people, opens the door to a new adjacent possible.'[28]

ANIMAL INTELLIGENCE AND COMMUNICATION

In building on the relational revolution afoot in the physical, natural and social sciences, animal studies is now using the concept of a relational universe, and our place within multiple relations within it, to revise our perceptions of the mental and communicative capacities of animals.[29] In the hierarchical model of the universe which DeMello outlines, in which humans have perceived themselves as superior to animals because of their intelligence, powers of reason and language, animals are deemed to have a limited capacity to feel, reason, communicate and be aware of their own death. But, from the 1960s onwards, a revolution occurred in research into the mental, communication and emotional (or affective) capacities of animals.[30] In discussing this 'revolution', DeMello distinguishes between 'modern ethology' in animal studies, concerned with cognition, emotion and self-awareness, and 'comparative psychology' concerned with the environmental causes of behaviour.[31] The emergence of what she calls 'modern ethology', as Waldau says, can be traced to elephant studies and the ground-breaking work with rescued orphan elephants by Dame Daphne Sheldrick who argued that

Elephants are emotionally very 'human' animals, sharing with us the same emotions that govern our own lives, plus an identical age progression, the same sense of family, sense of death, loves and loyalties that span a lifetime, and many other very 'human' traits, including compassion. They have also been endowed with other attributes we humans do not possess, such as innate knowledge in a generic memory ... In such a long-lived species, there is also a lifetime of learning through experience, just as there is for humans.[32]

Attributing to animals traits of the kind that Sheldrick discovered in elephants fundamentally changes the way in which we perceive of them, appreciating, often for the first time, the depth of their mental, emotional and communicative capabilities. Bekoff and Pierce point out that 'animal sentience throughout vertebrate taxa is now a well-accepted fact, and the focus of discussion has shifted to just how far, taxonomically, sentience might reach.'[33] In illustration of their argument, they remind us that scientists have gathered evidence for sentience in octopuses, squids, crabs, reptiles, amphibians and fishes.[34]

At one level, the new understanding of the cognitive and emotional capabilities of animals has placed a greater obligation on humans to listen to them and to develop what Downer calls 'sound sense'.[35] The American photojournalist Bill Thomas argues that 'learning to listen is very important in developing rapport with all wildlife. Most of us hear far more than registers in our consciousness, simply because we shut out sound.'[36] For example, contemporary animal science has identified that the fox has twelve distinct adult and eight cub vocalisations and as many as twenty-eight groups of sounds.[37] Animal science commentator Jennifer Ackerman reminds us that 'all birds vocalize ... They call to warn of predators and to identify family, friends and foes.'[38]

But communication in the animal world places as much importance on sight as hearing. Contrasting the wolf and the dog, the literary scholar and animal cultural historian Susan McHugh points out: 'Whereas dogs communicate primarily through scent, gesture and, in the case of pack hounds, vocalization, wolves use mostly visual cues to coordinate their stealth-hunting techniques.'[39] And Ryan draws attention to the study of the behaviour of bees by the Austrian ethologist Karl von Frisch which much preoccupied the French psychoanalyst Jacques Lacan:

> When a bee returns to its hive after gathering nectar, it transmits an indication of the existence of nectar near or far away from the hive to its companions by two sorts of dances. The second is the most remarkable, for the plan in which the bee traces out a figure-eight – a shape that gave it the name 'wagging dance' [sic] – and the frequency of the figures executed within a given time, designate, on the one hand, the exact direction to be followed, determined in relation to the sun's inclination (by which bees are able to orient themselves in all kinds of weather, thanks to their sensitivity to polarized light), and on the other hand, the distance at which the nectar is to be found up to several miles away. The other bees respond to this message by immediately setting off for the place thus designated.[40]

Ryan points out that 'the bee comes to stand for the sign systems of animals in general that more directly relate to the material world than human linguistic signs' and opens up 'possibilities for other forms of meaning-making and world-making'.[41] It is this which is fascinating many animal theorists and scientists. Noah Wilson-Rich maintains: 'Bees rely heavily on vibratory communication ... [they] often walk upon one another, exchanging signals by body shaking ... these signals are received through hair receptors throughout the surface of the bee body, including the antennae.'[42]

The importance which we have assigned to human language is one of the reasons why we have not, until now, fully appreciated the capacity of animals to communicate. But, as a result of contemporary animal science and more careful attention on our part, we are beginning to realise the diverse means by which animals convey information. An increasing number of academic and popular publications emphasise how animals communicate, for example, through sound, display and semaphore and do so for a variety of purposes including advertising their presence, courtship, staying in contact with each other, and issuing warning signals. Usually, their modes of communication are adapted to their *Umwelt*: for example, whales exploit the high conductivity of water while species living near waterfalls or in contact with urban noise have exchanged acoustic for visual means of communication. However, as discussed in later chapters, the diversity of animal communication fascinates creative writers, environmental commentators and animal theorists alike not simply for its range and sophistication *per se* as the extent to which it demonstrates animal intelligence, savvy awareness on the part of animals and, above all, the capacity of animals to reason within biological and social parameters.

AN ANIMAL'S *UMWELT*

Understanding the diverse and sophisticated communication system among animals begs questions, as Downer says, around what has become one of the most significant areas of animal studies, 'how other creatures perceive the world'.[43] The philosopher and animal theorist Lori Gruen, stressing that we are in relationships with other animals in a shared universe, maintains: 'The process of figuring out what the perspective of a very different other might be is centrally important for Animal Studies.'[44] In animal studies, as the animal psychologist Alexandra Horowitz, drawing on the work of von Uexküll, says: 'An animal's *Umwelt*, or worldview, defined by her sensory and cognitive capacities as well as the environmental niche she fills, differs from that of humans.'[45] The extent to which animals have evolved perceptual abilities that exceed our own in order to survive in their ecological niches is a significant area of study to which numerous animal theorists, including Ackerman and Balcombe, have contributed.[46] However, as Horowitz cautions with human anthropocentrism in mind: 'What appears to be a seen behavior may thereby be incorrectly interpreted, its context misunderstood, or its meaning or extent misperceived.'[47]

Approaching animal–human relations through this contemporary understanding of an animal's *Umwelt*, Gruen has distinguished between 'empathy' and 'entangled empathy' 'in which we are attentive to both the similarities and differences between ourselves and our own situation and that of the fellow creature with whom we are empathizing' and in which 'we recognize we are in relationships with others and are called on to be responsive and responsible … to another's needs, interests, desires, vulnerabilities, hopes, and sensitivities.'[48] Thus, 'entangled empathy' in a relational cosmology is a means by which 'we are able to preserve the sense that we are in a relationship to and not merged into the same perspective'.[49] In this regard, 'entangled empathy' also reflects the affiliated interest in animal studies in overturning the predominant cultural taxonomies in which, as Amanda Boetzkes says, 'humans conceal animals in anthropocentric systems of signification'.[50]

Kurki emphasises that relational cosmology presents a much more complex reality than one which encourages us to think of the world as 'out there' because it causes us to see ourselves (as does contemporary animal studies) in deep sets of relations.[51] Within this framework, freeing animals from anthropocentric signifying systems enables animal studies to think in terms of the particularity of animals as opposed to the 'generality of their species designations and subordinated place in the natural world'.[52] This awareness of animal particularity reorientates anthropocentricism and calls into question the limits of human perspective. As Boetzkes says, in contemporary animal studies, it is the specific environment that animals inhabit that now sets 'the parameters for interpreting their behaviours, sensibilities, communication and consciousness' rather than the historical differentiation of species and the imposition of human cultural meanings.[53] Focusing on the particularity and sentience of animals, instead of simply dividing them from humans based on our transcendent capacities for thought, enables us, as Ryan suggests, to 'think about their relation in terms of material interconnections and embodied experience'.[54]

ANIMAL HISTORY AND PSYCHOLOGY

How animals have a history which has both shaped, and been determined by, human history, is a recurring theme in animal studies, providing insights into interspecies relations and the changing nature of animality itself. This animal approach to history enables us to think hard about how our concepts of 'animality' have come to be and how far they resonate with the relational world at large.

Uncomfortably for us, as Waldau says, at the centre of animal history are 'the myopias and disfunctions of the exceptionalist tradition and other human centredness'.[55] Animal history is unfortunately integrated with human history through ways in which our perceptions of them have contradicted or even denied the existence of a relational universe and how we have used them, forced them to live in captivity, and have imposed suffering on them to fulfil our own needs. The literary and animal studies scholar Elaine Walker stresses, for example, that the horse's relationship with humans has been generally coercive and cruel and suggestive of a world in which animals are objectified and devalued despite evidence of the horse's potential willingness to 'interact companionably with humans'.[56] As Walker says, the subtleties in the human–horse relationship wore away 'as war and commerce lacked sufficient time for the nuances of interaction to be fully worked out'.[57]

While Walker's account of the use of the horse in warfare links the oppression of animals with physical violence, she also focuses on the psychological trauma which horses suffer in this context, stressing that, as a 'flight animal', the horse is not 'an especially fierce or even brave creature'.[58] In being turned into a kind of battleship, the horse's innate animality – its character and traits – is abused and distorted: 'For them to go into battle requires a reversal of their natural instincts to flee from loud noise or unfamiliar, alarming activity with all the speed nature has provided.'[59] Exemplifying the nuanced and complex thinking which characterises contemporary studies of particular species, Walker sees the human employment of horses in combat as not only an infringement of their instinct to flee from such noise and chaos but the exploitation of their instinct 'to run with and stay close to the herd and to follow strong leadership ... regardless of their bewilderment or fear'.[60]

In exposing the extent to which the natural character and traits of animals have been distorted by human use and abuse, animal history, as Walker exemplifies, lends itself to psychoanalytic methodologies and perspectives. While many scientific fields such as ecology and astronomy have subverted a human-centred view of the world, psychology is a discipline that until recently has proved persistently human-centred even when associated with animals. Ryan, for example, draws attention to the significance of animals to the origins of psychoanalytic theory in uncovering the complicated ways in which animals become associated with conscious and unconscious human experience, and the role that animal figures play in childhood development.[61]

In attempting to explain human behaviour, especially cruelty, toward animals from psychoanalytical perspectives, animal theorists have pointed toward a hierarchical cosmology dominated by the kind of human exclusiveness, myopia and delusion that Waldau argues blocks out the concept of an alternative, interconnected world shared by all living beings and non-living forms that inhabit it. This distancing of humans from other living beings has been seen as leading to perverse and sickening behaviours. For example, in a discussion of the cruelty which horses have suffered, Walker suggests that in the image of the 'strapped-down, fiercely bitted "broken" horse with heaving flanks and bleeding sides' that aspect of human nature which 'seeks to dominate can find satisfaction'.[62] In pursuing this approach to human and animal relations, she follows the earlier ground-breaking work of Yi-Fu Tuan who maintained, primarily with reference to pets, that humans can find pleasure in subjugating domesticated animals: 'great is the temptation for the powerful to reduce their pets ... to simulacra of lifeless objects and mechanical toys – the sort of frozen perfection that only the inanimate can attain.'[63] And he, too, suggests that humans can obtain a sadistic 'pleasure' in subjugating animals:

> However, to some people, a dog's submission to command is desirable in itself. Power over another being is demonstrably firm and perversely delicious when it is exercised for no particular purpose and when submission to it goes against the victim's own strong desires and nature.[64]

But while Tuan argues that much of history from an animal perspective is based on their abuse and subjugation, he accepts that there is also evidence of positive relationships between animals and humans: 'Most people – most of us – do not object to being a "thing" providing it is an appreciated thing. There is, moreover, comfort in being a thing the value of which, being externally fixed, does not depend on internal striving.'[65] This hint that the relationship between the dominant human and the submissive animal might involve more than is allowed by the oppressor–victim paradigm is further developed by Ryan. While accepting that pets are not 'a *natural* feature of life' because they have never existed in the large numbers that they do today, he argues that 'focusing solely on the problems betrayed by pet ownership we miss the importance of our encounters with these animals'.[66]

However, psychoanalytic approaches to animal history have begun to recast the focus on the use and abuse of animals as objects to an appreciation of animals as the subjects of their history. In doing so, animal theory has begun to examine the animal–human relationship from the perspectives of power-play, an important field of study in social psychology. Drawing on the work of the literary scholar and animal theorist Erica Fudge, Ryan argues that the pet, from a psychoanalysis of the pet–owner relationship, becomes 'a producer, or subject' within 'the larger structural ways in which power dynamics play out'.[67]

But Ryan's argument that power-play between humans and animals is important to the history of domesticated animals begs questions about power-play among animals themselves which are only now beginning to receive attention in animal studies, usually in regard to herd animals. For example, Walker's scholarship on the horse reflects the developing interest in animal studies in the subject of leadership, but shifts attention from the stallion, on which discussions of horses as a herd animal are usually placed, to the lead mare and the concept of the passive leader,[68] thereby providing fresh perspectives on horses as social animals, while Philip Armstrong considers fighting among ewes as well as among rams in communities of free-living sheep,[69] again suggesting that as undomesticated animals sheep have a different social culture from those reared on farms. Animal history constructed on the subject of power-play between humans and animals or among animals, as depicted in a number of the texts discussed in subsequent chapters, contributes to the wider interest in animal studies in the social and corporeal continuities that cut across the traditional boundaries between humanity and animality. Bekoff and Pierce, for example, stress the broad acceptance in animal theory of the principle that humans and animals share 'a large repertoire of cognitive skills, patterns of behavior, social instincts, and emotions such as joy, pleasure, happiness, sadness, grief and despair'.[70] Resonating with this relational approach and outlook, Walker points out that the place of the horse in animal history is no longer solely focused on its role in travel, commerce and industry but now includes how, freed from the socio-economic pressures of human ambitions, it has once again become 'an animal with which humans can make a relationship that impacts upon our ability to handle and understand it'.[71] Following a different, but related, vein, Susan McHugh, in her history of the dog, emphasises how the dog has moved from possessing, at best, a 'separate but equal status' to humans to becoming 'an integral part of our biological, legal and more profoundly cultural conception of who we are'.[72]

In her study of the horse, Walker emphasises that the horse–human relationship should be a symbiotic engagement: 'Ways of training horses have changed over the years, often reflecting changes in humans' understanding of themselves, rather than horses.'[73] However, there are areas within animal history where changes in the way in which humans appreciate animals, especially in regard to their intelligence and capacity to adapt to their environments, have not brought about changes in human understanding of themselves especially from psychological perspectives. Two of these controversial areas of animal history – hunting and animal rights – are discussed in the following sections.

PSYCHOLOGY, POWER-PLAY AND HUNTING

Like predatorship generally, which later chapters address, hunting is a controversial subject which writers and animal theorists have displayed difficulties in tackling and rarely without ambivalence and contradiction, as is evident in Tuan's work. At one level, Tuan argues that hunting animals is deeply embedded in human nature, pointing out that 'for half a million years protohumans and humans have been not merely scavengers but active and increasingly skilled hunters.'[74] In other words, in Tuan's view, hunting behaviour is in the biological make-up of humans as much as their sociocultural history: 'The hunter's body and mind, and with them a disposition toward activity and unconcern for suffering, are thus an inescapable part of our heritage.'[75] Tuan, however, is writing in advance of the science of gene-culture coevolution, concerned with how far genetic inheritance is inseparable from culture, and tends to conflate biological processes and culture rather too easily. This is evident, for example, in his ready acceptance, without further commentary, of the work of the anthropologist S. L. Washburn: 'The extent to which the biological bases for killing have been incorporated into human psychology may be measured by the ease with which boys can be interested in hunting, fishing, fighting, and games of war.'[76]

Although animal history, when narrated from the perspectives of animals, lends itself, as we have seen, to psychoanalytic approaches, Tuan avoids discussion of predator and prey among other-than-human species (discussed in Chapter 6), and focuses on what he sees as the 'perversely delicious' sadistic satisfaction that humans find in hunting, maintaining that 'to become skilled hunters, humans must have taken a certain pleasure in their task of running down prey and killing it'.[77] To his mind, this 'pleasure' in tracking and killing manifests itself in the way in which hunting among humans has become 'a sort of game' and various methods of killing have become 'exciting and fun'.[78] Despite the ideological traditions designed to lift some forms of hunting above what he sees as a base level of humanity – for example, with fox hunting in mind, the 'modern-age aesthetic of red coats and of brass bugles flashing in the morning sun' – he points out that in general hunting 'retains its flavor of violence in mud, sweat, blood and death cries'.[79]

However, at this point of his argument, anticipating twenty-first-century interest in history from the point of view of animals, Tuan shifts the focus of his analysis from the human to the animal perspective – 'to the hunted animal, obviously, the chase is not a game but a matter of life and death in which the opportunities to escape are, more often than not, cruel illusions'[80] – conflating the two so as to break down the barrier between them. But controversially, Tuan sees the hunted animal, through the act of being hunted, as emerging from the historical, cultural taxonomy in which it has been placed and its natural characteristics and traits as valued from the perspective of the hunter. The hunt itself, he suggests, offers insights into the relationality of the world order. But it is not the kind of order that supports the vision among some writers and animal theorists, as in several of the texts discussed in this book, of animals and people living in peace and harmony: 'In theory, the hunted animal should be a worthy antagonist in speed and cunning, or ferocity. It must have a chance to escape or fight back. Otherwise the killing would simply be the work of a butcher, not of a sportsman.'[81]

Accounts of humans hunting and killing animals are often characterised by emphasis upon the meeting of two intelligences, which are not as different as non-hunters might presume. Rooted in admiration of the hunted animal's agility and movement (which ironically undermines the hierarchical thinking that ostensibly legitimates hunting to begin with), it may be that these hunting narratives, especially when wrapped up as Tuan suggests in long-established traditions, reflect not so much an encounter between species as the product of a cosmology by which humans see themselves as superior to animals. Discussing the hunting of birds, the Welsh country writer D. J. Williams observes: 'The woodcock is a difficult bird to get, they say, unless you have the secret of its sudden turn in flight but it is not nearly as bad as the snipe. The best way to bring down a snipe is to hit it straight after it has risen, before it begins its artful dodges.'[82] Williams slips between regard for the artfulness of birds in escaping their human predators and a pride in his knowledge of them as a hunter himself. It is interesting to juxtapose Williams's commentary with that of the contemporary writer and falconer Daniel Butler who is passionate about birds of prey. He offers us insights into working with hunting animals in what he calls 'questing'[83] that can only come from an experienced falconer:

> The simplest of walks is immeasurably enhanced by the hawk and the dog. I can vicariously harness the animals' senses. The hawk's eyesight and the dog's sense of smell are both infinitely better than my own, so by watching their behaviour in the field I see far more than I could ever hope to detect on my own. This is hunting, but more in the sense of questing than a chase culminating in a kill. Merely the intention of 'capturing' something on a walk opens one's eyes to a host of other observations.[84]

Within the wider disputes as to what is 'true' and 'untrue' about hunting, those who justify humans hunting animals are often perceived as denying the cruelty and secret pleasures involved. The way in which, as Tuan argues, the powerful find pleasure in turning domestic animals into 'simulacra of lifeless objects' is reflected in the process by which deer heads, for example, become 'records' – in effect 'trophies' – of a hunt. In his article on collecting the heads of deer that he stalks and kills, Graham Downing justifies his actions by his philosophy of hunting – 'I hunt to control deer for the landowner on the ground where I am privileged to stalk' – and the 'science' behind collecting heads: 'Measurement of heads does, however, provide an internationally recognised baseline of the quality of our wild deer, a recorded dataset against which the performance of populations can be assessed over time.'[85] However, it is also clear that Downing achieves pleasure in the way he can 'cross-reference' the heads on his wall with the entries in his game diary, enabling him 'to relive a particular outing' and in the way in which each head, 'carefully skinned, cut, boiled out, cleaned and mounted on a board', lays bare 'the story of the deer itself'.[86] Although he attempts to shift the focus of his account from himself to the lives of the animals within his narrative, they remain the objects rather than the subjects of the story. The pleasure that he describes resonates with the traditional practice of taking heads as emblems of the hunter's 'personal prowess' and with a longstanding 'aesthetic' interest in the 'sheer delight at the beauty of the antlers themselves – one of nature's wonders'[87] despite his disassociation of himself from them. The sheer delight which he describes in displaying deer skulls and entering them in competitions, warrants closer attention, as Tuan's theoretical work on hunting suggests, from a psychoanalytic perspective.

However, of equal interest to animal studies is the predator and prey relationship among animals which is often depicted in the popular media to demonstrate how animal life is red in tooth and claw. But contemporary animal theory is becoming sceptical of the popular depiction of a violent animal world, placing more emphasis on the cooperation rather than the conflict among animals. In doing so, it has begun to recalculate the statistics behind the alleged extent of the predatory behaviour supporting particular ecosystems and food chains and is presenting a more harmonious picture of animal life.[88]

Although there are examples of writers and theorists, demonstrating diverse views on humans hunting animals, seeking to focus on being hunted by humans from an animal's experience of it, they frequently exemplify the difficulties in doing so and resort to maintaining the human perspective. This bias is reflected in the amount of work devoted to hunting between humans and animals, in, for example, adventure stories and rural memoirs, compared to that concerned with hunting among animals (even allowing for the many popular media depictions of animal predators). However, this emphasis on humans hunting animals has drawn attention to another controversial theme within animal studies related to it, animal rights, the topic of the next section.

ANIMAL RIGHTS

As animal studies as an academic discipline has become absorbed into a broad spectrum of cultural history, psychological and biological sciences, law and creative projects, the representation of animals as a subject of enquiry has become more nuanced, as Gruen says.[89] Through the discipline of animal studies, scholars from a wide range of fields have engaged in dialogue around topics such as animal intelligence, reason and emotion, social organisation and animal cultures, but also around animal rights and the ethical claims that animals make of us, topics as controversial as hunting and animal farming with which they are integrally connected.[90]

Waldau identifies three movements in animal rights. The first wave, dating back to the nineteenth century, he argues, uses the legal system and traditional legal ideas and methods to reduce serious harm to animals and features a continuum from 'welfare' to 'rights'.[91] This wave has come under scrutiny in contemporary animal studies from several perspectives. Acts of Parliament, from 1822 onward, outlawing cruelty are no longer seen simply as the product of a society becoming more compassionate to animals. As the sociologist and animal rights scholar David A. Nibert argues, institutionalised cruelty to animals, along with discrimination against women and ethnic minorities, was addressed because it was perceived as inconsistent with the expansion of capitalism and an increasingly sophisticated commercial society.[92] Moreover, the emphasis in animal Acts and in animal protection literature on what might be termed 'cognitively impressive' and 'companion' animals is no longer seen as bringing about much significant change in our understanding of animality *per se*.

The second wave has more support among animal theorists, differing from the first in looking to a more robust system of animal rights than one reliant on traditional legal ideas and methods and having a better understanding of the psychological as well as the physical realities of the lives of animals. According to Waldau, this is a consequence of a larger 'moral revolution' focused not simply on specific rights for certain animals, such as chimpanzees, elephants and reptiles, but on banning ownership of animals altogether.[93] Tom Regan, reflective of relational thinking about the world which animals and humans inhabit, argues:

> Like us, animals have certain basic moral rights, including in particular the fundamental right to be treated with the respect that, as possessors of inherent value, they are due as matter of strict justice. Like us, therefore ... they must never be treated as mere receptacles of intrinsic values ... and any harm that is done to them must be consistent with the recognition of their equal inherent value and their equal prima facie right not to be harmed.[94]

But his arguments do not satisfy all animal theorists. When he maintains that all animals with a certain complexity of conscious life have a value that cannot be reduced to their usefulness to humans, others, such as the political theorist Alasdair Cochrane, have found his notion of inherent value too mysterious and ethereal.[95] The importance of Cochrane's contribution to the controversy over animal rights is his differently nuanced argument that, since animals have no investment in freedom as such, they have no rights not to be kept or used by humans, but they have rights not to suffer and not to be killed.

An important difference between Cochrane and Regan's work is that while both advocate the well-being of animals, Cochrane prioritises the importance of the well-being of individual animals over an 'aggregate well-being' and argues that animal rights should be grounded 'in something tangible and concrete'.[96] In doing so, he adopts an 'interest-based' approach which avoids drawing up a definitive list of abstract animal rights and insists that the concrete rights of animals must be worked out in particular contexts: 'the interests of animals need to be identified; their strength needs to be evaluated; those interests need to be balanced against the burdens they impose on the putative duty-bearers.'[97] To an extent, Cochrane is a controversial voice in animal studies in that while he insists that animals 'have compelling rights that impose strict limitations on what we may permissibly do to them in a range of contexts', he suggests that animals may not have 'a general right never to be used, owned, or exploited by human beings'.[98]

Different cosmologies have structured models that we have used, as Ryan says, to identify, operate and relate to other animals and legitimate the belief that animals are 'naturally designed for utilisation by humans'.[99] The approach to ethics in contemporary animal studies is more reflective of the way in which, as Smolin argues, that in a relational universe, ethics must be integrated with nature and must be part of the responsibilities that in this context we assume for all life.[100] In effect, Smolin provides the means by which ethics and animal welfare can be linked in an understanding that our boundaries, vulnerabilities and ethical commitments for others are determined by our awareness of a relational cosmology.

ANIMAL FREEDOM AND CAPTIVITY

In twenty-first-century animal studies, the concept of a relational universe which we share with many other life forms, brought about a general reorientation of human and animal relations and informed a critical, ethical reconstruction of the many contexts in which we encounter animals. One of the most pressing of these for Waldau is animal husbandry, a subject of further discussion in Chapter 2. In his view, it emblematises the extent to which animal history has involved the subjugation and suffering of animals to meet human needs and the role of animal science, even veterinary medicine, in promoting, or insufficiently questioning, this.

When viewed through an ethical framework which reflects the relational nature of life on our planet, the farming industry, as Waldau says, reveals 'the astonishing and varied ways humans have to dominate, harm, and subordinate other animals' and this is especially the case in what he calls the 'large food production industries (also known as agri-business)'.[101] But, ironically, the transformation of animals into meat and other food products has been a key factor in ensuring their survival, albeit as market commodities. Central to this theme in animal history is the contradiction between how the basic material needs of agricultural animals are met (through, for example, vaccinations, medications, hormones, pesticides and automatic feeders) and how their subjective needs as living beings are often ignored.

The agricultural industry (discussed in Chapter 2), zoological gardens (discussed in Chapter 4), and the domestication of animals as pets (discussed in Chapters 7 and 8) are brought together in animal studies around the ways in which the concept of 'captivity' has changed along with that of animality itself. While, as Lori Marino points out, captivity is generally conceived in terms of 'the physical circumstance of being confined in space or in movement', in animal studies it has come to be seen as a state of being.[102] Reflecting the developing interest in animal studies in power structures and psychoanalytic approaches, exemplified by Tuan, Marino points out: 'captivity occurs when there is a self-directed creature capable of independent intentional actions, and her movements, choices, and actions are subject to the control of another who benefits from this control.'[103] From the interplay of these psychological dimensions, a deeper understanding of captivity emerges in animal studies whereby, as Marino says, 'captivity is a condition of powerlessness over one's options'[104] and is experienced in a range of locations – for example, zoos, marine parks and aquariums, circuses and travelling shows, private homes – but each of them involves restrictions and loss of control for the animal along with forced interspecies interaction, intrusion and monotony.[105] While accepting that the impact of captivity on a wild animal depends on the situation in which they are held, Marino develops Tuan's analysis of it in a way which reflects the movement in animal studies from animal rights as a means of preventing death and harm to an obligation to ensure that the captive animal experiences the best possible subjective life and has opportunities to 'thrive or flourish' and 'be free to express the characteristic nature of their species'.[106] How far this emphasis has become established within and outside animal studies as an academic discipline is evident in a statement from Lesley Griffiths, rural affairs minister, on the publication of the Welsh government's Animal Plan for Wales (November, 2021): 'I'm very proud of what has already been achieved in Wales in animal welfare. But there is more to do. Our long-term ambition is for every animal in Wales to have a good quality of life.'[107] Marino and other animal theorists enable us to better understand what is meant by that important phrase 'a good quality of life'.

Locations, such as zoos, in which animals are confined are the subject of debate and controversy in animal studies because, as Marino says, 'more often than not, captivity for wild animals no matter how good the veterinary care or how well intentioned the captors, will, by definition, be incompatible with thriving.'[108] Informing Marino's telling phrase, 'by definition', is a view of the universe in which the environment is not distant from its inhabitants but one in which they develop traits, skills and dispositions that allow them to live satisfying lives as members of particular species.

The distinction between 'domesticated' zoo animals, born into human society and dependent on human care for their well-being, and animals captured in the wild is a subject of much debate in animal studies. In a characteristically nuanced contribution to this debate, Cochrane argues that 'taking possession of a wild animal – say, by going into the countryside and trapping him – runs contrary to the animal's interests in not suffering.'[109] To his mind, captured animals kept in zoos or private collections, unlike animals bred in captivity, suffer by being removed from their familiar habitat and social network, made to feel threatened and kept in fear of their lives, as a consequence of which they grow frustrated at not being able to escape. Thus, Cochrane feels able to support 'radically restructured zoos which display certain species of captive-bred animal, and which respect every aspect of those animals' well-being' as institutions which are 'harmless and violate no rights'.[110]

ANIMAL WELFARISM, POST-HUMANISM AND ENVIRONMENTALISM

The voice of protest and defiance in animal studies, which, as noted earlier, Bruce Boehrer and Molly Hand identified, has its roots in the discipline of ecology as it emerged in the 1960s that the ecologist Paul Sears has described as a 'subversive science' because of the way in which it has challenged 'the assumptions and practices accepted by modern societies'.[111] But, as Waldau, points out, within and affiliated to animal studies, there are many fields – primatology, bird studies, marine studies, elephant studies and companion animal studies – that have subverted the notion of human exceptionalism and 'provided key perspectives on the profound truths of our membership in the interconnected, inviting universe all animals occupy'.[112] Animal science has moved on since the founding of the discipline of animal studies in the late 1980s and the 1990s, from accepting the ancient duality of humans and animals to discrediting human exceptionalism as 'not only antiscientific, but also antiecological'.[113] Conservation and management of the environment are important themes in animal studies but, in the wake of the emphasis in the natural sciences on a relational universe, the focus has shifted, as Timothy Morton maintains, toward ecological thought as involving a different orientation to the world, 'the thinking of interconnectedness'.[114]

This concept of interconnectedness is important to animal studies because, as Kurki points out with reference to social studies generally, social theories since Marx have postulated abstract social categories which have tended to detach us from the world.[115] In this respect, animal studies is one of the disciplines which situates itself within what has come to be called post-/critical humanism which, as Kurki says, sees humanism 'as a tradition of thought, or an ideology' in which humanity is 'a unified and unique species ... that stands apart from interspecies interdependencies'.[116] In an attempt to think beyond traditional humanism, achieve a better understanding of 'interspecies interdependencies' and to 'get at the sense of the relationality, the totality, and interconnectivity' of the universe, Kurki borrows the term 'mesh' from Timothy Morton, which she sees as dynamic and infinite in size and detail.[117]

However, although ecological thinking, according to many animal theorists, is underpinned by the concept of 'mesh', others regard aspects of ecology as controversial. Waldau, for example, maintains: 'Discussions of broad-sounding topics like "sustainability" often remain so insistently human-centred that they amount to what can be thought of as "environmental speciesism", that is a framing of environmental and conservative programs solely in favor of the human species.'[118] This subversion of human exceptionalist strands of environmental and conservation science has caused animal studies of late, as Waldau says, to re-examine the extent to which ecological and philosophical thinking in the discipline has been inadvertently influenced by 'ethical anthropocentrism'.[119] Bekoff and Pierce similarly maintain that they would like to see more scientists move away from being advocates for 'welfarism', which they regard as operating 'in the service of a variety of industries', and 'become more positive advocates for the animals themselves'.[120]

Thus, in summary, animal studies as a discipline alerts us as to how our assumptions about, and attitudes toward, animals may be based on outmoded cosmological conceptions, scientific discourses and sociocultural modelling that have been discredited and/or surpassed. In a cosmology inherited from Newton, animals have too often been seen as part of a world of things in which spatial and temporal boundaries have been defined according to our image of ourselves as special, intelligent and superior to other life on the planet. In thinking about animals from a relational cosmological perspective, animal studies challenges the ways in which we have conventionally thought about animals, the assumptions behind this thinking and our wider understanding of the planet from an animal's agenda, *Umwelt* and cognitive and emotional capacities. Writings about animals often critique our cosmological, scientific and sociocultural assumptions about them in ways that encourage us to think creatively and open us to different ethical and political perspectives and understandings of intelligence. Through this more creative thinking, based on contemporary animal and natural sciences, concepts such as animal, human, community, cosmology and context emerge, as in animal studies generally, as problematic. In reflecting on them and how they have been deployed in modern Welsh literature and culture as part of wider discussions of animals, birds and insects, the following chapters open up alternative histories, science, theological structures of thought and power relations.

2

Rethinking Animal Contexts: Rural and Industrial Wales

Drawing on cultural histories, animal theory, literary works and a range of cultural and educational artefacts, while comparing life for animals and human attitudes toward them across different centuries, this chapter attempts to rethink rural and industrial Wales from an animal's perspective. Chapter 1 noted that the contexts in which we encounter, and live and work with, animals have assumed increased importance in animal studies. But 'context' is both a graspable and an imagined 'reality'. As animal theorist Derek Ryan has observed, animal studies is a discipline about 'encountering many animals in thought'.[1] This is very applicable to the way in which rural Wales has been conceived over the last six hundred years or so.

The Welsh poet and scholar Anthony Conran points out that in Welsh medieval literature, the Welsh countryside constitutes an imaginary 'anti-image' to the gentry and the great house and to the culture and hospitality associated with them: 'Instead of the lord, there is the outlaw, the thief, the outcast; instead of the house, there is the glade and birchwoods … instead of the hospitality and feasting of the great house … there is the ritual of the birds, the feasts of love … the wantonness of the wind that bloweth where it listeth.'[2] In medieval poetry, rural Wales is a place of darkness and secret activity. For example, Llywelyn Goch ap Meurig Hen speaks of 'the forests' gloom' and for Dafydd ap Gwilym the birch wood is a place of 'trysting'.[3] In this regard, they anticipate the psychogeographical approach to the Welsh countryside of the author of twentieth-century country memoirs D. Parry-Jones who similarly identifies what he calls the 'countryside unconscious':[4]

Woods are places of mystery, they certainly do not extend their myriad hands out to invite, at least to any place of safety and security ... The wood hides – and hides perhaps too many gruesome secrets. One's reaction towards woods is natural and primitive ... a wood or a forest is surrounded in our imaginations by fears of the unknown, and brooded over and inhabited by spirits of sinister character.[5]

But running through his writings is the psychological impact of the environment not simply on human inhabitants but animals and birds:

You saw the little animals which had made it to their way home and which suddenly startled, shot off, seeking the protection of some object to peep at you shyly and suspiciously from behind trees, tumps, bushes and boulders. The weasel ran into the nearest heap of stones and turned round in his hole to look at you; the birds flew into the branches of more distant and darker trees, there to sit tight and watch your moves and try to divine your intentions. The rabbits halted at the mouth of their holes, sitting bolt upright and keeping an eye on you over their shoulders. Here the vixen and her young lay out in the open and played together without the slightest trace of fear. In the evening the badger joined them, uttering his call, a sort of mixture of a dog's bark and the *wroch* of a pig – indeed we call him the 'burrowing pig' (*Mochyn daear*).[6]

He sees the wildlife in the remote interior of Wales, as did the medieval Welsh poets, as part of a 'living body quite unconscious of itself'.[7] In the discovery of habitats that have to be searched out, there is a strong sense of the self-importance of humans being disassembled as they experience being watched and tracked themselves. Cast as the intruders, they are studied carefully and quizzically by the animals they encounter and those they cannot see. And this is the experience also of the contemporary naturalist Roger Lovegrove who begins his impressive study of the red kite by conjuring up the secretive, rural landscape with which these magnificent birds are associated:

For here in Wales, the precious remnant population of kites is secure in the depths of a countryside which is itself steeped in mystery and secrecy ... on wild hills and in valleys of crags, tumbling streams and ancient woodlands it is as if an unseen eye is watching and the kite is wrapped in a protective cloak of Celtic mystique; on one hand fugitive from man but at the same time fiercely protected by him in remote farmsteads and lonely communities.[8]

The sense within medieval Welsh poetry, and within rural Wales generally, of what Parry-Jones describes as a 'living body quite unconscious of itself' resonates with the relational world which the natural and physical sciences are seeking to bring into human consciousness. In this context, psychogeographical approaches to the Welsh rural landscape, reflecting the way in which it is depicted in Welsh medieval literature, make an important contribution to Welsh animal studies, encouraging acknowledgement of the impact of the environment on animal as well as human inhabitants. In doing so, it anticipates the increasing interest in animal studies, as Chapter 1 observed, in animal history from an animal's perspective, to which I now turn in the following sections.

NONCONFORMITY

The unconscious of the countryside which stirs in the depths of D. Parry-Jones's being and which Roger Lovegrove feels as a 'cloak of Celtic mystique' might have ancient roots as far as the psychogeography of the remote farmsteads and lonely communities are concerned, but it also has more recent origins. As the literary scholar M. Wynn Thomas maintains: 'By the end of the nineteenth century, distinctive Welsh identity seemed inseparable from Nonconformity.'[9]

This was indeed the case in rural, north-west and west Wales. Nonconformity provided education and the beginnings of widespread literacy through its Sunday Schools and its academies while numerous periodicals helped provide a confident intelligentsia and train distinguished social and religious leaders.[10] It was responsible, as I have shown elsewhere, for bringing a distinctive, pacifist movement into existence.[11] But its impact on shaping the lives of animals and determining human attitudes toward them, in other words its significant role in Welsh animal history, has been overlooked.

The collection of short articles and photographs, *Trwy Lygad y Bugail* (Through the Eye of the Shepherd), by the mid-twentieth-century, Welsh-language evangelical writer Mari Jones reminds us that there were two aspects to nonconformity.[12] One side of it has been described by Thomas as 'joyless, grim, oppressive and fearsome'.[13] But the other, in which wild and domesticated animals featured, as Jones's work suggests, was culturally richer, with roots in the tradition of itinerant preachers and storytellers who drew on spiritual insights and skills honed with audiences of farm labourers in rural communities. Parry-Jones, recalling his experience of itinerant storytellers as a child, observed:

> I believe they were the last survivors of an ancient order, the story-tellers, the entertainers of the countryside. In the uneventful, placid, monotonous life of a book-less, paper-less, radio-less community, they provided, with their stock of age-long stories, satisfaction for that profound need of man, to be thrilled.[14]

This side of nonconformity produced, to borrow Thomas's words, 'exuberantly virtuosic oral narrators' who employed 'a proliferation of mnemonic devices'.[15] But how Welsh, especially Welsh-language, culture was able to produce oral narratives that embraced animal life was the result of the multifaceted nature of medieval Welsh literature which reverberated with the verisimilitude of animals, a reverent appreciation of their beauty and themes of enchantment and transformation.

However, Welsh preachers and storytellers, from the eighteenth and nineteenth centuries, also relied extensively on anecdotes and motifs drawn from the rural subculture. Human and animal relations provided preachers with easily accessible subject matter for their sermons while animal stories and anecdotes offered the chapel, in which nonconformity in the late nineteenth and the first third of the twentieth centuries was becoming 'increasingly intellectual and rational in character',[16] analogies to issues of faith, the scriptures and moral behaviour. But nonconformist preachers and storytellers, exuberant and virtuosic in one respect but sensitive and quietly perceptive in another, combined the analogous aspects of their stories with genuine pleasure in the beauty and colour of animals, indicative of the wonders of creation; in the elaborate bodies and behaviours of animals and birds carefully attuned to their environments; and in reflecting on the experience of encountering, and working with, animals.

How nonconformist preachers drew numerous analogies to faith and the scriptures from the countryside in which they were brought up is remembered by Parry-Jones when he recalls the legendary preacher Reverend Dafydd Evans: 'His college was the woods, the meadows and wide nature; his teachers the mountains, the rivers, the oak and the ash, the spider and the ant, the bees and the crows.'[17] From a lecture that Evans gave on birds, Parry-Jones recalled, even later in life, 'their lessons and example for man', and how Evans 'waxed eloquent on the good qualities of the wren as a mother' and the 'good points of father-wren too'.[18]

Although the analogies to humans and animals with which the preachers and travelling speakers couched their texts provided opportunities for moral storytelling and appreciation of the splendour and beauty of birds and animals, nonconformity also encouraged seeing the impact of the Welsh countryside on animals and relating their history from an animal's perspective. However, while the extent and diversity of rural Wales has been examined in regard to human settlement and development, its impact on animals and bird life is only now being appreciated.

ANIMAL HISTORY AND THE HUMAN SETTLEMENT OF RURAL WALES

To place the importance of the rural environment of Wales in context, it should be noted that the majority of the population is concentrated in the former industrial and mining areas of south and north-east Wales, but 88 per cent of Wales is characterised as agricultural or common land or forestry with 70 per cent grassland pasture and sheep and cattle grazing accounting for 35 per cent of active farms.[19] Since 2012, the economic value of the Welsh rural environment has been estimated as being in excess of £9 billion even though the average farm income remains heavily dependent on direct income support while farmers can never be certain what they will earn from, say, their lambs and calves, even six months ahead.

Historians, such as J. Geraint Jenkins, have tended to focus on how the scattered habitats and numerous small farms shaped the human and material culture of Wales – creating relatively isolated communities within which crafts and facilities were shared among homesteads – but ignoring their impact upon animal life.[20] In the communities which Jenkins describes, animals – predominantly, as today, sheep, cattle and working dogs – were the means by which humans met their individual and collective needs and around which crafts such as woollen manufacturing and leather production developed. In the relative isolation of these self-supporting localities, animals found themselves integrated as part of their immediate human community but utilised as a resource for food and for the local craft and rural industries. In this context, the animals – as the words 'cattle', 'poultry' and 'livestock' themselves suggest – were objectified and devalued, so that even their body parts and fluids – 'meat', 'wool', 'milk', 'eggs' – became mere commodities.[21]

The structure of rural Wales as a network of scattered, remote farmsteads impacted on animal welfare in a number of ways including farmers' access to knowledge. Animals were invariably the subjects of traditional husbandry, inherited (and sometimes outmoded) skills and word-of-mouth information. At the end of the nineteenth century, a body of agricultural literature was available in English but had to be cascaded to the remote Welsh-speaking communities. As Richard Moore-Colyer has pointed out, a number of short-lived, Welsh-language journals offering comments on agricultural and rural subjects were available in the 1840s and 1850s and although *Baner ac Amserau* and *Y Genedl Gymreig* were the most widely read newspapers among farming families by the end of the century, they devoted only a limited amount of space to practical farming and the agrarian content was mainly political.[22] Even by the 1930s, Moore-Colyer maintains, there were only four agricultural texts available in Welsh.[23]

The needs of Welsh-language farmsteads which were met by Welsh-language manuals is evident in the first examples that became available in Victorian Wales – James Law's *Meddyg y Fferm* (The Farm Doctor) and *Llyfr Coginio* (Welsh Cookery Book) – however, they also incorporated particular assumptions about, and attitudes toward, animals and animality. In translation, *Meddyg y Fferm* was aimed at those in Wales who live in the depths of the countryside, far from towns, whose animals found themselves dependent upon inappropriate treatments and medicines (such as folk remedies and charlatan animal doctors as depicted in Gwyn Jones's story 'The Green Island', discussed in Chapter 9). Such veterinary books introduced ways of thinking about animals which, in seeing them as patients, was close to human medical texts but at the same time distanced them as objects of the veterinary gaze.

Law's *Meddyg y Fferm* begins with 'Effaith Meddyginiaethau, dognau &c' (Effective Medicines, portions etc.) through which, depending on the finances and enthusiasm of the farmers, anaesthetics, antiseptics, anodynes and antacids (together with an explanation of how they might be used and in what portion) were made available to them, often for the first time.[24] But the sharing of specialist veterinary knowledge with farm owners and workers was based on recognition that their livelihoods were dependent upon the accurate diagnoses and treatment of animal disease and injuries. As such, the veterinary manual supported, rather than challenged, the ubiquitous objectification and use of animals in the interests of human society. The remaining chapters of Law's book are organised around ailments, such as those associated with insects, feed, the heart, digestion and feet. Within this framework, reflecting the medical attitude toward humans at the time, animals are objectified as problems, perceived anatomically (in the text and through the illustrations) and discussed in a medically neutral language which renders them social-psychologically detached.

At one level, the way in which the book is organised along similar lines as a human medical textbook challenges the human and animal binary, suggesting that animals, too, have a right to care as sentient beings. But, taken together, the Welsh veterinary manual and the Welsh country memoir tread a similar, narrow path between seeing animals as sentient beings and as serving human society.

While Law's *Meddyg y Fferm* targets farmers on remote farms, *Llyfr Coginio* is aimed at the women in these homesteads perceived as in need of guidance and advice. But this Welsh-language, cookery and house-keeping volume, viewed from a Welsh perspective, is once again not as straightforward as it seems. It emerged from a particular historical context in Wales which can be traced to 'Brad y Llyfrau Gleision' (The Treachery of the Blue Books) (1847) when a report into the state of education in Wales scandalously and controversially attacked the Welsh language, nonconformity and the alleged immorality of the Welsh people. Welsh women were accused of being slovenly and improvident as wives and ignorant and injudicious as mothers. The impact of the report led to the publication of *Y Gymraes* (The Welsh Woman) which in addition to articles on marriage and religion included advice on cookery and housekeeping. Issued too close to the controversy around Welsh education and morality when many Welsh people might have felt that turning to such publications only seemed to endorse the 1847 reports, the magazine was unsupported and closed after only two years. However, when the controversy had begun to die, the publishers of Welsh-language cookery and housekeeping books like *Llyfr Coginio* clearly felt that they might unashamedly claim to provide for the needs of 'holl ddosparthiadau merched ein gwlad' (all classes of our country's women)[25] as still partly defined by that invidious report of the 1840s. The success of such books helped enable the revitalisation of *Y Gymraes*, under the editorship of the writer and north Wales temperance campaigner Ceridwen Peris (Alice Gray Jones), years later in 1896 which was published until 1934.

In the context of encouraging animal history from an animal's perspective, Welsh-language cookery books, like the Welsh-language veterinary manuals for farmers, only continued the objectification and devaluing of animals, as sources of food and labour, rather than their recognition as sentient beings. In doing so, they sought to strengthen the cultural link between animal husbandry and home-based butchery, which was traditionally seen as a man's responsibility, by suggesting that women needed to acquire better butchery skills. Thus, *Llyfr Coginio* is copiously illustrated with drawings as to how to arrange various cuts of meat from the oven for carving and there are four full-page illustrations of butchered, hanging carcasses marked in Welsh so as to show the position of the different joints that are cut from them. As in most Welsh-language cookery books of the period, and as a counterpoint to the Welsh country memoir, the living animal (possessing consciousness and able to feel enjoyment and to experience fear and suffering) is absent. It is replaced with a carcass that is subdivided into 'specialist cuts' employing a terminology that is so remote from the original animal at some points that further pictures are needed to relate the one to the other.[26]

The insistence in Victorian Welsh cookery books that women acquire basic butchery skills is deeply ironic when read through the lens of contemporary animal studies. One of the most controversial arguments against the slaughtering and butchering of animals is its link, which emerged in scholarship in the 1980s, with violence committed against women. It can be traced to William Hogarth's four printed engravings, *The Four Stages of Cruelty* (1757), in which the protagonist tortures a dog, beats a horse, and then seduces, assaults and murders a young woman, and to Anna Sewell's *Black Beauty* (1877) where, as Deborah Morse says: 'The representation of Ginger as a broken female horse calls to mind the familiar literary trope of the fallen woman who dies a prostitute in the streets. Ginger is "used up by men," who say they must get their money out of her flesh.'[27] In this respect, it was not by chance that Britain's first serial killer Jack the Ripper (in 1888) was suspected of being a slaughterhouse man and reports said of one of the victims: 'She was ripped open just as you see a dead calf at a butcher's shop.'[28] The feminist exponent of animal rights Carol Adams, arguing that the culture around meat-eating encourages expectations about male power and virility which are manifested in misogynistic attitudes toward women, points to a range of pornography in which women are described in terms that evoke the slaughter and consumption of animals.[29]

However, women's writing about the butchering skills which their foremothers acquired often shows regret over animals killed for food by or for men, as is evident in Jean Earle's 'Jugged Hare'.[30] Earle was born in 1909 and grew up, like her father's lover, in the shadow of books such as *Llyfr Coginio*. She remembers her father's lover making him his favourite dish of jugged hare and how she smoothed the hare's dishevelled shot fur before gutting it. But, maybe with the encouragement of Welsh cookery books in mind, Earle also remembers the pride which some women took in their culinary and butchering skills.

The promotion and support for the objectification of animals in Welsh-language cookery and veterinary books not only exemplifies this practice *per se* but exposes the thinking behind it which permeated rural and urban Wales. In a discussion of the Welsh poet R. S. Thomas (whose interest in birds and in the new relational science is discussed in Chapter 6), M. Wynn Thomas glimpses a rural world which does not so much contrast with as reproduces in its own terms the capitalist structure of commercial towns and industrial centres.[31] However, from an animal perspective, human and animal relationships in both rural and urban communities are characterised, as animal scholars like Paul Waldau have argued, by the assumption that 'living beings can be treated by humans as mere commodities', by 'the exclusivist notion of speciesism', by 'myopias and self-inflicted ignorance' and by 'disingenuous, self-serving denials of other animal's sentience and complexities'.[32]

Animals have generally been excluded from the history of rural Wales. But when narrated from an animal perspective that history is seen to include cultural forces, rooted in literature and nonconformity, that encourage appreciation of an animal's worldview. However, these histories exist alongside others, centred on animal husbandry, in which animals are seen not as sentient beings but as a source of food and other commodities. It may be that animal history pinpoints conflicts between different cosmologies, one based on a Newtonian universe and human exceptionalism and the other reflective of a relational universe in which the hierarchical boundaries between humans and animals are broken down. This conflict between different cosmologies and the different attitudes toward humanity and animality and modes of behaviour which each promotes becomes especially evident in post-war agriculture in Wales and the animal history of industrial Wales which the following sections examine.

POST-WAR ANIMAL FARMING

Agricultural textbooks about post-Second World War farming have emphasised the change in animal husbandry from a local-national operation to one on a global-international scale.[33] But in Wales, the reorganisation of animal farming to what came to be seen as 'animal production' continued to occur mainly within a local-national framework (reflecting the Welsh historian David Williams's notion of a 'spirited partnership'[34]) retaining at least a modicum of localised farming and resisting the segmentation of larger, global agricultural industries.

However, the technological, economic and social changes in the second half of the twentieth century placed agricultural animals in a less domesticated industry in which farms, as Jenkins says, became economic units independent of their neighbours.[35] The lives of farm animals, as the nature of farms themselves, changed as a result of Whitehall policies and the 1957 Agriculture Act, a response to the escalating cost of agricultural support. As Moore-Colyer points out, it directed production grants and other forms of financial assistance to improvements in agricultural efficiency, specific enterprises and farm managerial capacity.[36]

David Williams maintains that animal associations and societies became 'channels through which the agricultural revolutions came in Wales'.[37] But the concentration of populations in large industrial belts put pressure on animal husbandry and the Welsh countryside through these associations to improve the quality of herds, breeding stock and the meat into which animal carcasses were to be turned. In the process, animals became simply that, a part of a process, and the gap between animals and the humans who used them widened. As in the case of the renowned Black Welsh Mountain Sheep, for example, farmers were encouraged to think of their breeds in terms of their prolificacy, their maternal characteristics, their capacity for rapid growth, and how easy they were to keep.[38]

Not surprisingly, then, a distinctive characteristic of modern farming has been the introduction of new technical discourses which disguise its impact on animal welfare. In a book that was more controversial than perhaps even he realised at the time, the Welsh farmer and journalist Roscoe Howells describes how initiatives by Welsh farmers included 'slatted floors' on which cows walked uncomfortably while their excrement and urine fell into a pit below, saving on the cost of floor covering; 'cubicles' around the side of a covered yard in which cows were only free to move to and from their silage; and the 'barley-beef' technique in which cattle were fed mainly on barley without the need for a 'store' period and sent to slaughter much earlier.[39] According to Nibert, assuming a global perspective, such changes in farming practice emphasised 'systematic factors' and not 'the agency of individual human and animal actors'.[40] These new systematic factors litter Howells's uncritical use, and promotion, of a business and economics discourse – for example 'managing', 'systems', 'problem solving', 'compositional quality', 'pool price', 'store cattle' and 'fat stock' – that denies agricultural animals their sentient being. Wholeheartedly embracing late-twentieth-century farming as a business in which animals are an economic resource, Howells's book depicts an anti-image to traditional farming.

However, the Wildlife and Countryside Act 1981 marked the beginnings of a turn from modern agricultural production toward, as Moore-Colyer says, 'a greener agenda embracing environmental protection and sustainable (if not organic) farming methods'.[41] This was greeted by the public as a reasonable response to 'the perceived environmental damage wrought by the intensification of the previous three decades'.[42] But an animal agricultural history of Wales might see this period as one in which the increased emphasis on animal welfare and rights was perceived negatively by the farming communities that felt they were under siege from 'the antics of the Animal Liberation Front, the hunt saboteurs and the campaigners against the transport of live animals'.[43]

The contemporary holistic approach to environmental standards, food supply and animal health and welfare, in which farming is only one element in maintaining the natural environment and supporting sustainable tourism, can be traced to the European Union Agri-Environmental Regulation (1992) and the Common Agricultural Policy (2003).[44] Within this new context, the farming industry is having to be more ecologically aware, more respondent to environmental change and more conscious of the opportunities and threats highlighted by reports such as *Farming, the Environment and the Welsh Uplands*.[45] It is now broadly accepted that the natural resources on which we depend (including soil, water and air) are poor and declining and that farming, especially unsustainable farming, is implicated in this. Biodiversity reports (such as 'State of Nature 2020' and 'State of Birds in Wales 2018') highlight alarming declines in the numbers of farmland wildlife species associated with the loss of mixed farming and the destruction of habitats and, in Wales, these include many upland species such as curlew, golden plover and black grouse. *Farming, the Environment and the Welsh Uplands* suggests that future grants should be deployed so as to encourage farming that is appropriate to the sustainable potential of the land including adjusting stocking levels and the restoration and maintenance of habitats.[46] Animal studies, engaging with the social and economic realities of farming, is interested in models of, for example, what sustainable stocking might look like and the report highlights some key areas that are central to the ecological themes of animal studies: agro-ecological practices based on the application of ecological processes to food production such as organic farming; the efficient production and marketing of nature-friendly products; developing payment for ecosystem services and schemes; and land serving activities such as woodland creation.[47]

Chapter 1 noted that the voice of protest and defiance in animal studies has its roots in the discipline of ecology as it emerged in the 1960s in which it was perceived as a subversive science that challenged many traditional assumptions and practices.[48] The importance of environmental reports which follow the focus in animal studies, environmental sciences and ecology on a wildlife perspective lies in their inclusion of the impact of farming on nature. This, in itself, is evidence not only of the way in which we are rethinking farming *per se* from a relational perspective but the thoughts behind different farming methods.

However, as far as some animal theorists are concerned, the fact that agro-ecological initiatives have not been actioned until now is a reflection of flaws in our education system generally. Waldau, for example, reflecting on the way in which a better balance, globally, between human and animal interests has been too slow coming, maintains: 'An examination of educational traditions regarding other-than-human animals attempted through the lens of Animal Studies can prompt the noteworthy conclusion that both formal, institutionalized education and informal education have often been far too narrow-minded.'[49] In contemporary animal studies generally, the narrow-mindedness, which Waldau identifies, is perceived as too ready a willingness to accept what is essentially an outmoded, non-relational view of the universe, based on now largely discredited assumptions, such as human exceptionalism, the divide between humans and animals and the separation of humans from nature. To Waldau's critique of how animals, animality and ecology are handled in educational curricula, we now must add from Kurki, in the wake of the relational revolution in the natural and social sciences, 'a radical rethinking of not only science but also of views on ourselves, history, and our processing in the world'.[50]

SLAUGHTERHOUSE HOLD

A lingering image in the countryside and in urban Wales of the views of ourselves and of animality that animal studies seeks to reset, of the thinking behind human exceptionalism and of the hierarchical divide between humans and animals is the slaughterhouse. Chapter 1 observed that animal studies compels us to address the dark and disturbing aspects of human–animal relations including how we have used animals, how they have contributed to the so-called development of human societies and how we have abused them.[51] From an animal perspective, Nibert has suggested that 'the "domestication" of highly social animals – which developed out of hunting them – was no partnership at all but, rather, a significant extension of systematic violence and exploitation.'[52] In addition to the secret countryside hidden by extensive vegetation and difficult to access because of a lack of accessible roads, there is another hidden countryside of factory farms and abattoirs. As Ryan says, this means that humans generally only encounter the 'stark reality of animal suffering and exploitation … once these animals have, for various reasons, been killed'.[53]

We have already seen that animal theorists broadly accept that animals have the right not to be killed and that we should develop food production that involves the least number of animals being slaughtered. In England and Wales, during a survey period 29 January 2018 to 4 February 2018, a total of 19,718,680 species were slaughtered including: 35,343 cattle, 1,245 calves, 244,305 sheep, 176,887 pigs, 18,012,455 broilers, 803,006 spent hens, 147,750 turkeys, 402 goats, and 67 horses.[54] And we have also seen that animal theorists generally accept that animals have the right not to suffer, so our farming methods should cause the least suffering to the least animals, including field animals. In the survey period, the majority of species were stunned before slaughter, including 99 per cent of cattle and 97 per cent of calves (mostly by captive bolt), 75 per cent of sheep (mainly by electric head stunning), 86 per cent of pigs (mainly by high concentration CO_2) and 70 per cent of broiler chickens (the majority gas stunned). However, 25 per cent of sheep and 10 per cent of broiler chickens were slaughtered by non-stun halal methods.[55] But all of this does not include the trauma which animals suffer in being herded, transported and having to wait to be stunned. And the journalist Jane Jones has noted that, in 2017, the animal rights charity Animal Aid issued a report alleging that illegal abuse was occurring in 93 per cent of slaughterhouses in the UK.[56]

In November 2021, the Welsh Government published its *Animal Welfare Plan for Wales* which is intended to introduce a country-wide model, including improving the professional training and qualifications of animal welfare inspectors, in order to improve, monitor and enforce animal standards. As Jane Jones maintains, one of its key aims is to require all abattoirs to have CCTV in order to prevent the mistreatment of animals and poor practices and standards.[57] The bill is not without controversy and some animal practitioners have warned, as Jones says, that it doesn't go far enough and are not convinced that CCTV will necessarily prevent animal abuse.[58] She points out that some animal protection groups have drawn attention to research which shows that surveillance does not always reduce the mistreatment of animals and that the charity Animal Aid, which has exposed animal cruelty at abattoirs with CCTV installed, is calling for footage to be monitored by an independent body.[59]

There are many unrestrained depictions of animal slaughter in contemporary literature and art across the world. But one notable Welsh poem that employs this level of vividness without compromising the subtly of its writing warrants more critical attention than it has received, Frances Williams's 'At the Butchers'. The title suggests that being at the butchers is as innocuous as being, say, at the grocer's shop, a clothes boutique, or a pharmacy. But this assumption is swiftly and graphically undermined:

>Meat hangs on hooks,
>Stiff and heavy amongst the smell of sawdust
>...   the carcase
>Hangs between animal and meat, is
>Neither, too living and too dead.[60]

The suspension of the animal between 'living being' and 'meat' is encapsulated in Williams's book in the drawing of a suspended pig's head on the opposite page to the poem. The pig's snout is pushed close to the viewer and the head, with its eyes closed as if in a moment of dream, is arranged in suspension between 'pork', as dead flesh, and a pig as a sentient being. Throughout the poem, the 'butchers' is suspended between a shop and an abattoir and between killing and the beauty of art and nature as if to bring forth conflicting dimensions of the human sensibility: the pig's veins are like a 'coat of lace about the body'; 'the snout is wrapped in a paper twist'; the butcher's apron is patterned 'with flowers of blood' and the trays are rows of bargain-price-labels 'like butterflies'.[61] These images distract from the realities of butchery, as the butcher's jovial whistling hides the nature of his daily routine. At the end of the poem: 'He glances at a severed head / And they gaze at each other / With a mutual blankness.'[62] In one regard, the most disturbing aspect of the poem is not the savagery but the 'blankness', implying a nothingness in the soul, and the abject sensibility needed to undertake this kind of work.

The dichotomies in the human sensibility between its capacities, on the one hand, to appreciate animals as sentient beings and to recognise symmetry and beauty and, on the other hand, to butcher and revel in slaughter pervades a diversity of cultural works including mid-century school textbooks. *Gwersi i'r Safonau*, for example, includes exercises based on a picture of a market in the rear of which carefully arranged pig carcasses hang at the butcher's stall in front of trays of indistinguishable cuts of meat to which the accompanying text draws attention: 'cygyddion yn dangos porc, cig eidion, a chig myharen' (butchers are displaying pork, ox meat and meatballs).[63] However, this textbook also reflects an evolving, more holistic approach to farming in the twentieth century evident in the way in which fruit and vegetables are presented in the foreground with the aplomb of the harvest festival and, unlike the meat on the butchery counters, are all clearly depicted. As Carol Adams points out, the impact of the First World War encouraged a diet of milk and vegetables along with bran, bread, barley, porridge, potatoes and greens and the interwar years became the 'Golden Era of Vegetarianism'.[64]

An illustration of a grocer's shop (in which three women are customers and three men serve) displays hanging carcasses, fowl and bacon joints against its back wall. But in the foreground, the shopfront's aesthetic arrangement of sausages, rashers of bacon and legs of pork extends into, but is offset by, loaves of bread, bananas, cheese and a large tray of apples, again suggesting how the people's diet between the wars tended toward grain, fruit and animal products other than meat. However, toward the rear of the shop, the multifaceted human sensibility (which came to the fore in the War) is epitomised by the female customer who, poised between the hanging bacon and fowls and a meat slicer, is associated with complicity in the slaughter of animals. But she is also complicit in the way in which animals are objectified, devalued and killed for other resources apart from food by the animal fur she is wearing around her neck.

In this respect, *Gwersi i'r Safonau* might be seen as based on a conception of humans and animals in a universe that is pre-relational. They are actors, as Milja Kurki says, within 'a world of discrete objects which move and inter-act against a background'.[65] This is true also of Cynan Jones's novel, *Everything I Found on the Beach* (2011).[66] As in Williams's 'At the Butchers' and *Gwersi i'r Safonau*, animals are devalued and objectified as meat or as providers of other animal-based products and the novel reflects a cosmology which enables slaughter and violence. Although, with the exception of the graphic depiction of the killing of rabbits, most of the descriptions of violence in the book is kept at a distance, human debasement and the killing of animals is seen as integral to the exploitation of one group of humans by another and to capitalism. Like Jones's fiction as a whole, *Everything I Found on the Beach* is a 'noir' novel concerned with the social periphery, the criminal underworld, illegal activity and low paid, arduous employment. The abattoir is analogous to the capitalist society of western and central Europe which is failing its citizens, including the two main protagonists whose livelihoods depend on the killing and use of animals for food. Grzegorz from Poland, who works in a slaughterhouse, receives undeclared income from fishing and Holden (Hold), who spends his days baiting prawn pots with scad and herring, is forced to accept cash-in-hand jobs to make ends meet, such as shooting rabbits for a restaurant.

The body of a drug dealer found on the beach with his fingers missing, the discovery of drugs after the killing of the rabbits and the numerous allusions to the slaughterhouse emphasise the interrelationship of violence and criminal activity in the novel's underworld. The animals waiting obediently in line at the abattoir to be stunned are analogous to Grzegorz and Hold sleepwalking into drug trafficking, oblivious of the consequences. Throughout the novel, apathy toward animal slaughter and butchery and the reliance upon them in the food chain are integrated with indifference toward the social and personal consequences of drug-taking. The failure of Grzegorz's compass when he is at sea trafficking drugs is an analogy to the way in which his adopted country has lost its moral compass, exemplified in the decrepit house in which he lives with 'Polish Out' scrawled on the brickwork.

Kurki points out: 'Not only do human communities engage in wars and subjugation of some humans to the benefit of others, but they also engage in destructive patterns of consumption and relentless restructuring of relations between humans and nonhumans.'[67] Many texts in which the human subjugation and the slaughter of animals is analogous to the subjugation and genocide of one racial or ethnic group by another anticipates the argument in contemporary animal studies for politics that, in Kurki's words, rethinks 'relations and relations beyond states, beyond societies, beyond things' and opens us up to 'possibilities of thinking anew cosmologically'.[68]

One of the most interesting contemporary poems to employ this kind of framework is the Welsh writer Emyr Humphreys's 'Bullocks'. The poem is based on a literal observation of cattle that are free to roam a European town before being rounded up and driven to pens for slaughter. At the heart of the poem is the realisation of the bullocks as sentient beings: they have a capacity to enjoy the countryside – 'Up to their knees in grass / Stuffing their large heads / Into honeysuckled hedges'[69] – but also to experience terror: 'driven / All nostrils wet with fear / Towards the iron pens.'[70] The phases of the farming cycle are seen from the animals' point of view: the enjoyment and obvious pleasure in pasture in the summer, the implicit confusion and bewilderment they experience on being driven to the iron pens and their fear when they reach the abattoir. As sentient beings, they have the rights, as discussed in Chapter 1, not to suffer and not to be killed.

But, this literal representation of animal life, and the way in which the abattoir hangs over their lives like the sword of Damocles, is in creative tension with the poem as a symbolic narrative. The cattle's fate is determined by 'State Security', suggesting totalitarian regimes and, especially, the Shoah: 'No rescue is possible / In final solutions.'[71] Their 'clownish faces'[72] resonate with the way in which Jews were represented in anti-Semitic Nazi propaganda. The innocence of the bullocks in the summer is analogous to the way in which some Jews in Germany sleepwalked through the years preceding the War: 'Sticky globes of innocence / Their rolling eyes / Can't read the rules.'[73] The advancing 'columns' driving the 'population' before them alludes to the invading German troops and the 'units for slaughter' suggest the Nazi death camps. The Canadian scholar Peter Kulchyski offers an analysis of contemporary farming that is particularly apposite to Humphreys's poem and provides further insight into it: 'Capitalist modernism has produced the industrial farm, a form of living animal in which a concentration-camp existence exposes the utter ethical rot at the core of contemporary life.'[74] As Humphreys stresses, again with the Shoah in mind: 'They inherit nothing, / Except the butcher's knife.'[75]

Kurki maintains that cosmological assumptions are important because they define 'not only our role, our status as "us" but also the kind of collaborations, ethical commitments, and political communities we build'.[76] This may be illustrated by two poems which take very different approaches to how our roles and status are influenced by our cosmological assumptions: Gillian Clarke's 'The Field Mouse' and Emyr Humphreys's 'Turkeys in Wales'. But they also engage with the kind of questions asked by Donna Haraway who, observing that 'the themes of race, sexuality, gender, nation, family, and class have been written into the body of nature', asks: 'How do material and symbolic threads interweave in the fabric of late twentieth-century nature for industrial people?'[77] 'The Field Mouse' juxtaposes a cosmology evidenced in the war that raged in Bosnia in the 1990s in which 8,000 Muslim men and boys were murdered in Srebrenica.[78] This stands in contradistinction to the cosmology represented by the child in the poem who rescues an injured field mouse and which emblematises living things bound together in harmony and peace: 'the children kneel in long grass / staring at what we have crushed'.[79] But there is an irony in *Root Home* from which this poem and Clarke's commentary are taken which shows how hard it is to separate out and hold on to a relational cosmology given the conflict and killing at the heart of nature. In Clarke's mind, grey squirrels are demonised within a negative cultural taxonomy not unlike the Muslims in Bosnia: 'Every morning from the bathroom window I note with horror tree rats – grey squirrels – scuttling ... I wish them gone. They are alien beasts, the enemies of young trees and nesting birds.'[80]

Humphreys's 'Turkeys in Wales', ostensibly concerned with the supply of poultry to County Council establishments, does not pretend to be other than an analogy which undermines the specific nature of the poem's subject matter and its humour. Written with the First and Second World Wars in mind, the selection of birds for slaughter is analogous to military conscription which is thereby deconstructed and scrutinised in a way characteristic of pacifist writing with which Humphreys, as a conscientious objector in the Second World War, was all too familiar. People with influence are able to delay or avoid their conscription:

> Their cold combs
> Are colourless and flaccid
> Their long necks
> Shredded with age.[81]

But the young conscripts, 'comrades in fresh feathers', without influence, age or recognition, are 'snatched / And sacrificed'.[82] The older, strutting birds are also analogous to the elderly, decorated officers, especially in the First World War, who distanced themselves from the fighting:

> Their feet are decorated
> Like their feathers
> With fading orders
> And birthday honours.[83]

In using animals in an analogous relationship to human militarism, Humphreys draws on traditional human–animal power structures in order to undermine human exceptionalism. His poem 'Dream for a Soldier' is an argument for humans to step outside the exceptionalist tradition which has given them a god-like status over nature, animals and other humans exemplified by the cock pheasant which the soldier watches in his dream 'march like a guardsman through the tall bluebells'.[84] The poem is not simply a critique of the way in which humans construct analogies of birds to support their own sense of self-importance but the dialectic that exists between different analogies which as cultural constructions have little to do with the birds themselves. The soldier's projection of the grandeur of the military onto the pheasant is contrasted with the cultural significance of another bird: 'We shall be unarmed and harmless as doves.'[85] The way in which humans, within cultural taxonomies of particular animals, assert their authority, and priority, over other animal species is encapsulated in a further image from the soldier's dream which Humphreys himself may have seen on one of his rural walks: 'the fence adorned / With a carrion crow and the pinned out pelt of a weasel.'[86]

The way in which the meat industry exemplifies human exceptionalism and runs contrary to the concept of a relational universe has become one of the key themes in animal studies. But a plethora of arguments has emerged for an end to meat production, based on numerous ecological and human health care factors. Thus, consideration of what would happen if animal farming were to disappear has become a subject of debate both within and outside academia. Alasdair Cochrane contributes to the controversy by comparing the animal lives saved if animals were no longer farmed to provide humans with food with the loss of field animals through the preparation of fields for arable farming and the mechanised harvesting of crops.[87] Pursuing an interests-based approach, Cochrane suggests that field animals might be said to have fewer rights than animals such as cattle, sheep and pigs in which human communities have a larger investment.[88] But as opposed to the duality of animal and arable agriculture, he treads a third way, suggesting that humans have an obligation to end farm practices that cause animal suffering and to practise agricultural methods, whether in animal or arable farming, that cause the fewest animal deaths.[89]

However, Cochrane's nuanced arguments concerning the end of animal farming are very different from the stark controversies around meat-eating when this subject first acquired significant attention in the Victorian and Edwardian press. Many of the contentious issues involving animal farming are not as contemporary as we might think, as will be discussed in the next section before I turn to another controversial topic.

VEGETARIANISM AND VICTORIAN WALES

In 2017, the Vegan Society suggested that 3.25 per cent of the UK population were vegetarians, although the National Farmers' Union (NFU) counter claimed, apparently without recognising the boundaries between them, that only 1 per cent were vegans.[90] Links between animal farming and climate change apart, arguments against the meat industry in the twentieth and twenty-first centuries based on the cruelty which is inflicted on animals and on health reasons can be traced to the Victorian and Edwardian periods when they provoked considerable controversy in the local Welsh press. The increasing interest of the press in vegetarianism during this period not only publicised some of the debates concerning the pros and cons of eating meat but helped open up new perspectives on animal history, opportunities for better appreciating animals as fellow living beings and the possibility of more meaningful relationships between animals and humans.

However, press interest in history from an animal perspective did not emerge at once. Vegetarian and 'food reform' societies in the 1880s were more closely concerned with human health than animal welfare issues and the implications for animal history remained implicit. In 1884, *The Western Mail* reported briefly that a meeting of vegetarians at Merthyr maintained that, for health reasons, 'much less meat should be consumed'.[91] A much longer article on vegetarianism at the Health Exhibition in the same year, in the *Flintshire Observer Mining Journal and General Advertiser*, centred on the argument, current among vegetarians and food reformers at the time, that humans were really 'a fruit-eating animal'.[92] Although the article interestingly accepts that humans are animals, it refrains from pursuing arguments against meat-eating *per se*. It emphasises the potential drawbacks in humans giving up eating animals, and focuses on the science and the careful selection of vegetables that was deemed necessary to ensure that humans did not lose what it calls 'the transforming power of the animal',[93] referring to the benefits of animal protein for muscle mass, strength, bone density and body health. By the turn of the nineteenth century, the middle and upper classes enjoyed expensive home-produced meat while imports made possible by refrigerated steamships enabled the working classes their weekly roast.[94] The idea that meat-eating has a 'transforming' power for humans became very important in ensuring that men, especially those from undernourished poorer classes, were fit enough to enlist for war – the Boer War (1899–1902) and the First World War (1914–18).[95] With the outbreak of the First World War, supplies of meat were deemed essential to sustain soldiers in the trenches and there many working-class men ate more meat than at home. One vegetarian officer, who survived without using his rations, calculated that he had avoided consuming 'at least half-a-ton of meat that was due to me in rations, and at least a hundred and fifty pounds of bacon missed turning my stomach into a pig cemetery'.[96]

While meat-eating was generally seen as essential for sustained, manual work, the local Welsh press increasingly reported the vegetarian argument that abstaining from meat was beneficial to human health which in turn looked to disassociating human dietary needs from future animal history. An article in the *South Wales Echo* (September 1898) purported to have evidence that during the south Wales coal strike, colliers were forced to eat more vegetables and less meat and, as a result, illness and the death rate among them 'diminished to a significant extent'.[97] The following month, the *South Wales Daily News* published correspondence arguing for a vegetarian hotel in Cardiff along the lines of one already established in Birmingham.[98] The *Evening Express* (November 1903) reported that a meeting of vegetarians at the Friends' Meeting House in Cardiff, attended by a guest speaker from Manchester, debated whether vegetarianism led to a reduction in drunkenness among the lower classes that was in turn linked to 'ill-feeding'.[99] But later in the Edwardian decade, the *Prestatyn Weekly* (February 1908) offered a more profound interpretation of the benefits of abstaining from 'flesh-eating', suggesting that it 'undoubtedly affects character'.[100] Drawing on arguments from the Bible against 'the eating of blood', the article anticipates late-twentieth-century thinking about a relational cosmology in suggesting that this abstinence was essential to the dawning of a new 'Golden Age' in which 'man, animals, plants, the whole creation' would be interconnected.[101]

The argument that meat-eating affects character drew on a wider enthusiasm from the late Victorian period for psychology which, as discussed in Chapter 3, generated interest in the emotional and cognitive capacities of animals, especially in connection to their capacity to experience suffering and pain. The rearing, slaughtering and butchering of animals for food has long been linked to the instinct for war and violence, as we have seen, but never as dramatically as by the late-nineteenth-century vegetarian movement. Anna Kingsford, discussing the Women's Peace Conventions, bemoaned: 'These poor deluded creatures cannot see that universal peace is absolutely impossible to a carnivorous race.'[102] Commenting on a lecture on war and meat-eating given to the Fabian Society, shortly after the outbreak of the First World War, the pacifist editor of the *Woman's Journal*, Agnes Ryan, observed: 'Here was a new spiritual force at work in the universe … She clearly stressed the idea that wars will never be overcome until the belief that it is justifiable to take life, to kill – *when expedient* – is eradicated from human consciousness.'[103]

The twenty-first century Vegan Society, with an emphasis on dairy products rather than meat-eating, emphasises the stress they cause to animals.[104] It is an argument which was first mooted in the Victorian press in the wake of increased interest in the suffering of working and agricultural animals (discussed in Chapter 3) and the emergence of stronger pro-vegetarian and food reform societies. Then a shift in emphasis from the benefits that humans derived from a meat-free diet to the consequent improvements in animal welfare produced a backlash which only underlined how far some correspondents were removed from the real lives of agricultural animals. In a report on a meeting in London of what it called, somewhat sardonically, 'flesh eschewers', *The Aberdare Times* (May 1888) found many of the resolutions unconvincing. It noted, with scepticism, how 'science, in the persons of the most distinguished medical professors, had a habit of strongly recommending mutton chops' and how some of those who attended argued incredulously that 'the lives of these animals are probably pleasant to them, seeing that in order to keep them healthy they are well fed and cared for, their deaths are painless, and it is by no means evident that their existence would be more enjoyable if they were left to die of lingering old age.'[105] This kind of incredulity was countered forcefully by those with knowledge of animal abuse. In covering a locally delivered lecture by G. C. Wade (Provincial Secretary for Wales, Vegetarian Federal Union), *The Carmarthen Weekly Reporter* (October 1899) highlighted his support for 'the cause of the animals, dwelling on the cruelty of the cattle-ships, the driving of animals to slaughter, the horrible method of killing calves, the destruction of beautiful birds for the sake of their feathers ...'[106]

A full history of vegetarianism and animal history in Wales has yet to be published. However, it is clear that the extent to which vegetarianism has adopted an animal-centred or human-focused agenda has varied. This undoubtedly exacerbated the way in which vegetarianism has been misunderstood, sometimes deliberately so. In their counter argument to the claim of the Vegan Society in 2017 that dairy products caused stress to animals in the farming industry, the NFU might be accused of side-stepping the real issue in maintaining that the problem was that farmers did look after the animals and did produce food in a healthy manner but that this had not been publicised effectively.[107] It left Samantha Calvert able to argue on behalf of the Vegan Society that it is 'not possible to take animal products without suffering' and to point out that 'male calves get slaughtered because they have no purpose within the dairy industry' and that 'cows are distressed by the removal of their calves'.[108]

Although, as Colin Spencer points out, vegetarianism in the last quarter of the Victorian era and through the Edwardian period remained a solidly middle-class movement,[109] debates around vegetarianism and food contributed to an increased awareness of animal welfare and helped open up a realistic understanding of animal history. Images of humans and horses from the First World War trenches, and subsequent battle fields, served to develop this consciousness as did the catastrophic images unleashed in the late twentieth- and early twenty-first centuries of large-scale disasters that have become embedded in Welsh culture, and in the farming industry more generally, to which I now turn through the work of Gillian Clarke.

PYRES ON THE DOORSTEP

At the time this book was written, the Minister of Rural Affairs declared an all-Wales Avian Influenza Prevention Zone (3 November 2021) after bird flu, caused by viruses that have adapted to birds, had been confirmed in poultry and wild birds in north Wales. Avian influenza is one of the most frequently occurring diseases among farming and wildlife, which dates to the last quarter of the Victorian era when it was known as fowl plague. Losses from sporadic but contained outbreaks in the second half of the twentieth century were minimal, but since the 1990s, the high density of poultry farming has led to outbreaks that have taken the lives of millions of birds.

It is impossible not to discuss animal history in (but not exclusively) Wales without remembering the mass slaughter of agricultural animals which was brought about by industrial and natural catastrophes to which humans, reluctant to cease anti-environmental practices, contributed directly or indirectly. These disasters include not only outbreaks of avian influenza but more cataclysmic events such as the Chernobyl tragedy of 1986, over which the nuclear power station, like the slaughterhouse, might be seen – as by many environmentalists – as a menacingly haunting symbol of human exceptionalism, and the outbreak of Bovine Spongiform Encephalopathy (BSE), ten years later, which led to the prohibition of beef exports to Europe for a two-year period.[110] But, even more so, the Welsh countryside, like other rural areas, is still haunted by the mass slaughter at the beginning of the new millennium brought about by foot and mouth disease, a highly infectious, notifiable viral infection that can be spread by contact with infected animals, contaminated farming equipment, clothing, feed and wildlife and requires extensive vaccination, trade restrictions, quarantines and the culling of both infected and uninfected animals. In 2001, there were 2,000 confirmed cases of foot and mouth disease in the UK, wiping out generations of cattle and sheep breeding.[111] In Wales, one million animals were slaughtered (between 6.5 and 10 million in the UK) with the army being drafted in to help and, for every confirmed case, surrounding farms and communities were forced to cull their own animals[112] and many farms and rural businesses were ruined: 'Clouds of thick black smoke from blazing animal pyres and the pungent smell of disinfectant became part and parcel of everyday life across large swathes of the Welsh countryside.'[113] The final case was confirmed in Wales at Crickhowell, Powys, in August 2001 but it was not until January 2002 that Wales was declared free of foot and mouth.

The 2001 crisis gave rise to an especially haunting poem sequence, Gillian Clarke's 'Making the Beds for the Dead', in which the mass slaughter of farm animals to curb the outbreak emerges as a disturbingly perverse, inverse image of a relational universe. In the sequence, anti-images divide and multiply over and over again like the foot and mouth virus itself: 'its arithmetic heart / bent on sub-division, multiplication.'[114] Invoking an insect as 'the double mirror of itself',[115] the image turns out to be integral to the overall structure of the sequence. The legitimate, regulated business of Welsh animal farming is inverted in the double reflection of, for example, 'meat dealers banking the profits' and places 'where they don't fill in forms / to take a sheep to market'.[116]

The foot and mouth virus renders the countryside with its plague-ridden farms as an apocalyptic image – 'the lorries and the fires, the hooded men, the smell'[117] – and throughout the sequence is suggestive of the Shoah. Government vets and others associated with the mass killing are conceived as outsiders and reminiscent of the agents of National Socialism in Germany in the 1930s and 1940s: 'the ministry men', 'strangers dressed to kill', 'a man in a field with a rifle', and 'strangers at [the farm] gates'.[118] From their perspective, the farmers who refuse to cooperate are a negative, obstinate presence:

> A decent man, the farmer loves his beasts,
> refuses to call home the suckling sows,
> refuses to lure the easy creatures
> with the voice they know, buckets of meal.[119]

The refusal to cooperate resonates with the long tradition of rural Wales as a site of dissent and the 'ministry men / dressed to kill' which the farmer 'faces out' resonate with others (such as soldiers and police officers) whom protesters in Wales have had to confront, for example, over agrarian disputes, war, the status of the Welsh language and the closure of mines. The killing and burning of corpses carried out by, or under the supervision of, strangers is contrary to the normality of the countryside developed around a network of people who know, and maybe have grown up with, each other. At one level, an important part of this normality is the care that the farmers have for their animals as sentient beings: 'In the yard Dai Esger quiets / each one with voice and hand, / before the gun.'[120] But, at another level, the mass slaughter draws attention to the killing around which all animal farming is based.

The slaughter of animals for food and other commodities, and the licence which this end result sometimes gives to their use and abuse, is one of the disturbing aspects of animal history which, like the presence of the slaughterhouse itself, as some animal theorists have suggested, is kept somewhat secretive and almost hidden. Like hunting and animal rights, it is inevitably one of the most controversial areas of animal studies, often ridden with ambivalence and contradiction, but, as we have seen, it is also one to which animal theorists, such as Cochrane, are taking increasingly nuanced approaches. The slaughter of animals brought about by industrial and natural disasters and the culpability of humans, directly or indirectly, present us with inverse images of a relational universe. They disturb us as cataclysmic reminders of the inevitable consequences of human exceptionalism, myopia and refusing to reject non-relational worldviews. But, like the way in which the slaughter, as depicted in Clarke's poem sequence, is handled and how some act to turn the impact on animals to their own advantage, they remind us how entrenched is non-relational thinking and attitudes toward animals. Thus, one of the most disturbing aspects of animal history is the extent to which the recurrence of exclusivist speciesism, in which animals are regarded as commodities, and the replication of capitalist structures across rural towns and industrial centres are entangled

ANIMALS AND THE INDUSTRIAL COMMUNITIES

Given the geography of Wales and the extent of its rural hinterland, farming and agriculture will inevitably have pride of place in the animal history of the country. But horses played an important part in the development of industrial Wales and of the towns, some later cities, and the industrial belts through their involvement in drawing cabs, in haulage and in work above and underground in the mines and quarries. According to the RSPCA, in 1878 there were about 200,000 horses and ponies at work in British mines, although, due to the mechanisation of the coal industry, by 1913 this figure had decreased to 70,000.[121] Due to the particular geology of the Welsh coalfield, in which the coal was relatively easy to cut and often fell out in large blocks that required transport vehicles with a capacity of one or two tonnes, Ceri Thompson points out that most of the animals used in Welsh collieries, unlike others in the UK, were horses rather than ponies.[122] Many histories of collieries in the UK have inevitably focused on disasters in the industry from a human-centric perspective. Rosemary Preece, for example, acknowledges: 'Not the day to day attrition which left a family fatherless, a young widow struggling to make ends meet, or a mother losing sons, but the major explosions and inundations which led to much heroism and communal public guilt.'[123] The history of the coal industry from the perspective of animals has not always received the attention that it deserves and does not reflect the interest in them showed by the Victorian and Edwardian press (discussed in Chapter 3). It is one of the animal histories which particularly makes uncomfortable reading in revealing the suffering that animals endured to meet human needs.

Arguments have been made that in some circumstances pit horses and ponies were treated with kindness and a modicum of understanding but usually in histories which are more human than animal focused. Illustrating her text with photographs from the National Coal Board of underground stables showing 'clearly the effects of good management in well-built stalls and whitewashed walls', Preece maintains: 'Pit ponies are remembered both with affection and annoyance by those who had to work with them, their personalities and temperament being as varied as those of their drivers.'[124] She does not question that the photographs are from the National Coal Board, does not pursue the ambivalence of the attitudes toward the horses – 'affection and annoyance' – and blames the animal's temperament for their behaviour, failing to recognise that they suffer both physical and psychological captivity and are deprived of opportunities to live according to their natural traits and characteristics.

Coal owners and managers defended the use of horses as essential to mining before mechanised haulage. But animal groups and others (such as the Pit Ponies Protection Society), as Thompson – writing from the animals' perspective – maintains, saw the use of horses underground as inhumane. The RSPCA published numerous pamphlets including one entitled 'The Sufferings of Pit Ponies', with a picture of a horse bearing its injuries from the mines, and another, in 1933, 'Pit Ponies and Colliery Horses: The Facts'. The former declared: 'Remember horses are kept for years in tomblike darkness underground that you may have comfort.'[125] As Thompson says, horses selected for underground work had a life expectancy of only eight or nine years and around 7 per cent were killed in accidents.[126] However, while industrial history has tended to focus on the working conditions of the miners – in 1938 colliers were granted a week's annual leave which was increased in 1948 to two weeks – the changing conditions of colliery horses, in which they were granted that time above ground, has been often overlooked.

Reports of the effects of the holiday on colliery horses anticipate the emphasis in contemporary animal studies on the concept of 'captivity' as a psychological as much as a physical confinement, reminding us (as noted in Chapter 1) that to thrive or flourish animals have to be free to express the natural characteristics of their species. As one account from the 1960s remembers: 'When they got out on top they were put into horse boxes and taken to the lakes in Cwmtillery where they were released into the fields. Then they knew they were free – running, kicking and jumping – just like excited kids on holiday!'[127] Thompson's commentary on this account also anticipates the concept of 'entangled empathy' in contemporary animal studies, discussed in Chapter 1, which requires us as humans to be attentive to both similarities and differences between ourselves and our own situation and that of the fellow creature with whom we are empathising. While Thompson compares the released horses with children on holiday, he does not forget the characteristics and traits of horses as a herd animal: 'The horses' first instinct was to establish a pecking order among the new "herd". In some collieries the horses' shoes were removed before bringing them to the surface, to prevent injuries if a fight broke out.'[128] This detail is emblematic of an approach to animal rights – that we have an obligation to protect animals from harm – while the account of the horses' behaviour suggests another of the demands in contemporary animal studies, that we have an obligation not simply to protect animals from harm but to ensure that they have the opportunity to achieve the best subjective life given their species. Reports of cruelty to pit horses and ponies in the Victorian and Edwardian press, and the changing perspectives on animal suffering reflected in them, are discussed in detail in Chapter 3. But an important aspect of animal history in industrial communities which is often overlooked is their involvement in human recreation and community identity. Colliery horses were shown at local horticultural and agricultural shows, as well as at national events such as the Royal Show, competing with each other for 'champion horse'. For many people, this was their only brief encounter with a colliery horse or pit pony. As Chapter 1 pointed out, in contemporary animal studies the location in which we encounter animals is deemed important. In this context, the public encountered horses which, as Thompson demonstrates, were often little more than advertisements for particular collieries.[129] But we have already seen that contemporary animal theorists stress what is important in such encounters is the impact on how the human and animal relationship is perceived. Thompson suggests that only a minority would have recognised that show horses lived an untypical and privileged life – kept on light duties to preserve their appearance – and were intended to mislead the public over the quality of life of those horses which did work underground.[130]

It goes without saying that the employment of pit horses and ponies exemplifies entrenched non-relational thinking and attitudes toward animals. However, not all animals in relationships with humans in the industrial belts were robbed of opportunities to live according to their natural traits. In the late nineteenth century and in the first half of the twentieth century, keeping and flying pigeons was a widespread hobby in working-class, especially mining, communities. In south Wales, brightly coloured pigeon lofts, each capable of housing up to thirty birds, lit up the landscape, but what characterised pigeon keeping was the relationship between the keeper and their birds which has largely been ignored.

Pigeon keeping has generally been perceived as a male enclave, offering men an escape from the domesticity of the house and a sense of dignity and purpose which their work denied them. But, as the social historian Martin Johnes points out, the hobby, like working-class masculinity itself, was more complicated than that.[131] Johnes's paper provides insights into the relationship between birds and humans (examined in Chapter 6) and into animal theory's perspectives on captivity, care, dominance and affection (introduced in Chapter 1 and discussed in more detail in Chapter 7). Short-distance racing was popular among pigeon keepers but the birds had to be treated gently and cared for if they were to return to the loft.[132] In this sense, the relationship between the pigeon fancier and his bird overturned some of the stereotypical divides between 'femininity' and 'masculinity'. As Johnes points out, there was considerable affection between pigeon fanciers, as they became known, and their birds whose emotions, behaviours and weaknesses they came to know well. A bird's return depended on a mutual bond with its owner as much as the provision of a comfortable loft and food. From the perspective of contemporary animal theory, the birds were recognised as sentient beings but also, unlike colliery horses, were given opportunities to flourish and thrive according to their natural traits and characteristics. Moreover, the male fancier's emotional investment in his birds, according to Johnes, helped him develop a tenderness which positively shaped his relationships at home, offset the physical demands of work and brought the family together.[133]

In working-class culture, the pigeon became a symbol of the knowledge and devotion of the trainer, the emotional life of which working or unemployed men were capable and the spirituality which they craved in their lives and which the chapel and nonconformist literature worked to provide. In Menna Elfyn's 'Colomennod Cwm' (Pigeons in Ebbw Vale), the pigeons are a symbol of a close, chapel-based community:

> Sawl colomen ehedodd o'r dalar i'r nos
> a tharo pell lannerch gyda'r sôn dan ei phig
> am segurdod y lofa a'r gymuned glòs?[134]
>
> How many have flown into the night from this acre,
> striking a distant valley with a message –
> the silence of the mine and its close people.[135]

Not only pigeon keeping, but sport involving animals in industrial Wales, especially horse and dog racing, helped bound communities, classes and genders together in the late nineteenth and early twentieth centuries. The racecourse at Ely, in Cardiff, opened in 1855 and when the first Welsh Grand National was held there in 1895, watched by a crowd of 40,000, the racecourse acquired a significant role in binding not only communities but a nation together. However, in the first half of the twentieth century, attendance began to decline, while that at greyhound racing, which had stronger local origins and was more important to community identity in many respects, increased. A century later, the tables have turned. There is one independent greyhound track, with a race meeting once a week, although there are plans for it to become a Greyhound Board of Great Britain track, racing four times a week. There are now three well-known racecourses in Wales: Bangor-on-Dee, which held its first steeplechase meeting in 1859, hosts about fourteen jump racing fixtures each year; the Chepstow racecourse, at the other end of the country, where the first meeting was held in 1926 and which now hosts the annual Welsh Grand National; and, more recently, in the west of Wales, Ffos Las Racecourse, Kidwelly, opened in 2009 on the former site of Europe's largest opencast coal mine.

The greyhound has a long ancestry as a hunting dog which can be traced to Egypt, Greece and Rome. By the Middle Ages, it was highly prized by the nobility as a hunter and, in Wales, its value in coursing was acknowledged in the tenth century by the laws of Hywel Dda which made killing a greyhound a crime punishable by death. Throughout nineteenth-century industrial Wales, there were coursing clubs that arranged meetings open to its members whose dogs might participate in a number of stakes which were reported in the press (for example, at the Sully Coursing Meeting, the Cog Stakes for all-aged greyhounds and the Hayes Stakes for puppies[136]). More open coursing events, such as Greyhound and Terrier Coursing at Merthyr, extended the invitation to breeds of dogs that had established a reputation in other blood sports, and in doing so suggested the cruelty and the commodification of breed involved in coursing which the Welsh local press as community papers seemed satisfied to condone.[137] Privately arranged coursing matches between dogs were a feature of industrial community life and of such local interest that they were sometimes covered in the press, as in a match at Pontnewynydd which carried a bet of £5.00 a side. Assuming that the participants were known locally, and implying that dog coursing and the associated rivalry was a masculine activity, the press reported that the match 'took place in a field at Pontnewynydd, on Monday, between Mr Thos. Edmunds's dog and Mr Henry Tutton's bitch, resulting in an easy victory for Mr Edmunds's dog'.[138]

However, in both industrial and rural communities in the nineteenth century, coursing with dogs, especially greyhounds, was pursued alongside other recreational activities including badger baiting and dog fighting. The cruelty of these activities, in addition to the horrific deaths of the hunted animal and of injuries inflicted on the dogs that were forced to fight each other, lay also in the way in which the dogs were trained – coursing dogs were given the taste for blood in tearing small animals apart. Such pursuits commodified dogs – the traits and characteristics of competing, especially successful, animals were applauded by participants – and borrowed from agricultural shows the importance of breed, a concept which was itself influenced by commercialisation, class, the rise of leisure, the Victorian penchant for classification based on evolutionary thinking, gender attitudes and human exceptionalism. From the second half of the Victorian period, greyhounds from industrial communities were entered in local agricultural shows, underscoring the porous nature of the boundary between industrial and rural Wales, and the results announced in the press.[139] The early Victorian dog shows were very different from later events and part of lower-class entertainment culture of the 'Fancy' that reflected the way in which blood sports, involving sport and gambling, was based on classifying dogs in terms of a taxonomy and hierarchy and even, like human freak shows, included exhibitions of the spectacular and grotesque. The dog shows that became popular in the later Victorian period were influenced by the founding of The Kennel Club in 1873 (The Welsh Kennel Club was established in 1896 with Edward, Prince of Wales, as President), which also operated the national register of pedigree dogs and 'aestheticised' the physical characteristics of different breeds by which they were subsequently defined.

Modern greyhound racing in Wales, as in the UK generally, developed from and supplanted dog coursing which involved hounds that caught their prey by speed and sight rather than by scent. Welsh press coverage of a sale of greyhounds in the mid-1880s suggests the importance of speed to coursing while implicitly pointing to a sport in the future focused on the race between dogs rather than a kill at the end: 'As they were a racing looking lot capital prices were obtained.'[140] In west Wales, the distinction between coursing and sporting dogs became a legal controversy by the end of the nineteenth century. A case at Carmarthen Police-court, involving an unmuzzled greyhound at a railway station, had to be adjourned for a fortnight while the magistrates considered the defence that the greyhound was a sporting rather than hunting dog and was exempt.[141] However, it was not until 1928 that organised greyhound racing in large arenas was introduced into Wales at the City Stadium in Cardiff (it was introduced into England two years earlier from America, where the first greyhound race was held in 1912). It was popular in the period before the Second World War and in the two decades following it, providing not only release from day-to-day hardship for the working class – offering bright lights, an exciting night out and plentiful betting opportunities – but, as Daryl Leeworthy points out, a commercial novelty which brought new investment vital to economic recovery.[142] In 1934, the sport became even more profitable and popular with the passing of the Betting and Lotteries Act, which allowed stadiums and racecourses to operate their own totalisators, and made oncourse betting legal for the first time. The boom picked up after the war and lasted into the 1960s when live coverage of horse racing and high street bookmakers seduced the public away from dog racing and many tracks closed.

One of the most impressive stories by a Welsh writer concerned with dominance and affection in greyhound racing, and the way in which they are regarded by the betting community, is discussed in Chapter 7. It resonates with the contemporary focus in animal studies on the welfare of the dogs which tells a very different kind of story from pigeon keeping, including the extent to which they are subjected to deliberate or indifferent cruelty, held in captivity and are prevented from achieving a flourishing life. Allegations made in a report by The League Against Cruel Sports in 2014 alleges that racing greyhounds spent 95 per cent of their time in small, barren kennels without social contact; others were housed in pairs but kept constantly muzzled; many did not receive basic health care; and industry sanctions against those who mistreated dogs were feeble and ineffectual.[143] A survey of greyhounds and lurchers entering local authority pounds in Wales found that in a one-year period, 140 abandoned greyhounds were collected by local authorities (2,800 in Britain) and that, a major animal welfare problem exists.[144] As evidence of how looking at the role of animals in sport from their perspective is changing human–animal relations, at the time of writing, a petition fronted by Hope Rescue, Pontyclun, to ban greyhound racing in Wales has over 21,000 signatures and the support of three members of the Senedd.[145]

Through its focus on animal histories, literary texts and other cultural and educational artefacts, this chapter has sought to revise the way in which rural and industrial Wales have been perceived. In summary, the development of animal farming in scattered farmsteads throughout the large rural hinterland; the diverse use of animals in urban and semi-urban areas and in the industrial belts during the time of heavy industry; and the ways in which some areas have remained remote and secret enough to provide habitats for wild, and sometimes rarely encountered, animals and birds are not unique to Wales. But they are characteristic of it. The mistreatment of racing dogs – by the twenty-first century, it has become a major animal welfare problem – and the cruel abuse of colliery horses working underground (discussed in Chapter 3) make an uncomfortable contrast to the care bestowed by racing pigeon hobbyists on their birds. As does the difference between the way in which farm animals have been bred for slaughter and/or abused by mechanised farming and the greater respect which they have been shown in agri-ecological farming methods. The varied experiences of animals and birds betray different attitudes toward animality, themselves associated with the impact of particular conceptions of the world in which we live, which will be pursued in the course of this book. An article in the American *Atlantic Monthly* (2015)[146] demonstrates the way in which conceptions of animals as objects in a hierarchical universe conceived by human exceptionalism currently exists alongside alternative viewpoints, focused, as Marc Bekoff and Jessica Pierce describe, on 'championing the peaceful coexistence and harmony of animals and people'.[147] Moreover, in placing animal history in its numerous, diverse and changing contexts, Bekoff and Pierce remind us of what Steven Johnson has described as 'the adjacent possible': 'The past and present prepare us for any number of futures ... The strange and beautiful truth about the adjacent possible is that the boundaries grow as you explore them.'[148]

It is appropriate to conclude this chapter with the work of Bekoff and Pierce because, while animal history can rightly shame us, it also provides examples of positive relationships between animals and humans of which they speak. How far the 'adjacent possible' in relationships between animals and humans was explored and promoted by the Victorian and Edwardian Welsh press is the subject of the next chapter

3

EMERGING ANIMALITIES IN THE VICTORIAN AND EDWARDIAN WELSH PRESS

Stories in the Victorian and Edwardian press constitute the beginnings, however small, of history from an animal's perspective. But, as Paul Waldau has cautioned of animal history,[1] while the press reported testimonies to our humanity, it also published graphic representations of cruelty. Not simply appeasing the sadistic fantasies which the popular press had nurtured since the 1850s, this coverage was often intended to address the ills of human exceptionalism which the nineteenth century had begun to recognise, to reinforce human obligations toward animals and to expose the shame which animal supporters and protection societies maintained that animal abuse brought on the nation. In the Victorian and Welsh press, we are forced to confront the extent to which our culture, our language and our thoughts have become distanced, as Ryan says, from animals and from our own animality.[2]

Chapter 1 observed that in the first wave of the development of animal rights in the nineteenth century, traditional legal ideas and the legal system itself were employed to reduce harm to animals and curtail practices which were deemed incompatible with the expansion of capitalism and a commercially sophisticated society. But in nineteenth- and early-twentieth-century Wales, nonconformity influenced the way in which animal rights were configured through its concept of a higher culture in which Christians sought to establish themselves as superior to animals. This argument for human exceptionalism had a particular resonance for Welsh-language society after 'Brad y Llyfrau

Gleision' (The Treachery of the Blue Books) in 1847. In their allegations of immorality and poor education, they suggested that the Welsh people did not have a sufficiently refined culture to transcend what the more austere side of nonconformity perceived as negative traits shared by animals and humans.

The Welsh press used cases of animal cruelty to draw attention to wider anxieties about the nature of humanity, animality, social stability and the breakdown of conventional social boundaries. For example, the *South Wales Daily News* (December 1891) reported a litigation in the County Court, Cardiff, over the invasion of a private garden by sheep. In the story, they are described as 'powerful animals', 'strange' and 'unfamiliar', overturning the way in which they have been depicted in the Judaeo-Christian tradition as passive and compliant.[3] They signify a threat to the garden as a symbol of order where the classification of plants for retention or for disposal as 'weeds' is analogous to the selection of animals for breeding stock or for fattening and slaughter by farmers and shepherds. Moreover, the way in which the sheep are described by the plaintiff echoes the way in which certain animals in Wales at this time were categorised as undesirably 'wild' or 'forbidden', words which resonate with the way in which the 'oppressive and fearsome side' of nonconformity, as M. Wynn Thomas describes it,[4] conceived of animality.

One of the most controversial cases in this respect was reported in the *Weekly Mail* (August 1907), concerning a proposal from the Welsh Pony and Cob Society to the Board of Agriculture that the fields of Radnorshire were threatened by 'undesirable stallions and other such male commonable animals'.[5] While in animal husbandry it might be deemed necessary to cull animals to protect a herd, other species or the balance of the environment, it will always be perceived as controversial because of the subjective decision making involved. In this case, the Society's report begs questions about the criteria whereby some animals are rendered 'desirable' and others 'undesirable'. In labelling stallions as undesirable, the society implies that it wishes to protect its mares, as Edwardian parents might have wanted to protect their daughters, from males, and/or that males have violent, uncontrollable traits. But whatever is being implied, the wider cause of concern is the way in which language can be deployed in the stigmatisation of an identified 'Other' (as several decades later became all too evident in the eugenics of Hitler's *Mein Kampf* which makes explicit references to animal husbandry). The kind of language and terminology employed in the Welsh Pony and Cob Society projects a human-centred taxonomy on to animals which denies them their identity as sentient beings and establishes a signifying system which reinforces the way in which animals may be defined differently from humans. As the Agricultural Commissioner for Wales, C. Bryner Jones, demonstrated in the years preceding the First World War, the use of the term 'undesirable' entered Welsh farming discourse in connection with the 'drafting', or 'selection', of desirable from undesirable animals according to their physical characteristics (again anticipating, despite Hitler's vegetarianism, *Mein Kampf*).[6]

It goes without saying that there must be locations to which animals are denied access in the interests of human and nonhuman animal safety. But the distinctive language in which the Welsh press couched such issues left animals open to abuse and violence rather than care and protection. For example, in reporting the prosecution of a captain of a steamer who brought two calves from Russia into the country, breaching the Foreign Animals Order of 1910, the *Cambria Daily Leader* (October 1914) employed the headline 'Forbidden Animals'.[7] This term suggests that 'forbidden animals', like 'undesirable animals', have a different status, different rights and a different place in the natural order from other animals.

THE NATION'S VICE

The *Pembrokeshire Herald and General Advertiser* (February, 1909) carried a report of an address by Miss Constance Warner on behalf of the RSPCA (the SPCA was established in 1824 and the 'Royal' added in 1840).[8] It suggested that not only were the number of cases of cruelty increasing, but that the RSPCA and the courts were developing a taxonomy of cruelty based on the nature of the animal's suffering, the duration of that suffering and the extent of human involvement in it. In many respects, in a small, community-oriented country like Wales, this approach proved successful in combating animal cruelty. A year after Miss Warner's presentation in west Wales, the *Weekly Mail* (June 1910) reported a reduction in the number of instances of cruelty not only through prosecutions but the raising of public awareness of animal welfare by the RSPCA.[9] The story particularly commended the Society's success in reaching the drivers of horse-drawn cabs in Cardiff through documented instructions and through lectures as part of social evenings.

Miss Warner's talk, which began by calling to book fashionable women for wearing furs and feathers without thought as to where they came from, marked the beginning of thinking about animal welfare as the barometer of the psychic and civic health of the nation. In recalling cases of gross cruelty, Miss Warner did so in a way which encouraged her audience to reflect on what animal abuse revealed about humanity and the civic nature of the country. For example, she pointed out that sheep were still being branded on the nose and recalled the case of a man throwing two dogs down a mine shaft where they were left for eighteen days; maintained that decrepit horses were being transported overseas for slaughter without food or water; and alleged that there were slaughterhouses allowing children to witness its work as if to pass the practice of animal cruelty from one generation to another.

As noted in Chapter 2, slaughterhouses provided especially disturbing manifestations of human exceptionalism and indifference to animals as sentient beings. For much of the nineteenth century, they served as emblems of the way in which farm animals were perceived as only of value as part of the food and fuel chains.[10] Most of the employees in the Victorian slaughterhouse were men and the implication in Miss Warner's talk that masculinity and animal cruelty were linked seems to have been recognised by the *Pembrokeshire Herald and General Advertiser*, which juxtaposed their account of her talk with a case from County Cork, under the headline 'A Barbarous Outrage', in which a gang of moonlighters were reported as having taken revenge on two girls for speaking to the police, cutting off their hair with shears and pouring tar over one of them.[11]

Throughout the late Victorian period, cases of cruelty to animals, including those from outside Wales, were depicted in the Welsh press as a national sin, with the *South Wales Echo* (1896) reporting a case in London against a cab driver for 'cruelly torturing a horse by working it while lame' as 'a disgrace to humanity'.[12] The *Weekly Mail* (November 1904), under the headlines 'Suffering Animals' and 'Two Bad Cases of Cruelty at Newport', reported two linked cases of lame horses being led to Newport Cattle Market.[13] Clearly, these cases were selected for inclusion in the newspaper for the nature of the injury and the extent of the horses' suffering – they were walked eight miles – and for the evident indifference of the men involved. The extent of the injuries was stressed in order to establish that this was a case of 'gross cruelty': one of the horses 'had his hoof turned right over by the weakness of the tendons, and the animal was obliged to step on the fetlock joint'.[14] However, the main focus of the reports is not simply on the physical injuries which the horses suffered but on the extent of the pain which they had had to endure and on their capacity to feel suffering as intensely as humans. One horse was said to be in a 'very distressed and perspiring condition'; the 'sweat was dropping from it' and he was 'lifting his near forefoot from the ground, and appeared to be in great pain.'[15]

Resonating with the way in which the press was beginning to report cruelty generally, these particular allegations exemplified how the coverage of cruelty to animals, and particularly to working horses while injured, had changed over the closing decades of the nineteenth century in several respects: by extending coverage of cases of animal cruelty as a reflection on the nature of 'humanity'; by associating cruelty with 'torture'; by emphasising the responsibility of owners as well as their employees for the welfare of their animals; and by linking good animal welfare to national and civic pride. In this wider conceptualisation of what needed to be done to protect animals, especially working animals, from harm, there are the beginnings of the second wave of the movement toward animal rights which, as noted in Chapter 1, went beyond protection to providing animals with the best possible subjective life.

Chapter 1 observed that late-twentieth- and early-twenty-first-century animal rights theorists such as Alasdair Cochrane have argued that animals have the right not to be killed and not to be harmed and that husbandry and working systems should be designed with these rights in mind. Although these rights were not implemented fully until a century later, reports of cruelty in the Victorian and Edwardian press were inclined to suggest that these were among the basic rights to which animals were entitled. They also anticipated contemporary animal rights' theorists on the importance of grounding animal rights in something tangible and concrete and imposing strict limitations on what we may permissibly do to them in a range of contexts. For example, the *Chester Courant and Advertiser for North Wales* (May 1901) reported a case against two Welsh hill farmers charged with 'causing horses to be ill-treated by withholding from them proper and sufficient food'.[16] The case involved a Welsh rural tradition which allowed owners of ponies to enter into a contract with owners of mountain land to graze their ponies and how, within this convention, there was no clear demarcation of responsibilities. In the heavy snow of winter, there was no shelter and little food but each of the men involved argued that the other was responsible for providing them. The RSPCA, with as long a reach into rural north Wales as the industrial south, reported that the dead horses 'were mere bags of bones'.[17] In cases such as this, where animals suffered because of insufficient forethought, the boundaries between animal cruelty and accidental death became blurred but, once again, they also reflected negatively, in specific, tangible terms, on the character of Welsh rural life.

Thus, in the Victorian and Edwardian press, cruelty to animals is integral to the beginning of a complex and nuanced understanding of animals as sentient beings, promoting the recommendation coming from the courts that the severity and duration of an animal's suffering should be the criteria by which the crime is judged. But alongside this changing view of animals and animality, how animals were treated was beginning to be seen as an indicator not only of humanity but the civic standing of a nation or region.

HORSES AND PIT PONIES

The way in which the Victorian and Edwardian press linked civic pride to the way in which animals were treated was not unique to the late nineteenth century. Although the horse has enabled human development across the globe, it was revered nowhere more so than in medieval and pre-modern Wales. As Elaine Williams points out, the Roman occupation introduced new equine bloodlines into Britain resulting in larger, more vigorous hybrid horses.[18] Not simply the value placed on horses in early modern Wales, as Williams suggests, but the care that the Welsh had for them is evident from as early as 950 CE when 'riding a horse with a saddle that galled its back could incur a fine of four pence, a figure that would be quadrupled if the skin was broken'.[19] By the medieval period, the horse had acquired an important role and presence in Wales, enabling the transformation of travel and trade.[20] However, it was then that horses began to be seen not with the nobility with which the laws of Hywel Dda invested them but as work animals.

Maybe under the influence of Anna Sewell's Victorian novel *Black Beauty* (1877), which was available in Welsh soon after its English publication,[21] but also reflecting the reality of rural life in Wales, mid-twentieth-century recollections of childhood in a farming community included more about human relationships with horses than any other animal. D. Parry-Jones's *Welsh Country Upbringing* includes a section entitled 'The man who loved horses', an account of a small holder who, given 'all the ploughing and harrowing the holding required', longed for a horse of his own:

> He was as I said, extravagant where horses were concerned, he was extravagant too, in the language with which he addressed them. He spoke affectionately and confidentially to them ... Why shouldn't a man speak in terms of admiration to his animal, and whisper in its ear sometimes words of regard and affection, even at times employ a little exaggeration as to its value in gold.[22]

The relationship between this man and his horse exemplifies the emotional bonds that can be developed between humans and animals. But, in his account of his country upbringing, Parry-Jones recalls the extent to which war entered into, and shaped, horse breeding in south-west Wales, in the desire for horses that were not only suitable for the battlefield but reflected the pride and grandeur of the regiment: 'In west Wales of those days farmers bred a clean-legged, tallish light horse ... They were very much sought after for the army, and horse fairs at Llanybyther and Lampeter were swept clean by army buyers, German and French as well as English.'[23] With the breeding of horses for a very different kind of purpose from agricultural work – not that that was always easy on the animal – not only did the relationship between horses and humans change in rural Wales but the way in which the horse was perceived as a marketable commodity.

However badly horses were treated as cab horses on city streets or in war, this was as nothing compared to their lives underground. As noted in Chapter 2, according to the RSPCA, in 1878 there were about 200,000 horses and ponies at work in British mines.[24] Despite the emergence in the Victorian press of a better understanding of animals as sentient beings, the use of horses in the coal mines exemplified the way in which cruelty toward horses intensified with the extent to which they were perceived as cogs in the vast industrial process. The importance of levels of production and of the efficiency of the mines in meeting industrial targets became more significant than the horse as a living being with whom humans might establish the kind of relationship which Parry-Jones remembers from his country childhood.

As Ceri Thompson points out, 'until the 1880s, the welfare of colliery horses and ponies were left to chance.'[25] Thereafter, legislation designed to protect them was introduced in 1887, 1911, 1949 and 1956. For the most part, these Acts are reflective of what animal studies has categorised as the first movement in animal rights (as explained in Chapter 1) in which the legal system and traditional legal ideas and methods were invoked to reduce serious harm to nonhuman animals. However, in the 1949 and 1956 Acts, which became known as 'The Pit Ponies Charter', there are the beginnings of a concept of animal rights concerned not only with protecting animals from death and harm but with ensuring that captive animals experience as fulfilling a life as possible.[26] This shift from thinking about protection from harm to the quality of the individual horse's life runs as a leitmotif through Victorian and Edwardian press stories about colliery horses.

Given the dependence of industrial Wales on horses in coal mining (discussed in Chapter 2), it is not surprising that colliery accidents involving them, and their working conditions, were regularly reported. Chapter 1 highlighted arguments in contemporary animal studies for the importance of the advocacy of animal rights to be grounded in tangible and concrete contexts. On the evidence of the Victorian and Edwardian press in Wales, this approach can be traced to the way in which the conditions of horses and ponies in the collieries were reported, which came to a head during the First World War. For example, *The Amman Valley Chronicle and East Carmarthen News* (November 1916) reported allegations from the House of Commons that 70,400 horses and ponies were used in coal mines in the UK, of which 4,870 were killed as a result of accidents and disease and 10,880 injured.[27] South Wales was listed as one of the regions recording the highest number of deaths (86 per 1,000) and injuries (193 per 1,000). However, it is sometimes difficult to discern whether the mistreatment of animals in mines was reported to make colliery owners, and the nation as a whole, more aware of the sufferings of colliery horses and ponies or to alert readers to how London was repeatedly trying to disparage the Welsh nation.

Scepticism in the Welsh local press over the objectivity of English reports of animal cruelty within Welsh collieries was not confined to journalists, as exemplified by the controversy generated by a piece of correspondence, apparently grounded in tangible and concrete terms, in *Baner ac Amserau* (July 1910).[28] The letter, allegedly based on information obtained from a 'collier friend', addressed conditions underground before highlighting the 'cruelty of a frightful character [that] is practised upon horses'.[29] Economic pressures to improve coal output increased the stress on colliers, which was in turn transferred to the horses and ponies who, enduring conditions which would never have been permitted in tenth-century Wales, were brutally flogged and forced to drag loaded trams through places lower than their height, leaving their bodies horribly injured. Their suffering, according to the correspondent, was extenuated by inadequate, filthy stabling, from which they acquired 'masses of festering sores', and insufficient rest periods. Three days later, *The Rhos Herald* (July 1910) provided more details of the deliberate animal cruelty, alleging that horses were kicked, cuffed, beaten with staves and pick shafts, deprived of food and water and were deliberately blinded and in one case had their tongue cut out.[30]

Turning for a moment to how the past pervades the present, it should be noted that, although horses are no longer employed in coal mines, the animal rights charity Animal Aid has alleged that such cold-blooded cruelty occurs in twenty-first-century slaughterhouses. On the publication of its 2017 report on abuse in slaughterhouses in the UK, Isobel Hutchinson of the charity maintained: 'It really is a very widespread problem, and in terms of what we found, it's not just technical breaches and incompetence, but really appalling deliberate violence. We filmed animals being punched, kicked, deliberately being given electric shocks, even cigarettes being stubbed out on them.'[31]

In the early twentieth century, the Edwardian press was well aware that the abuse which animals endured and which they exposed, like the Animal Aid report one hundred years later, brought the Welsh nation into disrepute. Unsurprisingly, the Edwardian press articles did not go unchallenged. *The Merthyr Express* (September 1910) published correspondence arguing that 'opinions may differ as to the alleged ill-treatment of ponies' and urging caution over taking the word of one miner over half-a-dozen humanitarians and colliery officials while recommending that evidence from miners themselves be brought before The Royal Commission on Mines.[32]

Reports of the suffering of colliery horses and ponies in the press were often placed in a wider context that highlighted the more general cruelty of which humans were capable, redolent of Walker's address on behalf of the RSPCA in February 1909. Under the headlines 'Pit Ponies Maimed' and 'Shocking Monmouth Outrage', *The Cambrian* (August 1909) reported that a number of ponies (put out in a field as a result of stoppage at the Powell-Duffryn Company colliery) were the victims of appalling and sadistic cruelty. Two of them were stabbed through the heart and five others 'shockingly mutilated', 'gashed across the neck and other parts of the body'.[33] The story demonstrates the difficulty in reporting this kind of cruelty, which turns on a fine distinction between exposing what animals suffer and providing examples of gratuitous violence. In the article, these horses and ponies are converted into spectacles of horror. But there is an implication in the story that, due to human kindness and consideration toward animals, they had been enjoying a respite from conditions underground, being returned, albeit temporarily, to the freedom to express, and enjoy, their natural traits and characteristics.

Thus, the emergence of urban and industrial history from an animal's perspective can be traced to the Victorian press and nineteenth-century protectionist literature. They promoted change in the way in which cruelty toward animals was perceived, increasingly focusing throughout the century on, for example, horses as emotional and feeling subjects and the capacity of animals to suffer pain, and depicting the mistreatment of animals as reflecting badly on the nation and humanity in general. But a further significant development in the coverage of cruelty to animals in the Welsh press, in the 1890s and the first decade of the twentieth century, was a shift from simply summarising the facts to empathising with the animal as victim. In this respect, the Victorian and Edwardian Welsh press anticipated the wider psychologically oriented approaches to animality of the twentieth century.[34]

The psychology of animals was discussed in a number of local papers in the Edwardian era and was the subject of a feature about nervous animals run in the combined *County Observer and Monmouth Central Advertiser, Abergavenny and Raglan Herald, Usk and Pontypool Messenger and Chepstow Argus* (May 1904).[35] Under the headline, 'Nervous animals', these papers reported that 'deaths of animals from "nervous upset"' were not uncommon, and were to be found among 'very different classes of animals'. The evidence presented in the article is drawn from different locations from different parts of the world and the causes of 'nervous upset' vary from natural events, such as thunderstorms, to the conditions within which animals are transported and, in some cases, the impact of their capture. The article implies a shared psychology between humans and animals and, as if to reinforce the point, it is juxtaposed with an advertisement for everyday ailments among humans, the first of which is 'nerve pains'. The advertisement is illustrated with a female hand and finger touching a spot where the product is to be applied perhaps suggesting that nervous disorders are associated with women rather than men and aligning animal nervousness specifically with female psychology.

To place the concern of the press with animals as emotional subjects in a wider context, it should be noted that, during the first half of the twentieth century, the notion of animals having a nervous disposition and the capacity, like humans, to be unsettled by natural and unnatural phenomena around them was a recurring theme not only in the press but in the Welsh country memoir. For example, Parry-Jones describes accompanying a young heifer to the town market: 'The rough shouting of this early morning, the barking and heeling of strange dogs were enough to upset it, and did upset it.'[36] The use of the word 'upset' implies that he might be talking about a child as much as a young animal and, as his account progresses, this becomes explicit: 'The strangeness of the place, the smells, the crowds, the strange cattle, the lowing and bellowing that filled the air must have terrified almost out of its senses this child of the peaceful, silent uplands.'[37] In another book recollecting his childhood, Parry-Jones observes: 'Horses shied at everything in those days. Despite miles of walls and palisades alongside the railways, some of the old horses simply refused to come to terms with them.'[38]

In summary, the Victorian and Edwardian press reveals the beginning of changes in the ways in which humans perceived animals and animality that are now prevalent in animal studies. These include an understanding of animals as emotional beings that are responsive to mental as well as physical trauma. As will be discussed in subsequent chapters, these new approaches to animality were developed by twentieth-century- and twenty-first-century writers whose work reflects an increased awareness of animal cruelty, of the ills of human exceptionalism, of greater recognition of the capacity of animals to suffer and feel emotions, and the grounding of animal rights in tangible and concrete contexts. In some respects, the way in which animal suffering was reported in the press paved the way for the use of animal stories, blended with science, by twentieth-century- and twenty-first-century authors arguing that animals have rich emotional lives and are capable of experiencing joy, empathy, grief, anger and love.[39] These themes were undermined but also developed in different ways and in different contexts in accounts of the use of animals for entertainment in circuses, travelling menageries and zoos as well as in adventure literature, which are the subjects of the next chapter.

4

EXOTIC PETS AND SPECTACULAR ENTERTAINMENTS

Interest in exotic animals is focused on what in animal theory is generally conceived as the 'imaginary' and the 'symbolic'. At one level, in the Victorian period and the early twentieth century, the public exhibition of exotic animals symbolised the success of empire but, at another level, they suggested what was thought to lie at the edges of human rationality and consciousness. As Yi-Fu Tuan suggested, animals who provided humans with entertainment in, for example, circuses, zoos and menageries, served as manifestations of human imaginary fears and insecurities rooted in a distant psychic history: 'Wild and awesome nature assumed both vividness and specificity in the shape of wild animals and monsters.'[1] Exotic animals present the human imagination with highly charged images which, as Derek Ryan maintains, 'turn out to be all too human': 'In many instances they are either stand-ins for human concerns, or they are used primarily to confirm, by way of contrast, a specifically human worldview.'[2]

However, the suggestion that exotic animals served as 'stand-ins for human concerns' begs questions about how far, and in what ways, the human imaginary can penetrate the 'Other' which animals inhabit. Luce Irigaray, on whose work Ryan draws, asks: 'How can we talk about them? How can we talk to them? These familiars of our existence inhabit another world ... I project my human imaginary onto them.'[3] Projecting our concerns onto animals widens the gulf between us, especially when the highly charged images that then infest our psyches are manifestations of our phobias. In the Victorian period and the first half of the twentieth century, public interest in animals and insects on which diverse phobias were projected was catered for by the press in short features, sometimes only a single paragraph. These 'reports' often combined scientific knowledge with pandering to common phobias about particular species. For example, the *Barry Herald* (September 1898) could not avoid suggesting that 'immense swarms of spiders' and their webs would soon cover the 'whole country' and that it would not be possible to 'walk very far without coming in contact with gossamer'.[4] Having aroused childhood fears of creepy-crawlies, the paper contributed to arachnology in a more level-headed way, drawing attention to how the migration of swallows and September's wetter climate provided spiders with more small insects for food but also encouraged wonder and enthusiasm for the size of the spider webs and the agility of their weavers, 'half volant, half aeronaut'.[5]

While the Welsh local press encouraged public enthusiasm for nature, it also burgeoned late Victorian and Edwardian interest (further fuelled by overseas adventure stories for young adults) in the colonial discourse around the 'different' and the 'unnerving'. The *Welsh Gazette and West Wales Advertiser* (December 1910), in a paragraph headed 'Huge Spiders', reported on a spider to be found in houses on Trinidad, with a body 'as large round as a penny' whose 'eight horrible legs spread themselves out to a circumference the size of a cheese-plate'.[6] The story is as interested in inflaming the arachnophobia of its Welsh readers as promoting the difference of the Caribbean. Breeding pairs are said to live undetected in the corners of cupboards and ceilings, the female 'clasping her white egg-case to her body by her forelegs', only to emerge at night when they might hunt cockroaches and be heard 'crunching [their] prey'.[7] However, this was not always the case: a feature in the Welsh press (February 1904) on 'Immense Spiders' in the mountains of Ceylon and India, for example, emphasises the size of the spider and its vast webs but is as impressed by 'the bright yellowish silk' and by the beauty of the spider itself, 'being bright gold or scarlet' with a covering of 'the most delicate slate-coloured fur'.[8]

Stories about ants in the Victorian press frequently fed readers' interests in the exotic and the savage. For example, the *Weekly Mail* (January 1894), under the headline 'Eaten Alive by Ants', reported how a woman who was suspected of having caused the death of a child by witchcraft in Pondoland, was covered in grease and bound to a tree in the middle of an ant hill and eaten alive.[9] However, for the Edwardian period onward, features on ants in the local press were as likely to be inspired by myrmecology as myrmecophobia. As Paul

Waldau, observing the developing interest in animal science in insects as social animals, suggests: 'Children often notice that insects are fundamentally social creatures. In both formal and informal education, reflective humans eventually encounter the science-based view that many social insects are genetically inclined to give their individual lives readily for the sake of the community.'[10] But in the Victorian and Edwardian press, the colony building of ants was frequently analogous to imperialism, colonial projects and slavery from the ancient human empires onwards. For example, the *Denbighshire Free Press* (9 December 1905) reported on ant colonies in which 'alien queens [are] duly fed and reared by the workers of the invaded colonies', where 'the workers die off, leaving a colony of foreigners' and where 'new comers make raids, and capture more to supply their place' than in 'an ordinary case of slavery'.[11]

Thus, the Victorian and Edwardian press addressed scientific interest in insects, and their complex, social world, because they mirrored the imperialist project. But it also pandered to phobias with an eye on what was perceived as lying at the edges of human rationality and of so-called civilised society. These different aspects of reporting about insects were also manifested in the way in which larger animals from overseas were increasingly exhibited on the street, as part of circuses and in zoos and travelling menageries.

STREET MONKEYS

From about the 1870s, exotic animals from overseas had a significant part in Victorian and early-twentieth-century entertainment reflecting the successful expansion of Empire and the project of British imperialism.[12] As the cultural historian and museum curator Rachel Poliquin points out, animals were 'a tantalising ingredient in this Western fashioning of colonial otherness'.[13]

Within the cultural context of the 'Other', Desmond Morris points out that monkeys have had a chequered history: despised as evil in the ancient Western world, regarded as sacred in ancient Egypt, revered as a monkey god in Hindu religion, depicted as shameful and disgusting in emblem books of the sixteenth and seventeenth centuries, used satirically in eighteenth- and nineteenth-century Europe and elevated in status after the Darwin debate in Oxford in 1860.[14] Organ-grinders, accompanied by a costumed capuchin monkey that was trained to collect coins, frequented Victorian street culture and monkeys proved popular in zoos, streets and cafes because they resembled humans and, as Morris says, humans appeared to enjoy 'their intelligence and playfulness', 'their expressive faces and their ability to manipulate small objects in a human manner'.[15] But, as Tuan also reminds us, they were invariably a popular attraction because, through their 'easy sexual behaviour', monkeys in zoos and menageries gave licence to an otherwise 'forbidden' voyeurism.[16]

In his novel *William Jones* (1944), the north Wales, Welsh-language writer T. Rowland Hughes provides a memorable anecdote of a relationship between a south Wales man and a street monkey. Initially, the monkey arouses fear and a sense of the uncanny in the human animal he resembles: 'He felt something rubbing the side of his neck and looked down at his waistcoat. A long, long tail hung down it and Huw sat motionless, terrified of moving even his eyes lest they made a noise.'[17] Subtly, this passage is developed around human phobias relating to animals. The monkey's long tail might remind the reader of a few of the species of which people are most often scared, such as snakes, rats and mice.

Huw's monkey was originally owned by an organ-grinder but, after his owner's death, he 'adopts' it, becoming known himself as Huw-Monkey which underscores the similarities between humans and this particular species especially. Before Huw makes his decision, the constable and others come to the house to remove the animal but, as in the comparable scene in Gwyn Jones's 'Take Us the Little Foxes' (discussed in Chapter 7), they find that the two have established a mutual bond:

> the monkey was squatting in the middle of the table feasting on all the apples, plums and sweets in the house; and it was quite evident that he and Huw were great friends. When Will-P'liceman tried to grab the animal it leapt on to its hospitable benefactor's shoulder and looked suspiciously at the man in uniform. It may be that similar uniforms had frightened the monkey more than once before; be that as it may, Will was admittedly a rather nasty bit of work. Huw said nothing, but when the constable stepped forward to lay hold of the monkey he quietly pushed him aside and took his new pet out for a turn in the garden.[18]

Hughes examines the relationship between Huw and the monkey from a number of perspectives. Huw's monkey is both an imaginary – reflecting back to humans a mirror image of themselves – and an insight into the kind of relationship humans might achieve with animals and among themselves. But, put on display, the organ-grinder's monkey is objectified and devalued as a living being. At a symbolic level, Huw's monkey brings 'home' the wildness of empire in a domesticated form. However, Hughes also uses the domestication of the monkey in a way that anticipates the interest in contemporary animal studies, observed in Chapter 1, in animal cognition, emotion and self-awareness and how animals have established intelligences that are different from, but no less effective in their own niche environments, than human intelligences.[19] But Huw's monkey, through his relationship with Huw, reveals that he has capacities, also, to think, reason, remember and recognise particular individuals.

Hughes's anecdote raises additional questions around the monkey's captivity, which again anticipates contemporary animal studies and contributes to the understanding of captivity as psychological as well as physical. As noted in Chapter 1, once conceived in terms of physical confinement, in animal studies it has come to be seen as much in psychological terms.[20] Read against this redefinition of 'captivity', the innovative depiction of Huw's monkey and the novel's interest in its emotional and cognitive capacities become all the clearer. The ethology evident in Hughes's account complements, and extends, for example, Morris's more social-history oriented commentary on organ-grinders' monkeys.[21]

The emphasis on the psychology of Huw's captive monkey begs questions about how our literary animals, as Ryan says, 'are always already on our own terms, mediated through human language and weighed down with cultural assumptions' but confront the 'material and conceptual asymmetries in human and animal life'.[22] Hughes's depiction of the monkey is focused on the conflict between his instinct to escape and his desire to maintain human company; how the fear of some humans – in this case those in uniform – and recognition of kindness from others has been instilled in him; the way in which his species, like humans, are able to 'read' people; and how the extent of people's 'humanity' can be judged by the way in which they relate to animals.

In some respects, the street monkey in Victorian society emblematised an emergent ambivalence about captive animals as cultural symbols, as manifestations of socio-psychic fears and as sentient beings having to endure the psychological as well as physical realities of confinement. In a society in which criminals and the mentally ill were incarcerated, they reflected pervasive, uncomfortable social realities, but not to the same extent as circuses and how they were reported in the press.

CIRCUSES AND THE WELSH PRESS

Animal circuses are no longer a part of Welsh life. After a fourteen-year campaign by the RSPCA, the Wild Animals and Circus (Wales) Act was passed by the Senedd in 2020. The length and tenacity of the campaign reflects the extent to which animal circuses had become lodged in the popular imagination, evidenced in the extensive and positive coverage they had received in the press for some considerable time, and the role that the captivity and subjugation of animals had assumed in the human psyche. Few statistics exist for the number of circuses and menageries touring in late-nineteenth- and early-twentieth-century Wales. However, it was not only the existence of travelling circuses with animals but reports of them in the late Victorian and early-twentieth-century Welsh press that defined them for their interest in the exotic, in animal intelligence and in the as yet untapped potential value of animals to humans. Through their popularity, evident in the size of the audiences who attended them and the positive ways in which they were reported in the Welsh press, there is little doubt that circuses helped shaped Welsh attitudes to animals outside as well as in the circus.

Competition among circuses in Wales led to pressure for more spectacular shows and novelty acts pushing the boundaries of animal training. An advertisement for the Lord George Ginnett's Circus at the People's Park, Pontypridd, in *The Pontypridd Chronicle and Workman's News* (September 1891) boasted of bringing together 'two great collections' with an emphasis on the 'exotic', on animals which the public at the time may never have encountered except in picture books or magic lantern shows – elephants, bulls, bears, monkeys and kangaroos – and on extremes of size: 'Pongo the only and largest Gorilla in Europe' and 'the stud of tiny ponies'.[23]

The way in which circuses presented their collections provided a framework which smaller and less extravagant animal shows adopted. For example, an article on 'Gigantic Animals', in *The Aberystwyth Observer* (May 1894), opens with reference to the Cart Horse Parade in London which featured two bays, described as 'gigantic animals', a phrase that marvels at their exceptional size and which renders them as 'exotic' as large circus animals.[24] The bays are celebrated in the paper because they stand eighteen hands high, weigh a ton and are capable 'of driving a weight of over four tons in addition to their driver'.[25] In stressing their spectacular appearance (in the show, they were adorned like circus horses with decorative harnesses and plumes), the article describes them as 'mammoth horses', juxtaposing species from different periods of history. But their size does not simply render them visually exciting, they are useful in utilitarian terms. They are not products of nature for their increase in height and weight over a usual carthorse has been brought about mainly through diet and selective breeding and cross-breeding 'in just proportion in a particular animal'.[26]

Such articles appeared to give licence to humans, through manipulating animal cross-breeding, to intervene in and assume control of nature. The use of words like 'gigantic', 'mammoth' and 'exotic' to describe the carthorses begs questions, as this article points out, as to 'whether the limits of size which Nature seems to have set to the growth of particular species is really as fixed and arbitrary as might appear'.[27] This human intervention in nature resonates with the world of farming in twentieth-century Wales which sought to make adjustments to animals and animality to satisfy human economic, nutritional and even fashionable needs.

Elements even of twenty-first-century animal shows, such as farm animal competitions, military tattoos, sheepdog trials and police animal displays, can be traced back to the animal circuses of the Victorian period. The references to the spectacular events in the article on Ginnett's Circus imply noise, movement and chaos which would normally upset animals: 'Rides of death through all the performance of the circus riders' and 'the Fall of Rome'.[28] But the implication is that the animals, like military and police horses, have been trained to ignore the bombardment around them and suppress their nervousness.

Victorian circuses had a significant role in encouraging greater enterprise in the use of animals. The Lord George Sanger's Circus, performing on the Sophia Gardens Field, Cardiff, impressed the *South Wales Daily News* (June 1894) in the spectacular nature of its offering and its willingness to push back the human–animal boundary: 'Unlike the generality of circuses, the programme here is not merely a few items of bareback riding, acrobatic contortions, and cross bar trapeze evaluations, enlivened by the usual clowning.'[29] The emphasis on the number and diversity of animals, on the exotic and, above all, on military campaigns is admired with no thought to the pressure and suffering imposed on the animals. Noteworthy, the predictable and safe acts involve humans while the new and daring performances feature animals: 'the colouring given by the introduction of elephants and camels with mounted guns', 'the military'-like dash and the booming of the 'mounted artillery' and re-enactment of moments from 'the fateful Soudan campaign'.[30] If, as discussed in Chapter 3, animals can be disturbed by natural events such as thunderstorms, and certainly by their capture and conveyance, the impact of mounted artillery and booming cannons on them is unimaginable. Ironically, given the distinction throughout between humans and animals, the article opens with a report of the 'continuous stream' of people to get into the marquee which eventually turned into a herd in which one person was crushed, a woman shaken and children 'suffered a good deal'.[31]

A report of the Royal Italian Circus, coming to Andrews Hall, Queen Street in Cardiff, in the *Evening Express* (February 1909), stresses the number, diversity and exotic nature of its menagerie: '200 performing ponies, dogs, monkeys, goats, and the renown Malay bear, "Madame Batavia," and the historic baby elephant, Queen Alexandra's pet, "Jumbo Junior"'.[32] But if the implied ordeals of capture and transportation were not enough, the article begs further questions as to how much the animals might suffer. The circus stresses that its originality lies in the fact that all animals 'go through all the performances of human performers'.[33] But some of these spectacular circus acts also mirrored the way in which dead animals in the Victorian and Edwardian periods were dressed as humans and placed in human scenes by taxidermists. 'Madame Batavia' is said to have driven a motor car to the London Stock Exchange and to have danced at a Covent Garden Fancy Dress Ball; 'Jumbo Junior', riding a cab, has attended fashionable parties in London and is described as a musical prodigy; and 'Theresa' is introduced as the musical and calculating pony, while the show itself is based around 'the astounding cleverness of the dogs, monkeys and ponies'.[34] All of these acts are reported in the paper without any scruples and prepare an audience to leave the show with a delusional belief that their understanding of the capacity of animals, and of animal training, has been enhanced. The way in which circuses treated animals as objects in a 'living taxidermist display' is indicative of the cosmology that brought such events into being, which the late-twentieth-century cosmology of a related universe in which all living things are connected eventually supplanted, helping to bring animal shows based on human exceptionalism to an end.

The absent referent in many articles about circuses was the extent to which they promoted animals as inferior to humans and how their training reflected the superiority of the human in enabling animals to perform tricks. This absence is attributable to an insufficient awareness of the capacity of animals to suffer and to experience emotions. In this respect, Victorian and twenty-first-century concepts of animality are very different despite the new sensitivity toward animals emerging in the press of the day. The *Cardiff and Merthyr Guardian, Glamorgan, Monmouth and Brecon Gazette* (February 1869) reported a case from the Lambeth Police Court that it perceived 'highly important, as the facts would show, with regard to animals used in public performance'.[35] An RSPCA officer stopped a boy riding a lame pony that regularly performed at the Crystal Palace and the Lyceum Theatre. On removing rags and bandages, he found a deep wound on the off forefoot and two wounds, one on top of the other, on the near forefoot. The case reflects the changing approach of the Victorian courts, and the RSPCA at this time, to animal cruelty (discussed in Chapter 3) in which importance is attached to the severity of the injuries, the extent of the animal's pain and suffering, and the evidence of the indifference of the rider and the owner. The injuries were said to have been caused by a technique 'usually adopted by owners of performing horses, in tapping them against the legs, in order to urge them on to carry out the various tricks'.[36] Such reports, stressing the extent of the injuries inflicted on an animal, raised questions about the nature of humanity and encouraged reflection on the priority humans assumed over other species.

However, the Welsh press did occasionally turn the tables on circus audiences. The *Evening Express* (May 1909) under the headline 'Men v Animals' reprinted a feature from *Fly's* Magazine:

> It has often occurred to me that if, at the circus, we could put the men, women, and children in the arena, and the beasts and birds in the audience, the human performers would, compared with the rest, betray themselves as one remove only from paralytics. The jumping of those who make and break records on both sides of the Atlantic would move the flea and kangaroo to derision. The monkeys and the parrots would pity the climbing even of our sailors, who alone seem to have preserved a

mode of motion common enough in the era when men's feet were hands and a prehensile tail gave him better hold of the branches.[37]

The article begins by classifying animals as 'beasts and birds' in opposition to men, women and children. But once the positions of humans and animals in the Big Top have been reversed, animals are identified as individual species. However, even when exposed as less superior to animals than they think, humans are still deemed to have reached an exalted state above their original animality signified by their now very distant ancestor, who, the article stresses, once walked on four 'hands' and had a 'prehensile tail'.

In articles that are a combination of reportage and advertising, the Victorian and Edwardian press, which otherwise exposed the cruelty with which working animals were treated and encouraged appreciation of their capacity to suffer pain, appeared to go out of its way to argue that the training of circus animals was not cruel, as if it wanted to protect the entertainment available to the local community. In its report on the Royal Italian Circus, The *Llangollen Advertiser Denbighshire Merionethshire and North Wales Journal* (July 1914) emphasised the high regard in which its animals were held. In highlighting the performing seals, the paper stressed what it had obviously been led to believe by the circus itself: 'These animals have to be very carefully nursed and petted and are valued at £1000 each.'[38] A much earlier article in *The Aberystwyth Observer* (January 1872), reprinting a feature from the *Daily News*, highlighted the special qualities needed by circus 'tricks' masters and mistresses and the close relationship they had to establish with their horses if they were to be successful: 'Patience and courage conquer the temper without breaking the spirit, and the animals "with a temper" almost invariably develop the most intelligence.'[39] Here there are echoes of how 'benevolent' plantation owners might talk about their slaves but also an emphasis upon horses possessing intelligence, the quality Aristotle believed separated humans from animals and rendered animals inferior. As repeated often in the press during the years that followed, animals are said to be successfully trained not through cruelty but a positive relationship between animals and trainers: the trainer's 'resolution must be unquestionable, his patience not to be strained, his perseverance indomitable. He must have a quick perception of individual equine idiosyncrasy; and if his temper is not thoroughly under control, he may as well lay down the riding switch at once.'[40]

But, within such accounts, the 'absent presence' is the anti-image of the cruel, uncaring trainer. When they occurred, reports of cases brought against circus employees in the Welsh press in the late nineteenth and early twentieth centuries helped raise public awareness of animal welfare. Unlike those brought against workers in small-scale fairs and shows, these cases tended to result from irresponsible behaviour rather than intentional cruelty. But some of them beggared belief. Even the court admitted that a particular case which occurred at Brentford but was nevertheless reported in the Welsh *Evening Express* (December 1909) was 'unusual'. It involved a circus rider charged with 'driving to the common danger' after allowing twelve circus ponies for which he was responsible to run 'about all over the road', scattering pedestrians.[41] Although not a Welsh case, the story was no doubt of interest to the *Express* because it focused, as did much Welsh reporting about animality, on the boundaries between 'domestication' and 'wild'. In the Victorian period and the early twentieth century, the Welsh press appears to have welcomed stories in which circus animals reveal their true, untrained selves. In this respect, even aspects of Welsh coverage of the escape of the lynx from Borth zoo in the twenty-first century, to which I will return shortly, can be traced to the Victorian and early twentieth-century Welsh press.

Looking through a Victorian lens, stories of animals casting off their 'tame' veneer and revealing the wild nature they have not lost, and humans behaving as a herd of unfettered animals, are analogous to the perceived internal and external threats to human society at the time. Since the 1870s, outbursts of popular unrest, pockets of anarchist activity, assassinations and attempted assassinations of world leaders made Europe an insecure and unstable continent. In April 1900, the Prince and Princess of Wales were almost killed by a fifteen-year-old anarchist as they waited for their train to leave a railway station in Brussels.

TRAVELLING MENAGERIES

The most controversial animal shows in the Victorian period and in the early twentieth century were the travelling animal exhibitions with horse-drawn cages, wagons and caravans. The *Evening Press* (November 1898), in reporting an attack by lions on their animal tamer in the Bostock-Wombwell Circus and Menagerie's tour of the

French provinces, despaired that this was 'inevitable with the class of entertainment which these establishments provide'.[42] The paper alleges that this type of entertainment inevitably led to 'infuriated beasts', implying that in their search for ever more spectacular shows, animal trainers drove their animals too far.

Travelling menageries interrupted the normal routines of the communities which they visited, stimulating the imaginations of their audiences and providing a sense of excitement and, for a short while, even danger. The arrival of a travelling menagerie in a small Welsh town is depicted in Mary-Ann Constantine's short story, 'The Elephant at Tregaron':

> The wagons of Batty's Menagerie are creaking past cottages and July hedgerows, the lions and tigers and pythons and cockatoos and monkeys all jolted up and down inside ... People have come out of their houses to stare ... They halt in Tregaron, in the market square. They fill it with beasts and their minders, spilling over into the stables of the Ivy Bush and the Talbot. The wagons are pushed into the ring position and a few of the advertising boards are put up: this is only a temporary stop, overnight, but there's no point wasting an audience.[43]

The story is based on a myth that the corpse of a travelling circus elephant from Batty's travelling menagerie in 1848 is buried somewhere beneath the beer garden of the Talbot Arms in Tregaron, Ceredigion, which was the subject of a project initiated by an academic and her student from University of Wales Trinity Saint David in 2011.[44] One local historian, however, in a history of Llansawel claims the event happened on 16 June 1888, when a travelling menagerie called Bostock and Wombwells arrived in Llansawel to put on a show.[45] Bostock and Wombwells was one of the oldest, biggest and best of the menageries, unlike Batty's travelling menagerie of forty years earlier, but, given the poor condition of the roads in Victorian Wales, it frequently divided into several companies touring different parts of Wales.

Elephants were important to nineteenth-century circuses and menageries. But behind their presence in such entertainment shows was a wider, global problem. It is estimated that elephants roamed over about a quarter of the African continent, but the nineteenth century saw the beginnings of an intense ivory trade in which elephants were hunted and killed for their tusks, the loss of their natural habitat, and the capture of elephants alive for logging, circuses, zoos and religious reasons. By 1900, there were several million elephants in Africa but a survey conducted in 2007 estimates that there were less than half that number. The greater numbers were confined to specific areas such as southern Africa (about 300,000), East Africa (137,000) and only around 7,000 in West Africa.[46]

An important theme in animal theory is the parallels that can be drawn between the capture and use of elephants, and other exotic animals such as wild cats and monkeys, and human slaves. As Ryan observes: 'the circulation of lifestock in global capitalist markets, where they are transported around the world in severely cramped conditions only to be auctioned and slaughtered on arrival, disturbingly mirrors the "hellish" treatment of slaves in the "Middle Passage" as they were transported to the "New World".'[47]

But, as discussed at the outset of this chapter, large animals in the menageries and zoos of the nineteenth century emblematised the power and grandeur with which humans invested large animals. The Tregaron myth allegedly involved an elephant called Jwmbi, that had become a name for any large elephant after the African bull elephant, Jumbo, at London Zoo from 1865 to 1882, who stood thirteen feet high. Although, according to records at Swansea museum, the Llansawel elephant was named Lizzie, she was known in the menagerie as Madame Jumbo. But important as these elephants were for their size, it must be borne in mind, too, that they gave a sense of 'reality' and specificity to what existed as a generalised imaginary in the human psyche.[48]

Constantine's short story can be seen as engaging with the way in which wild animals from non-European continents have been seen in psychoanalytic animal theory as having an imaginary presence, originating deep in the human psyche, and a symbolic role. But Constantine places more emphasis on the way in which through the culture of the circus and the participation of their audiences, the elephant becomes a simulacrum. Audiences are important not only to the financial survival of the menagerie but to the fetishisation of animals from overseas as 'exotic' on which their capture and captivity depends. In Constantine's story, the interest which a small Welsh community shows in the menagerie's animals, and its participation in the fetishisation of them as commodities, provokes an angry response from a minister of religion concerned that his congregation might forsake Sunday worship. The story makes a controversial and unexpected connection between the exotic menagerie and Christ in that both are 'seen and touched and gone' and live on 'like any miracle in hearts and minds for years'.⁴⁹ A further link between the two is that the elephant which is supplanted by the fetishised, exotic 'object' and the human Christ who is supplanted by the fetishised and institutionalised figure of the divine Christ both come to the fore through the act of dying, a point which Constantine reinforces by having the animal die, as Christ was born, in a stable behind an inn:

> But for it to stop. To sink down on its knees and not get up, and to finish up somewhere as familiar as the stable behind the pub, dying of the weather or sorrow or lead-poisoning or the wrath of an unjust God, that is a cruel disenchantment for anyone to witness.⁵⁰

The buried elephant is the real, unfetished animal, as the initially entombed body of Christ was the human Christ. It is this unfetished elephant that lives on in the minds of those present at her death, as the human Christ remained in the memories of those who witnessed the crucifixion. Reflecting on the animal's grave, the concluding sentence of the story – 'Grass, and nothing to show'⁵¹ – is appropriately ambiguous, pointing to the anonymity of her grave (again like the tomb of Christ) and the absence of the menagerie show. The menagerie left the sick elephant behind in Tregaron, finally free of her slavery and her fetishisation. But the community gathered around the sick and dying animal is especially ironic as in animal studies, as noted in the discussion of Dame Daphne Sheldrick's work with elephants in Chapter 1, the capacity to grieve and mourn has been perceived as something which elephants and humans share and has opened up more work in animal theory around ethology.

Thus, travelling circuses provided the public with entertainment which made the exotic and the psychological imaginary 'real' and specific, but also simultaneously questioned human exclusiveness. They helped determine the way in which animals and animality were perceived outside and within them. But this might be said also of another institution, based on animal captivity, which has aroused as much controversy in animal studies and is the subject of the next section, the zoo.

ZOOLOGICAL GARDENS

Following the founding of the *Ménagerie du Jardin des Plantes* in Paris in 1793, the number of zoos in Europe in the nineteenth century grew to 300, with an estimated 150 million visitors, and in the twentieth century to 10,000 worldwide with an estimated 700 million visitors each year.[52] Many of the zoological gardens which were developed across port towns and cities after the opening of the London Zoological Gardens, in 1828, offered a more organised and refined environment than the travelling menageries were to do. Socially exclusive, they catered for the middle and upper classes and saw themselves as disseminating zoological knowledge. But this 'zoological' knowledge amounted to a human exceptionalist view of animality which underscored the perceived difference between humans and animals. In putting animals on display as objects against empty backgrounds, zoos reflected a Newtonian cosmology – in which things were perceived as moving mechanically in empty space[53] – as opposed to current scientific thinking in which everything is perceived as bound together through networks of relations.

Not only did the animal displays in zoos reflect the expansion of empire but many of their visitors worked in jobs and professions which the imperial project had created. The zoo provided face-to-face contact with the exotic animals which children and young adults read about in adventure stories, studied in textbooks and viewed in paintings or magic lantern slide-shows. As Poliquin notes: 'Large African predators in particular ... were metonymic of entire geographies, concentrating in animal form what made those distant landscapes so ferociously exciting, so *exotic*.'[54] However, although zoos provided children and adults with education and popular science and catered for polite society, there was another, more controversial, side to them. Zoos provided the 'reality' to the fantasy of the exotic and individualised animals that in popular mythology were depersonalised in homogeneous, often mythical, groupings. The 'wildness' and rarefied animality on display in zoological gardens – the name brings together the 'untamed' in the word 'zoological' with the 'domesticated' in the concept of 'gardens' – were analogous to what was presumed to lie at the outreaches of 'civilisation', of the rational mind and the humane. Animal theorists like Tuan remind us of a time 'lost in prehistory, when the fear of unknown forces was diffuse and more likely to take the shape of protean monstrous presences'[55] and have pointed out that deep in human history 'obscure beasts and monsters stood for the unknown and threatening forces of nature'.[56] Moreover, these zoos hid the truths about the capture, captivity and transportation of their animals which were analogous to the concealed truths about the slave trade. But they also reflected back to supposedly sophisticated humans (emblematised in the 'gardens') the wildness and animality that were within themselves.

More controversial were the less-refined zoos which doubled as entertainment parks and attracted a wider social class. They were principally performative spaces catering for a public that wanted to be entertained rather than informed. In them, exotic animals were even more likely to be exploited and abused than in the larger zoos. Their captivity and display were not so much about conservation and science as taught behaviours, compliance and, as discussed in Chapter 7, the concept of 'domesecration'.

From the late twentieth century onwards, the nature of zoos changed with more of an emphasis being placed on animal welfare. With this development, what the sociologist Adrian Franklin labelled the 'zoological gaze' also changed.[57] This change reflected the different view of animality from that which existed when zoos were first established. At one level, there is more awareness of the way in which humans and animals share the same planet. But in addition to this relationality, there is more interest in animal ethology and in captivity as a psychological as well as physical state of being. But a conviction remains that humans in their superiority over animals have the intelligence and capacity to save the planet.

These changes in what Franklin calls the zoological gaze are evident in the National Zoo of Wales, established by the naturalist Robert Jackson as the Welsh Mountain Zoo in 1963, when the Welsh Zoological Society assumed responsibility for its management and development. The National Zoo maintains: 'conservation remains at the heart of our ethos, and the future survival of animals and their habitats continues to drive us ever forward.'[58] Its mission reflects the educational aspirations of the better Victorian zoos but with more clarity and more animal-oriented interests: 'Today's best and most progressive zoos usually consider their main roles to be those of conservation, education, scientific study and recreation.'[59] The caveat 'best and most progressive' reminds us that while there are 'progressive' zoos, there are many, as in the Victorian period, that are not.

Of particular interest in contemporary animal studies is how convincing have been the various rationales – science research, preserving species threatened with extinction, education and entertainment – which have been devised to justify the existence of zoos. In charting their development from private menageries to public institutions, animal studies has become concerned that 'not only are the scientific merits of zoos overstated, but the benefits of containing animals for education and entertainment are also exaggerated'.[60] Despite the increasing focus on animal welfare and conservation in contemporary zoos, the emphasis on humans in some respects remains, evident, for example, in the focus on human education in wildlife and the dangers they face; the scientific study of animals in which the animal inevitably becomes an object of the scientific gaze; and on human recreation designed around animals. As Ryan points out, at the centre of this concern is the paradox to which the French philosopher Jacques Derrida first drew attention, that public zoos reflect both the exploitation of animals and human interest in them and that the model of zoos itself continues to be based on problematic power structures.[61] Thus, evolving from Ryan's Derridean approach, questions worth asking are: to what extent do zoos challenge the human–animal boundary, provide opportunities to rethink the human and animal relationship, see animals (and enable animals to be seen) as sentient beings with rights of their own and promote the interrelationship between different life forms?

From its website, the National Zoo is conscious of the narrow path zoos tread. For example, it admits: 'the best way to serve animals is in their own environment.'[62] This appears to be a nod in the direction of those who would argue for the abolition of zoos on the grounds that animals in captivity are denied the lives they would live in their natural habitats. However, the National Zoo recognises that this is not always possible and argues for the need to 'establish a reserve population far away from the dangers of the wild'.[63] But it recalls Victorian zoos in that one of its unique selling points is that it is home to animals, such as a pair of snow leopards, which are endangered but also spectacular with a significant public-pulling power.[64]

How far a reconstructed 'zoological gaze' has challenged or enabled a revision of human and animal cultural taxonomy is a moot point even though it has certainly revised, and continues to determine, the nature and location of animals in many zoos. The binary between the domesticated and tamed animal and the undomesticated and wild animal has remained a source of interest to the Welsh media if not Welsh culture as a whole. This came to the fore even in twenty-first-century Wales when a lynx which escaped from Borth Wild Animal Kingdom was shot, 'humanely destroyed', by Ceredigion council after the risk to the public was rated as 'severe'. If the animal's escape generated controversy in itself, this was as nothing compared to the arguments generated by its death.[65] The zoo's co-owner argued that the lynx might have been 'darted' and he saw the council's action as heavy handed. The park's response to the killing on its Facebook page implicitly, and unconsciously, invoked the way in which it blurred the boundaries between various cultural manifestations of so-called 'exotic' animality, such as the hunting of 'exotic' animals as game, the display of 'exotic' animals as a public attraction, the conservation of rare or overseas species, and the 'taming' or domestication of the wild: 'We are truly devastated by the hunting and killing of Lillith last night. For the past three weeks we have been tracking and attempting to catch her in a safe way.'[66] Some reports, for example from BBC Wales, appeared to invest their account of the lynx's escape with a drama and awe which readers have always found in stories of exotic animals in countries which were themselves rendered exotic, different and exciting: 'Lillith is believed to have escaped after making a "giant leap" over an electrified fence at some point in the last four weeks and was destroyed after the council said the risk to public safety had "increased to severe".'[67] The BBC account juxtaposes this verbal image of the lynx's dramatic 'wildness' with pictures of it sitting comfortably in its enclosure like a domesticated cat, an image reinforced by the repetition of the lynx's 'domesticated' name (a girl's name but also a demon in Jewish tradition, encapsulating the ambivalence around the Borth lynx).

ZOOS AND SCIENCE MUSEUMS

Although animal science has provided valuable information about particular species, without the broader discipline of animal studies issues such as the distortions brought about by cultural caricatures, the dominance of human exceptionalism and the invasive nature of animal research might have been unchallenged. Both these disciplines have a bearing on the zoological museum which combines the specificity of animal science with the cultural taxonomies of the exotic and of the spectacular exposed by animal studies. Gillian Clarke's poems 'Silent' and 'The Company of Bones', from *Zoology* (2017), based in a zoological museum, suggests that museum collections have been compiled, at least partly, according to the criteria employed by zoos. In the museum, skeletons of animals, like the living species in zoos, are displayed behind glass and labels that depict classifications, facts and figures. The classification systems signify the power of the human over the animal but the museum display also shares further characteristics with zoos and even circuses. The bones often belong to animals of extreme size (such as the gigantic mammoth or killer whale and, at the other end of the scale, the little golden lion) or are exotic and not seen in Wales outside zoos, such as the leatherback turtle, python, bear, reindeer or elk.

The title of Clarke's poem 'The Company of Bones' suggests that she sees herself as sharing her existence with that of other animals and that they share common and tangential evolutionary histories. The poem opens and closes with the same line: 'Orangutan, Chimpanzee, Gorilla, Man.'[68] While at one level, it suggests that humankind has evolved from the great apes to become superior to them, at another, it repositions humankind in its animal context. The bones are displayed in a way which, from one perspective, appears 'forensic'. But the poet discovers that behind the glass are sources of wonder: the golden lion is seen as a 'little dancer', it has 'beautiful bones', there are 'twenty-six joints in the engineered curve of its tail', and its ribs are a 'breathless cage'. The different bones behind or under glass – a mammoth's molar, wolf's mandible, bear's humerus, and reindeer's antler – suggest how animals should not be seen as 'primitive' to humankind or to other species in evolutionary history but as sophisticated adaptations to particular environments in specific periods of natural history. In this respect, Clarke reflects the interest in contemporary animal studies in thinking of cognition and intelligence in other-than-human terms and as manifested in how animals, birds and insects have evolved in response to particular environments and their own *Umwelt*. In the course of the poem, the glass behind which the bones are located becomes a symbol of the lenses through which they are viewed, which includes our perspectives and our language. Initially, the poet is separated from the bones by the glass, but at the end of the poem that gap is bridged, as the poet thinks about her own heart pumping her blood through her body.

WILLIAM GRIFFITH'S *ANTURIAETHAU CYMRO YN AFFRICA*

Interest in the exotic formed the backbone of another genre, exemplified in Welsh literature by William Griffith's *Anturiaethau Cymro yn Affrica* (Adventures of a Welshman in Africa) (1912). This Welsh version of the Victorian/Edwardian, English African adventure story, set in 'exotic' countries about which most people knew very little outside imperialist fiction, autobiographies of travellers and slide-shows, is threaded throughout with encounters with animals that are impressive on account of their size, their unusualness and the dangers which they pose to humans and other animals. And like its English counterpart, it takes the reader into a world which Poliquin describes: 'characterized by extravagant vegetation, colossal flowers, heavily perfumed fruits and exquisite birds, excessive heat and humidity, and dangerously large snakes, adders, and cats.'[69]

Griffith's work confirms recent scholarship on the Victorian and early-twentieth-century adventure story which has highlighted how the interplay of kinship and difference within the subgenre dismantles the logic of human domination in favour of recentring the animal.[70] This is illustrated in the way in which a number of human and animal encounters are depicted in *Anturiaethau Cymro yn Affrica*. For example, in Griffith's brief encounter with a python, the snake appears suddenly, transfixes an observer (a boy who is accompanying Griffith) and disappears quickly: 'wedi disgyn i lawr, ac yn mynd trwy y gwellt bron cyn gyflymed a mellten' ([it] had descended, and went through the grass almost as quickly as a thunder bolt).[71] The snake is a manifestation of what lies beyond human understanding and is a threat which transfixes the boy in a moment of danger and exposes the inadequacy of Griffith's response in raising his shotgun.

While both humans and snakes have the capacity to sense danger and experience fear, this is as far as the cross-species understanding extends in this encounter. Before this first meeting with a real python, Griffith describes it as alien and monstrous, as 'bwystfil rheibus' (rapacious beast) and 'creaduriaid erchyll' (hideous creature).[72] Resonant with Welsh nonconformist and biblical taxonomies of animals, the python is variously described as a snake (neidr) and a serpent (sarff); the two words are interchangeable throughout the chapter which is entitled 'Nadroedd a Seirff' (Snakes and Serpents).[73] The comparison of the snake with a serpent invokes the Garden of Eden and reinforces the python's association with evil. The description of the animal is designed to terrify readers at home, stressing its enormous size: 'rhwng deg a phymtheg troedfedd o hyd' (between ten and fifteen feet long) and 'o bymtheg i ddeunaw modfedd o amgylchedd' (from fifteen to nineteen inches in circumference).[74] One of the most frightening features of the encounter is that the python 'yn hogian oddiar gangen, gerfydd ei chynffon, ac yn union uwchben y llwybr yr oeddym yn ei droedio' (is hanging from a branch, her tail as if carved, and exactly above the path that we were treading).[75] Griffith has travelled into a remote area which might remind readers of secret, remote hinterlands at home (discussed in Chapter 2) but it is a much more uncanny and frightening location. The longer he is in Africa, the greater the enlargement of his *Umwelt* to include animals of which he was not aware, encouraging the reader to think about the limits and assumptions of their own *Umwelt*. The sense of wonder that writers experience in encountering animals and birds that they rarely see close-up often lies in their beauty. But the awe that pythons inspire in Griffith is connected with the snake's unusual capacities as a predator. The carefully observed description of the way in which pythons move swiftly to attack and immobilise their prey is imbued with wonder. Griffith focuses on how the prey moves unwittingly towards the snakes; how the pythons throw themselves down suddenly; how one end of the them is curled around the branch of a tree while their head is curled around the prey; how they lubricate the body of their prey with a slime so that it can be swallowed more easily; and how the prey is always swallowed feet-first.[76] The description is dramatic and intended to enthral and repel young readers, pandering to their delight in being safely scared. Griffith goes on to admit that he has seen several pythons killing prey, but he still marvels at how the snakes, slowly but surely, manage to swallow their prey by enlarging their mouths and their bodies.

As his *Umwelt* is broadened by his travels in Africa, Griffith disassembles the dominance of the human where every day he can expect to 'meet with snakes of every size, form and colour' (Byddem bob dydd, tray n y rhan yma o'r wlad, yn cyfarfod a nadroedd o bob maint, ffurf, a llun).[77] Becoming only one species among many and more aware of himself as potential prey, Griffith finds himself having to rely on intuition and embodied sensibilities as much as the potential predators around him. As he describes some of the potentially dangerous snakes which he may come across, such as the puff-adder and the night adder, he is now respectful of them, appreciative of the rhythms in their lives, of their own fears and of the effective ways in which they have adapted to their environment and its intruders. This is reflected in the way in which the language which Griffith employs changes so that he avoids intensely negative phrases such as 'creaduriaid erchyll' (horrendous creatures). As he focuses on how carefully he must walk, the thoughtfulness with which he must choose his clothes and the attention he must give to the time of day and the evening, the animality of his being is drawn closer to that of the snakes he might encounter. He becomes more appreciative of the extent to which many of these animals are attuned to their environments and how there are other-than-human ways of conceptualising intelligence, understanding and knowledge. This book is important to animal studies in the ways in which it deconstructs colonial taxonomies of animals through Griffith's increasing awareness of himself as another species in Africa.

In summary, the concept of the 'exotic' helped shape nineteenth- and twentieth-century perspectives of animals and animality and provided further examples of the ideologies hidden in language which animal studies has sought to deconstruct. Circuses, zoos, menageries and fiction and non-fiction set overseas reflected and further determined public interest in 'exotic' animals and the use of such animals in spectacular shows. The local press, as discussed in Chapter 3, was sometimes critical of human exceptionalism and its role in animal cruelty. But in reportage of circuses and zoos, the human assumption of superiority over animals generally went unchallenged, maybe because of the importance of circuses and zoos in reflecting the success of imperialism, in sharing with its audiences an interest in the 'Other' and in how the exotic had roots deep in the human psyche. However, with the changes in what has come to be termed the 'zoological gaze', with more focus on the capacity of animals to experience emotions and on the psychological suffering of captivity, animal menageries and circuses have been made illegal and zoos have assumed more of a role (possibly not completely convincingly from an animal's point of view) in conservation, education and animal science. These changes reflect the emergence of different views of animality which, once again, suggest that animals and animal–human relations need to be examined in the context of changing attitudes toward 'animality' and 'humanity' in the cosmologies of the time, a subject discussed in the following chapters through close reading of Welsh texts.

5

Brief Encounters

Most of us encounter wild or 'undomesticated' animals only briefly. But these occasions are important to contemporary animal theorists such as Derek Ryan because they provide opportunities for us to consider, and reconsider, their relationships with us.[1] Milja Kurki maintains, with reference to human exceptionalism and contemporary ecological crises, 'some thoughts are now increasingly unthinkable'.[2] Some of our key assumptions are, to borrow Kurki's words, 'historically powerful' but also – as contemporary critical studies of particular species demonstrate – 'historically particular', having their 'origins in monotheistic religions as well as their translations into secular ideas'.[3]

This chapter approaches human and animal encounters in a way in which they are being addressed in contemporary animal studies, with an emphasis, as Derek Ryan argues, not on 'rigid categories of human and animal being' but, in resonance with a cosmology that has no fixed, external frame of reference, on 'more fluid and transformative encounters'.[4] The importance of this approach lies in the way in which it allows animals to emerge from the cultural taxonomies in which they have been hidden but also, as Ryan says, in the 'shift away from preconceived divides between generalised abstract categories, such as "animal" and "human", and in its resistance to any ideal synthesis between them'.[5]

Rejecting rigid categorisations of 'animal' and 'human', animal theorist Paul Waldau has no doubts as to the need to think in terms of 'fluid and transformative encounters': 'Animal studies must contend with realist points of view in animal-focused discussions and yet also soar to questions about what other animals know and teach us.'[6] This is often the starting point for nature writers who encounter animals unexpectedly in the wild. Richard Gwyn, for example, recounting a meeting with a bear in the Canadian Rockies, confesses: 'Watching this animal, I was completely entranced, outside of time. I had been drawn towards the bear in a way that afterwards I tried to explain, but could not. Words failed me utterly.'[7] As is characteristic of much writing about brief encounters with animals, especially those whom we do not see very often, his focus is not only on trying to understand what has occurred but its impact on how he thinks about animals and the assumptions behind this thinking: 'I had not only learned something about the gaze that passes between human and animal, but equally about my deeper self – what I can only call the soul – and in a way I had barely considered before, but had always known.'[8]

The porous boundary between human and animal which has become so important in animal studies, as Chapter 1 observed, is crucial, as Gwyn's essay demonstrates, to fully appreciating the disruptive nature of such sudden encounters to a Newtonian cosmology composed of objects and things. As Gwyn says: 'Animals will not stay put in their allocated place. They have continued, without even trying, to make the boundary between their worlds and ours an unsettled and unsettling one.'[9] He goes on to confirm what we lose when we cut ourselves off from our fellow beings and from the way in which everything is interconnected: 'Every animal encounter of the kind that I have described evokes a reaction of loss, and reminds us of something that surpasses the individual and yet is somehow integral to our humanity.'[10]

Such thoughts inform and account for the significance which the brief encounter has assumed in a broad range of nature and animal writing, exemplified by Neil Ansell's account of his meeting with a stoat:

> It was a fine winter morning and I was sitting on my porch. The stoat came bouncing up the hillside like Tigger, alongside the fence. Just across my track was a boulder, and it hopped up on that, stood up on its hind legs and cocked its head from side to side, weighing me up, twitching its short black-tipped tail. And then, having seen enough, it bounded back down the field and was lost behind a turn in the fence.[11]

The characteristics of this type of writing include: the suddenness of the animal's appearance and disappearance; the appreciation of a fellow living being sharing similar emotions such as caution and inquisitiveness; the animal's capacity for weighing up situations and human intruders; the animal's confidence which allows for trepidation without being overwhelmed by fear; and the animal's knowledge of, and security in, their environment.

R. WILLIAMS PARRY

In Welsh-language literature, such brief encounter writing was developed in the early twentieth century by the poet R. Williams Parry. His place in the canon of Welsh-language nature poets was secured by the literary scholar Idris Bell who recognised: 'his deep and instinctive sympathy with all natural life', his 'keen eye for significant detail', his 'rare intensity of vision' and the 'magical felicity of language which enabled him to re-create a scene, more often, a single object or experience with startling vividness.'[12] As noted in Chapter 1, the process of figuring out the perspectives of 'others' might be centrally important for Animal Studies.[13] Of all Williams Parry's strengths which Bell identifies, the one which in particular anticipates contemporary animal studies and current rethinking of human–animal relationships in a relational universe is how he 'portrays the creatures of the wild not with condescension of a human observer looking at them from outside but as if he had himself shared in their life.'[14]

At the heart of Williams Parry's writing about animals is the importance (to employ the words of the French philosopher Merleau-Ponty) of 'situat[ing] ourselves within the being we are dealing with, instead of looking at it from the outside'.[15] Merleau-Ponty's concept has a subtly different nuance from Bell's critique of Williams Parry's work, stressing not only 'the shared life' between humans and animals, but an imaginative projection into the inner being and minds of animals. In this context, the concept of 'entangled empathy' introduced in Chapter 1 – in which we are attentive to both similarities and differences between ourselves and our own situation and that of the fellow creature with whom we are empathising – provides a further framework in which to discuss Williams Parry's writing.

One of Williams Parry's best-known animal poems is 'Y Llwynog' (The Fox) (1924).[16] Although the sonnet has been appreciated for almost a century for the qualities to which Bell drew attention, it repays further analysis from the perspectives that have been developed in contemporary animal studies: for example, 'entangled empathy'; the *Umwelt* of an animal; and the way in which everything is interconnected in a shared network. The first five lines of Williams Parry's poem function as would the octet of a traditional sonnet, providing a background to the subject which is normally addressed in the sonnet's sestet, but in this case in the remaining nine lines. The poem is structured around a moment of stillness (in which the fox appears) situated between the poet and his companions walking up the mountain and the fox's disappearance. The first five lines describing the slog up the mountainside and the summons of the church bells are concerned with religion as something that is conventional and routine but also the sense of a cosmology composed of objects and things.

However, everything changes radically with the appearance of the fox. The poet (and the reader) experiences a moment of rare spiritual insight, beyond the kind of nonchalant observation with which the poem opens. Paradoxically, with this moment of stasis, in which the humans and the fox are frozen, a new sense of movement and vivacity enters the language, capturing 'the two steady flames of his eyes' (dwy sefydlog fflam / Ei lygaid arnom) and the rich, red of his fur (flewyn cringoch).[17] The energy in the syllabic movement of the Welsh is more impressive than in most of the English translations I have seen, alerting the reader to the distinction between 'sight' and 'insight' and reflecting a relational rather than Newtonian and mechanical universe. Williams Parry's language invites the reader to participate in a spiritual, almost magical, event in which the beauty of the natural world, which appears somewhat veiled in the first part of the poem, is suddenly and breathtakingly revealed. The encounter between humans and animals is approached in a way in which, as observed at the opening of this chapter, contemporary animal studies sees as 'fluid and transformative' and as outside rigid categories, in a way that resonates with a universe which has no fixed, external frame of reference. It takes us to what the French philosopher Gilles Deleuze conceived as the threshold between 'thought' and 'unthought',[18] but in a way which rethinks what happens with the fox's sudden appearance. The poem stresses the importance of humans opening themselves to their position within the universe and to their own innermost sensitivities while retaining the lucidity and self-control to reflect on the impact of their experiences.

The appearance of the fox creates an inner state of concentration in both the fox and its human observer. Each is trying to 'read' the other, which underpins the emotive and psychic content of the poem. Thus, the human–animal encounter may be envisaged as having a horizontal physical plane, in which human and animal confront each other, but also a vertical, metaphysical plane which conflates the psychic-spiritual aspects of the encounter. Interacting with the animal, the observer interacts with the larger forces of the cosmos which bring form into being. This is the crux of much writing about brief encounters with animals in which the emergence and disappearance of them is analogous to the evolution and dissolution of form itself. In 'Y Llwynog', this is underlined in the closing couplet which compares the disappearance of the fox to the vanishing of a shooting star (Digwyddodd, darfu, megis seren wîb).[19]

The full stop in the final line of the poem, marking the disappearance of the fox and the shooting star, reminds us that the poet and his companions have been holding their breath since the fox first emerged. On the full stop, the pent-up breath of the poem is exhaled as the shape, colour and eyes of the fox remain with the observers, and hopefully the reader, in a kind of 'after vision'. In other words, the poem suggests that something beyond, yet embedded in, the material world has been internalised by the human while begging the question, is this also true for the fox? This is a sphere of human–animal encounter which recent animal theory has only recently begun to examine, through the internal psychology of animals (who even today are too frequently only conceived of as bodies), and, as a result of relational ways of seeing the universe, perceiving ourselves and other living forms not as distanced from the physical world but part of its materiality and energy.

'Y Llwynog' is a particularly interesting text to read through, and engage with, ideas in contemporary animal studies because it can be read on many different levels and readdresses the relationship between the human and the animal from different perspectives. In the background is the way in which animals in literature, folklore and popular thought have been invested with religious, cultural and aesthetic meaning. The fox has often been perceived negatively in popular cultural taxonomies, a subject to which Chapter 7 returns in a discussion of Gwyn Jones's short story 'Take Us the Little Foxes', but in this poem, the fox is an emblem of the beauty and spirituality at the heart of nature and also an emotional being. The poem captures, additionally, the mythologised, cautious, wily nature of the fox. Its eyes are as fixed on the human observers as their eyes are on it, prodding the reader to question (or marvel at) the extent of the animal's mental and reasoning capacities and how far these are at the heart of this particular encounter.

The meeting with the fox inspires the poet/the reader to revise the way in which foxes are thought about but also to rethink the nature of human perception and knowledge themselves. Whereas human–animal encounters are usually described empirically and analysed cognitively, there are other forms of knowledge on which creativity itself depends, such as intuitive and embodied knowledge. Embodied knowledge is physically experienced, felt more in the body than the mind, and in this poem the human perception of the fox is physically experienced, evident in the way in which the bodies of the observers freeze. The poet/observers do not simply witness the animal's cautious movements, instincts, intuition and nervousness but absorb them through their skin. From the animal's perspective, this fear is the product of its experience of humans which reflects the human taxonomy (the signifying system) into which the fox is generally placed, depicting it as vermin and a ruthless predator which will kill needlessly for the sake of killing.

The emphasis upon the eyes of the fox and the suddenness of its appearance and disappearance brings to mind the later poem 'The Thought-Fox' by the Yorkshire poet Ted Hughes (1930–1998).[20] Like Williams Parry's poem, it is carefully attuned to an animal–human encounter where the boundaries between the two are blurred, in their shared experience of fear, caution and mutual interest in each other, and the fox provides momentary insight into the wider order of nature. But in Hughes's poem, where the poet sits struggling with an idea, the fox is a symbol of the muse or imagination and the completed idea is more important than the disappearance of the fox. However, in both poems the importance of the momentary presence of the fox to the poet cannot be gainsaid. Hughes's poem brings to the fore the physicality of the fox, with an emphasis on smell, 'a sudden sharp hot stink of fox', and, as one would expect of a poet who had worked with animals in a zoo and with farm animals, the poet virtually tastes the animal's scent. But in Williams Parry's poem, possibly through the influence of nonconformist writings, the encounter is more spiritual. The poem's essential sense is sight not smell, emphasising the colour of the fox in a way which enables insights into the invisible beyond the immediate material world.

CONTRASTING SITUATIONS

Many of the brief encounters involving animals in literature and in nature writing concern humans. Fewer involve encounters between animals themselves and consider how they see each other. Often those that do are based on situations that involve a predator and prey as is the case with Williams Parry's 'Gwenci' (Weasel). Again, the poem deals with an animal that is often depicted negatively but in this case one which figures much more rarely than the fox in real human–animal encounters. Indeed, the weasel's low visibility to humans is reflected in the poem itself in which its presence is withheld for much of the text. When nature writers describe their observation of the usually secret weasel, it is with inevitable wonder at their speed and agility. Daniel Butler, a freelance writer and falconer living in rural Wales with a passion for predatory animals and especially birds of prey, recounts the precious moments that he has spent watching a weasel:

> I often watch her hunting up and down the sleepers as I wash the dishes. She is irresistibly active – constantly on the move, darting in and out of the gaps between the creosoted timbers to peer around for a few instants before slipping back into the labyrinth of hidden chambers.[21]

The first eight lines of the poem describe the poet and his companion's walk from the modern, urban world to the pre-modern, rural world, from a county road to a country lane, through a pig stile (giât mochyn), to a right of way across land, and to a sheep walk. The journey suggests not only how far into the animal world they have entered but how far removed from that world they were at the beginning of the poem. Through their walk, they remove themselves from the human signifying system into which animals are placed. The nub of the poem is the poet's discovery of a large, possibly dead, rabbit. After having clapped their hands and shouted and produced no response, they turn away to continue their walk.

If the rabbit had been another human, the poet and his companion would have behaved differently. The remaining six lines makes what the companion does seem careless and indifferent. The sestet is focused on the discovery that the rabbit is alive, only feigning death to fool a predator, and is considering its next move, preparing for that last possible moment, milliseconds away, when it might as well try to make a hop for it. The reason for the rabbit's fear is revealed with the emergence of the weasel in the last couplet when the rabbit finally tries to make its escape. The shock of the weasel's appearance is encapsulated in the energy and vivacity of the language. There is no compromise in the word 'sugnwr' (sucker); it conveys how the weasel's sudden, wrenchlike grip would send a jolt like shards of glass along the rabbit's spine and rush the life out of its body. In just a few details, Williams Parry demonstrates his capacity, which Bell commended, to suggest the weasel through only a few key features, in this case, the small head and white front.

The poem is about two encounters, one of which involves a human and an animal and the other, two animals. The poem situates the reader in the being of the rabbit and, reflecting accounts of animal suffering in the Victorian and Edwardian Press (discussed in Chapter 3) and anticipating interest in contemporary animal studies in ethology, suggests that animals are capable of emotions and self-awareness. But the poem goes further than implying that animals like humans are able to feel fear and suggests that the rabbit has the capacity to feign death, raising questions about the reasoning and intuitive capacity of animals.

In undermining the notion of animals as 'thing-like objects', which is how they are perceived in a Newtonian cosmology, as Chapter 1 says, the poem encourages us to think hard about interconnectivity, anticipating what Kurki describes as 'the notion of thoroughgoing relationality of all being and becoming in the mesh'.[22] 'Gwenci' takes the reader from animals as things to a wider interconnectivity through which our universe is revealed as a network of relationships. Thus, in 'Y Llwynog' and 'Gwenci', the environment is not a 'background' against which human and nonhuman things move, but one which human and nonhuman animals cohabit symbiotically. Both poems suggest our need to focus on the relationships, negotiations and structural entanglements we are 'of' as well as 'in'.

THE DELUSIONAL IMAGINATION

Kurki points out that 'when we realise that we live in a mesh ... our encounter with other beings becomes profound': 'Our cohabitants are strange in part because it is always difficult to "capture" them in their "essence", but most fundamentally, because strange strangers in relations, including ourselves, are always "porous", they do not exist "on their own".'[23] I turn now to a poem in which relating to 'strange strangers, relationally bound with us and yet not completely separate others either, is as tricky as it is interesting'.[24] Such writings probe the extent to which we think in terms of 'multiplicities of relationalities' or think of relationships 'as relations of things'.[25]

'The Badger' by Gwynn ap Gwilym, the son of a nonconformist Welsh minister, is concerned with the distorting perspectives which come into play when we think of our nonhuman cohabitants as 'strange strangers' to which we are not relationally bound. For this reason, the voice of the participant-narrator cannot be trusted, perceiving badgers as 'strange strangers' and focusing on what is perceived as their almost primeval awkwardness, 'strange tread', 'garbled jerk', 'rambling' and 'shaking'.[26] The awkwardness is not in the badger but the observer who is removed from nature and whose view of the natural world is increasingly delusional and unreliable: 'In my swift vehicle I was Arthur, haunting light's larcenist.'[27] In ap Gwilym's poem, the badger is not allowed his animal identity:

> he trod before me on his certain journey,
> like some relic from the temples of earth's old gods,
> or some corrupt idol pregnant with sin,
> and his grossness I could not comprehend.[28]

The observer's distorting imagination is in sharp contrast to Ansell's encounter with badgers in his nature writing:

> After the sun had set, but well before dark, a striped muzzle emerged from the underground lair and tested the air. It disappeared again, and I thought at first that I had been rumbled, but then a big boar badger came barrelling out of the sett, closely followed by two sows. They remained around their heavily trampled arena for a while, scratching and sniffing. Badgers move with a sinuous roll that belies their bulk.[29]

Acknowledging the characteristics which the badgers share with humans, Ansell permits them their animality. Thus, they are cautious, rely on their senses and are confident in their own skin when they are in the open air, free of the smell of predators. Ansell's language is much truer to the animal – 'a big boar badger came barrelling'[30] – which he captures subtly in the strategic repetition of the consonants, the rhythm and the energy of the description. While ap Gwilym's poem is based on the observation of a 'thing', Ansell's prose captures the interconnectivity.

WILLIAMS PARRY'S LEGACY

As examples of how the 'brief encounter' poem has been developed in modern Welsh literature, I turn now to three notable poems – Gillian Clarke's 'The Presence' and Hilary Llewellyn-Williams's 'Mole' and 'The Bee-Flight' – by two writers for whom the environment, as for Williams Parry, is not a background for human and nonhuman animal actions but constituted of multiple human and animal intra-actions of which they are a part.

An obvious difference between Clarke's 'The Presence' and Williams Parry's 'Y Llwynog' is that whereas Williams Parry encounters a fox on a Welsh hillside, Clarke notices a hare at the boundary between the domestic and the wild, 'between field and lawn'.[31] The liminal situation of the hare emphasises how, as a 'strange stranger', it is relationally tied to us but also separate from us. 'The Presence' resonates with contemporary animal studies in its interest in the diverse range of nonhuman life within urban environments and their burgeoning importance, as Waldau says, in helping those whose outlooks have been blinkered by a life within city walls to 'see how one-dimensional their understanding of life on earth is'.[32] But, as stressed at the outset of this chapter, human and animal encounters have as much a location in language and thought, which 'The Presence' deconstructs, as in a physical reality.[33]

Images have the power to attract as well as repel the human observer. But Clarke and Williams Parry are drawn to moments of reflection and stillness which have an inward-looking quality. 'The Presence', like 'Y Llwynog', stresses the stillness of the creature, how the animal holds the poet in its stare, how it impresses her with its colour (red-brown which is similar to Williams Parry's fox) and disappears as quickly as it arrived: 'There. Not there.'[34] The lasting impact of the encounter, which is implicit in Williams Parry's poem, is explicit in 'The Presence': 'a sense / that such a living thing once seen / in that sunlit space will never be gone.'[35]

Clarke's poem impresses on the reader the extent to which the human and nonhuman animal are of the same materiality in a relational universe within which both are insiders; through, for example, references to the way in which the hare's heartbeat halts, to the stillness of its limbs and how its presence 'stops the air'. The narrow boundary between ontologically very different spatial realities – the lawn and the field – emblematises the equally large difference, which is also in 'Y Llwynog', between 'strange stranger' and cohabitant of the same planet. But Clarke more emphatically enters this liminal space in order to deconstruct the attendant assumptions. Through its conception of the hare as a 'pulsing presence' and as 'something [that] powers the morning', with its breath as 'a mist on the air',[36] the poem, in effect, disentangles the notion of a relational universe as an entanglement of 'strange strangers', suggesting an interconnectivity between the season, the tree, the mist and the hare which the poet enters and shares. This interconnectivity becomes a condition in which an even deeper, spiritual stillness is experienced.

Hilary Llewellyn-Williams, a younger but less prolific Welsh contemporary of Gillian Clarke, defamiliarises small animals and insects, such as moles, bees and bats, which in the popular imagination are often perceived as 'strange strangers'. Her interest in them is in the way in which they challenge the limitations of the 'human' and extend our understanding of the relational mesh of which we are all part. As Chapter 1 observed, contemporary animal studies encourages us to think about animal, and not simply human, histories and increasingly about the porous boundary between them.

Although the mole has been trapped in large numbers, at the beginning of the twentieth century for its velvety fur and in later times as a pest disrupting agriculture and urban gardens, evidence of its tunnelling underground, through the presence of 'mole hills', is seen more often than the animal itself. Physically present, the mole has features which, to the human eye, render it a 'strange stranger' on account of its size, spade-like forelimbs with large claws, a pink fleshy snout and very tiny eyes. In her poem 'Mole', Llewellyn-Williams reclaims the animal in its own 'animality', suggesting its perfect adaptation to its environment, its depth of knowledge and an intuition which humans do not have. In this respect, it reflects contemporary interest in other-than-human 'intelligence', observed in Chapter 1, in the way in which animals develop, for example, sensibilities and modes of awareness in order to process and cope with the environments in which they live and in seeing animals in terms of their material interconnections and embodied experiences. The poem reflects contemporary animal science also in suggesting that even small animals, such as moles, have the capacity to revise our concepts of animality. As the poem exemplifies, the mole's life is lived in darkness and she relies on her whole body as a network of physical sensations: touch, smell, temperature, sound and vibration. Her body responds to a biological clock which has no external referent that she can see: 'toiling alone in the dark / her body shifts with the unseen year.'[37]

The poem approaches the mole as one of our cohabitants of this planet in a relational universe. Animal theorists have lifted the mole out of the cultural taxonomies in which it has been placed as a source of fur or a 'pest' and have emphasised its role in the ecosystem, preying on many harmful insect larvae, such as cockchafers and carrot fly, while its tunnels aerate heavy soil.[38] The closing lines of the poem – 'calmly ploughing about her own business / she sinks her shafts, subverting our sensations'[39] – are delightfully double-edged, referring to the undermining of physical foundations and the subversion of our preconceptions of ourselves as humans.

In brief encounter poems, there is a tension between the expressive autonomy of the animal and the human imposition of meaning upon it. At one level, the brief encounter poem, like contemporary animal studies, asks us to consider the animal itself. Literature and art about animals capture how the animal that is glimpsed in its natural habitat communicates to the observer through its sense of itself, its physical qualities and bodily presence.

As an onlooker, who becomes more and more a participant in nature, Llewellyn-Williams is brought 'out of herself' through her reflections on animals and insects, which involves her recognising that the environment is not a backdrop but an interconnectivity which she is 'of' and within. There are fewer better examples of this interconnectivity in the insect world than the evolution of the bee, which, as Noah Wilson-Rich reminds us, adapted 100 million years ago, with the spread of flowering plants across the world, from carnivorous wasps.[40] As Wilson-Rich says, the coevolution of bees and flowering plants, facilitated the diversification of the other.[41] Llewellyn-Williams observes in 'The Bee-Flight' that the insects inspired her at a moment when, unable to perceive the intra-action between herself and the environment, she thought 'there was nothing to fill me, nothing to speak to me':

> ...   Birds calling, then
> a humming past my ear, and again; brown bees
> sailing in from the sedges, dipping down
> into darkness, hollow mouth-oak, in and in
> with grains of new gold.[42]

As Chapter 1 observed, bees have a significant presence in contemporary animal studies, emblematising, through communication which places as much emphasis on sight as sound, an animal sign system that relates more directly to the material world than human linguistic signs. The uplift in the language when bees sail into the poem imbues it with the energy and movement of the insects. Llewellyn-Williams introduces not only bees but one of the mysteries about them that has troubled animal science for years, that the bodies of bees were simply too large to be supported by their delicate wings.[43] Eventually, animal scientists, humbled by having overlooked the very essence of the insect, discovered that 'the shape of the flapping wings produces air vortices at the leading edge, providing the additional lift required'.[44] The poem closes with an image of flight, 'the presence of flying bees',[45] almost as a signifier of how much there is in the brief encounter with animals and insects that is at the limits, and beyond the reach, of humans.

Contemporary animal studies has provided ideas and insights into our brief encounters with animals that suggest that the 'brief encounter' poem often has a relevance to our understanding and way of looking at animality that has not been fully recognised: freeing animals of the cultural taxonomies in which they have been hidden; causing us to revise our thinking about animals and our relationships with them; encouraging us to consider the ways in which animals perceive the world and the extent to which their sensory and cognitive capacities have been developed by their *Umwelt*; and enabling us to recognise the capacity of animals to feel emotions and to 'think'. 'Brief encounter' poems present the reader with changing, and changed, concepts of animality which reflect the difference between cosmologies. Within this context, they depict a shift from a view of animality determined by a cosmology in which animals are perceived as objects and as inferior to humans to one which is based on the interconnection between networks within the universe and on which the natural universe, as now perceived, is evolving.

Of the animals we encounter in brief moments but also regularly, whose animality has been extensively revised by contemporary animal science and animal studies, the most common are birds. Their role in animal and human relations and the way in which writing about them anticipates, reflects and expands upon contemporary animal studies is the subject of the next chapter.

6

Birds over Wales

The Royal Society for the Protection of Birds has advised that there are 83 million pairs of native breeding birds in the UK (19 million pairs fewer than when monitoring began in the late 1960s).[1] In Wales, species that are thriving include the red kite, house sparrows and stonechats while others, for example rooks, starlings, chaffinches and greenfinches, are in decline because of parasitic disease or the loss of enclosed pastures.[2] At least two species in Wales, the chough and the curlew, are on the path to extinction.[3]

Robert Bateman, Antony W. Diamond and Rudolf L. Schreiber remind us how, up until about the mid-twentieth century, birds were revered for their cultural, religious and aesthetic value to human life,[4] how we have been enriched and inspired by their beauty and freedom, and how we have been intrigued by the mystery of their migrations.[5] They have played a significant part in our early spiritual strivings, appeared in art as religious symbols, served as emblems of might and empire, acquired chequered reputations in folklore, been feared as ill-omens and respected for their fabled wisdom.[6]

Of the many approaches to birds in contemporary animal studies, one which is receiving much attention at the moment is the extent to which the 'animality' of birds – the characteristics and traits associated with them – has changed over time within, and across, cultures and how this reflects different cosmic assumptions. As animal theorist Paul Waldau observes, birds unite 'fascination with natural places and wild, free-living animals' with 'urban nonhumans' and in 'an often unrecognised way ... provide connections to other-than-human dimensions of life on earth'.[7] The ambivalence of his phrase, 'other-than-human dimensions of life on earth', invokes the special place that birds have had in human folklore, tradition and religion, but it also suggests the larger living and material world that is emerging from contemporary natural and physical sciences.

PORTENTS AND MYSTERIES

As far as Welsh writing is concerned, birds have a significant presence in the Mabinogi and in the Welsh, medieval 'llatai' – for which, the scholar and translator Rachel Bromwich says, 'no foreign parallels appear to exist'[8] – where they are invested, in Bromwich's words, with 'mystical reverence' but also reflect 'exact and accurate observation'.[9] Yi-Fu Tuan points out that, in medieval thought, birds were seen as resembling humans, in that they have two legs, but because they flew, they were also perceived as resembling angels.[10] These characteristics, he maintains, meant that birds were 'fit denizens of both the heavenly and the terrestrial paradise'.[11]

In medieval poetry, birds were revered for their sophisticated movement and control over their habitat. Dafydd ap Gwilym thought of the thrush as the prophet of the hillsides and of 'the wooded glen'.[12] On the topmost branches of the wood – 'the shining hazel-fortress' – ap Gwilym's mistle thrush is 'agile beneath his wings of grey'; elsewhere the seagull is 'light upon the ocean wave' and a 'swift, proud, fish-eating bird'; and the skylark impresses with what he calls 'the gentle feat of [its] grey wings' and the bird's capacity to climb so high as to become 'a splendid charm near the stars'.[13] However, as Tuan points out, despite their perceived ability to move in flight between earth and heaven, birds could not be allowed to fly free and, by the seventeenth century, they were associated with gardens and were caged so that humans might be entertained by their captive song.

Writing of human encounters with birds from the medieval period onwards opens windows to a world manifest in, but also beyond, the visible. Exemplifying the skilfully executed epistemological and cosmological shifts in medieval poetry, Dafydd ap Gwilym innovatively compares the feathers of the cock thrush to a 'chausible' (a robe worn by a priest) and, not faltering in his observation, sees the 'unpolluted' beauty of the 'sea-lily' as resembling 'the snow or the white moon' and 'a [white] page of brilliant texture'.[14] This creative approach to birds, fusing spiritual reverence with verisimilitude, is also evident in eighteenth- and nineteenth-century nonconformist culture which, as Chapter 2 observed, was strong throughout rural Wales, in pulpit preaching and in traditional Welsh storytelling. Through the stories conceived and circulated within nonconformist and Welsh-language speaking communities, a fairly sophisticated and multi-layered version of writing about birds (and animals) emerged in modern Welsh culture. This is evident in the twentieth-century evangelical writer Mari Jones's recollection of an encounter with a buzzard which, as D. M. Lloyd-Jones says in his preface to her book, draws on the stories and experiences of others as well as her own.[15] The account, like all evangelical and nonconformist animal stories, is reflective within a Christian framework and tagged to passages from scripture. This nonconformist-inspired writing integrated the experience of something profoundly spiritual with wonder at the beauty and complexity of animal life. The moral in Mari Jones's 'Y Boda' [The Buzzard] is based on her experience of watching the bird soar (in her mind's eye above pain and suffering) and achieve God's view of the world from on-high, but there is as much delight in the bird's capacity for flight and wonder at its agility *per se*.

BIRDS AS MESSENGERS

From among the many twentieth-century, Welsh-language, religious nature poems in which birds are analogous to human spiritual concerns but which also revel in their beauty and agility, Euros Bowen's 'The Swan' stands out. The swan is an awe-inspiring presence but also one of the birds whose history, to employ once again the words of animal theorist Paul Waldau, offers 'eloquent testimony to the breadth and depth of our human spirit' while reminding us of the indifference and cruelty of which humans are capable.[16] Unfortunately, although there are 32,000 swans in the UK, it has an amber conservation rating[17] and is at risk from, in addition to illnesses such as bird flu, the pollution of freshwater areas, poisoning from lead shot deployed as weights by anglers (even though its use is illegal), entanglement in fishing tackle, overhead power lines, predators such as foxes and vandalism by humans.[18]

The bird initially impresses the poet because of the way in which he appears to have attuned himself, as the priest-poet is seeking to do, to a solitary existence (presumably his mate has died): 'His solitude swims in the quiet of the water, / A pilgrim acquainted with sedges ... / As it goes its slow, bare way in the chill of March.'[19]

The encounter with the bird enables the poet to better understand how solitariness can define the animal as much as the human condition. However, the swan also enables the poet to find solace in the human capacity 'to see portents and mystery'[20] and, as part of that, to appreciate the beauty of the other-than-human world: 'To see colour and sinew, the flash of white / As the bare hills of the age are visited from heaven.'[21] Whilst respecting the bird's literal presence, the language, as in nonconformist writing about animality, increasingly tilts toward Christian discourse, speaking of 'heaven', 'soul', 'vigil', 'immaculate', 'flood', 'flash of white', and 'the flame of his beak'. In lines that appear to have been influenced by Shelley's 'To a Skylark' (1820), the swan's departure is the most dramatic part of the poem, capturing the power of the bird but also suggesting the ascension of Christ:

> A shiver ran through his wings, then stopped,
> And on a sharp beat he broke from the water:
> Slowly he went, then up to the high air,
> And the fire of his wings draws a soul from its cold.[22]

The different elements of the poem are brought together through the poet's developing appreciation of the 'portents and mystery' of the swan. In the concluding lines, the identification between the two is such that it is not simply the swan but the poet himself who is a soul drawn 'from its cold'.

While the swan invokes the ambivalence of avian and animal history, the curlew, as a bird that is threatened with extinction, is at least as much a poignant presence in the Welsh landscape. At one level, the 'Curlew' by Jeremy Hooker (an English-born poet who spent many years in rural Wales and became one of the leading exponents of Welsh writing in English) imbues the bird with a more emphatic sense of transcendence and spirituality than even Bowen's swan:

> The curve of its cry –
> A sculpture
> Of the long beak:
> A spiral carved from bone.
>
> It is raised
>   quickening
> From the ground,

> Is wound high, and again unwound,
> down
> To the stalker nodding
> In a marshy field.[23]

But Hooker's approach is much more embedded in the materiality of the world than Bowen's and resonates with what in animal studies is often perceived of as a 'planetary' perspective which Milja Kurki describes as emphasising 'the groundedness, ecological, material, shared, and multiplicitous nature of all being on the planet'.[24]

Hooker wrote of this poem: 'Every year the curlews would come back to the land of Mynydd Bach. They'd always return at the beginning of March and every year I would try to capture the haunting cry in words.'[25] In the light of how this particular bird is now threatened with extinction, this seems particularly ironic. In the poem, the curlew is important for what finds expression in sound, language and being: 'this life / Welling from springs / Under ground, spiralling / Up the long flight of bone.'[26] Chapter 1 observed, with reference to work by animal scientists and theorists, how animals and birds, in order to survive in their ecological niches, have evolved perceptual abilities beyond that of humans and Hooker conflates his sense of wonder at the curlew with a scientific understanding of how it is sensitive to vibrations beyond the human senses. Its probing bill is sheathed in living tissues, densely packed with microscopic touch receptors which are sensitive to the pressure-waves sent through the mud by the worms and molluscs below.[27] In writing 'Curlew', Hooker seems to have had in mind 'The Curlews of Blaen Rhymni' by the south Wales poet Idris Davies. Like Davies, Hooker stresses the echo in the bird's call – 'It is an echo / Repeating an echo / That calls you back'[28] – but he captures what is the essence of this echo: a sound that seems to emanate from the void, creating vibration, and communicating at a deep primal level.

In 'Curlew', the bird is a messenger that comes forth in the poet's search for a new kind of spiritual and material understanding of nature and his place within a universe in which everything is interconnected. For readers who are aware of the curlew's potential extinction, an absent presence in the poem (even though, as Daniel Butler says, other predators may be to blame for its predicament[29]) is the way in which the human exceptionalist orientation to nature has been responsible for damaging the planet and destroying its wildlife. In war poetry, and in Welsh pacifist writing, birds frequently fly in the face of this human exceptionalism which is seen as fuelling war and divorcing humankind from nature and from the eternal creative process of which everything is a part.

The prison sonnets of T. E. Nicholas (a conscientious objector who was imprisoned in the Second World War) inspired by Oscar Wilde's 'Ballad of Reading Gaol' are especially worthy of mention in this respect.[30] Like the medieval poets, Nicholas takes inspiration from birds, especially migrating birds: 'Between the bars my sonnets come from / bowers ... As birds fly homewards to their native climes' ('Daw fy sonedau taf drwy y barrau ... / fel adar yn dod adref i'w hen fro).[31] In the original Welsh-language version of this poem, instead of migrating to 'native climes', the birds return to the 'old country' ('hen fro'). This is unsurprising as, throughout the sonnets, Nicholas gleans inspiration from the Welsh rural landscape. But the countryside lay well beyond the urban environment which he could see from his prison cell in Brixton. As he laments in 'Through the Window': 'Naught is in sight but endless chimneys smoking / All walls with city's grime are daubed and dun.'[32]

The title of the sonnet collection, *Llygad y Drws* (The Eye of the Door) refers to both the spyhole in the door of the prison cell and the poet's mind's eye, as is evident from 'Through the Window': 'Beyond the walls are trees and flowers in legions, / The birds and hues and leaves on country steeps.'[33] Birds are important to him, as to the medieval poets of the 'llatai', as symbols of spirituality, freedom and purity of soul. The migrant swallow represented the resurrection,[34] and Nicholas, in 'The Urge', describes them wonderfully as 'living rainbows' and their song as 'music falling like a golden dew'.[35] They provide Nicholas with hope, inspiring him to think of the day when he, too, would fly south. But, as a symbol of the spiritual and the invisible embodied in the physical world, they also disassemble the sensibilities and intelligence of humans who have gone to war with each other.

As Bateman, Diamond and Schreiber say of the sparrow, 'the routine daily acts of take-off, level flight, turning, accelerating, slowing down and landing, are none the less remarkable for being in the repertoire of this wide-spread and frequently ignored little bird'.[36] At one level, this is an example of cosmic thinking that everything is so small and humble that we are lucky to be alive but, at another level, it is analogous to relational cosmology which underscores the preciousness and interaction of all life. In 'To a Sparrow', the bird which regularly visits Nicholas in prison is an emblem of hope through its 'bright singing' from 'a heart that knows no bars'.[37] In the narrow cell, the bird offers the poet, in his imagination, the opportunity to celebrate the sacrament, if only he had wine.

However, the hope that Nicholas finds in the sparrow is also inspired by its ability to navigate over great distances and return to where it has come from. As Jennifer Ackerman observes: 'That a sparrow transported far beyond its known territory seems to know exactly how to get back on course is one of the astonishments of the bird mind.'[38] In his mind's eye, Nicholas sees the bird flying over rural Wales, Dyfed's moorland, Great Frenni's height and the foreland of Ceredigion. There are no other moments in the sonnets when rural Wales is recalled so extensively and so precisely. Animal science and cultural myth are combined for the bird becomes, like the starling in the Welsh myth of Branwen in the Mabinogi, an emissary. In the Mabinogi, Branwen, imprisoned by her husband, the King of Ireland, teaches the bird her name and sends it to her brother who comes to rescue her. In 'To a Sparrow', the poet imagines that the bird, analogous to what he hopes is his (and the world's) capacity to get back on course, has come to him as a symbol from the Welsh heartland which promises freedom, encounters with animals in their natural habitats and a oneness with nature.

War is rooted in a cosmology which Kurki describes as having 'wedded onto the world of the image of the state and the political imagination that humans can exist only within and through the state' and in which '"the planet" becomes a "background" to our play "on it"'.[39] In 'Midnight', the German planes in an air raid, allow us in this cosmological order, to use Kurki's words, 'to continue to think that "we" are in charge of the world'.[40] The planes are a cruel, human inversion of the sentient being that offers hope and freedom in 'To a Sparrow'. This anti-image is developed in 'Disgust', in which the 'mechanical birds', amidst the screeching of sirens, the 'shooting searchlights' and the guns 'spitting death', bring about humanity's darkest hour.[41] Mothers with their children invoke the key primary need in human and nonhuman animals of caring for one's loved ones, which is supplanted by the cosmic politics which Kurki describes, and they become in their fear like 'madden rats'.[42]

The contrast between the machine and the avian world (as manifestations of two cosmologies, each responsible for a different human orientation toward the universe) is especially developed by two later

Welsh, English-language writers, R. S. Thomas and Leslie Norris. While the importance of birds to the cultural, religious and aesthetic aspects of human life remains a recurrent theme in their work, their writing anticipates contemporary animal studies in its shift of emphasis in favour of birds and humans sharing a relational world. However, the significance of birds in their work, the subject of the following sections, has not received the critical attention that it warrants.

A THEOLOGY OF BIRDWATCHING?

In R. S. Thomas's work, the machine, as in T. E. Nicholas's poetry, is a manifestation of human exceptionalism while the bird represents the profound interconnectedness that he discovered through his reading and his observation of birds, which becomes a kind of alternative theology. Joseph A. Quine in his rare study of birds in Thomas's poetry, neatly summarises the significance of the machine for him as a 'synecdoche for the industrialism, mechanism, and rationalism ... behind "the awful levelling process of modern uniformity and centralization"'.[43] In other words, it stands in contradistinction to the 'search for natural authenticity and being, for material and spiritual reciprocity [which] underlies Thomas's poetic vision'.[44] In 'Swifts', 'The 'phone's frenzy / Is Over' and 'There is only the swift's / Restlessness in the sky' and the poet's wonder at 'the geometry of their dark wings'.[45]

As Quine points out, Thomas began birdwatching during his early ministries in rural Wales in the 1940s – his 'Bird Book' consists of over fifty years of birdwatching notes[46] – and he turned to birds and birdwatching as a direct response to how the machine was transforming the character of the land and mechanising its people.[47] Of particular importance in the development of this aspect of his life and work was his period at Aberdaron, on the tip of the Llŷn peninsula, where he was able to enjoy streams of migrant birds.[48]

Quine points out that for Thomas: 'The Machine was changing the human relationship with the earth, setting a cycle of disconnection, exploitation and destruction in motion.'[49] However, to employ Quine's words, the sense of a relational world with which birdwatching provided Thomas, restored 'the wild, mysterious, and unknown' and opened the potential for 'intimations of the eternal'.[50] In this respect, Thomas's work looks over its shoulder to the English Romantic poets, especially Coleridge, but ahead to the natural and physical sciences of the twenty-first century. Unusually in a brief encounter poem, in 'Swifts' Thomas ponders not only his response to them but their response to each other: 'Sometimes they meet / In the high air: what is engendered / At contact?'[51]

In Thomas's poetry, the birdwatcher is both a reality and an extended metaphor. In the contemporary natural sciences, the human, as Kurki says, is 'connected with other beings – animal, vegetable and mineral'.[52] In Thomas's mind, birdwatching is, as Quine says, an activity in which to rethink the spiritual and material.[53] However, more than that, it provides opportunities to rethink not only the concepts of 'material' and 'spiritual' but the traditional thinking which has given rise to them. Through the experience and the figure of the birdwatcher, Thomas conflates several types of knowledge – cognitive, imaginative, intuitive and embodied – in which he experiences, as Quine says, the 'revelation' of God at the embodied, sensory level'.[54] But Thomas's poetry also reflects relational cosmology in that it is not about being 'embedded' in the world because such a notion, as Kurki says, 'would reflect a kind of separation from the world as a "background"'.[55] The birdwatcher is a manifestation, and a metaphor, of how everything in a relational universe is intra-active and in coexistence with other beings.[56]

Thomas's poetry is not simply concerned with the birdwatcher as synecdoche but the 'theology' of birdwatching which, as Quine says, involves the 'regrounding of religion and the opening-up of ideas of God'.[57] In their shared need for the qualities of stillness, imagination, unobtrusiveness and wakefulness, the expectedness of birdwatcher, priest and poet are interconnected, as in 'Moorland': 'expecting a presence. It is where, also, / the harrier occurs, / materialising from nothing.'[58] In Thomas's experience, birdwatching brings forth the presence of God, like the hawk gliding over the moorland, but as part of the eternal creative process in which everything is interconnected. The revelation of God at this embodied, sensory level, points to a cosmic theology which in turn embraces a theology of the stratified biosphere (in which the uppermost layer, biologically filled with gases and water vapour circling the globe, is vital for life) and of the habitat in which every wild animal and plant occupies its own ecological niche in the environment. But birds, Thomas says, have their appearance and disappearance: 'here a moment, then / not here, like my belief in God.'[59] The linking of the disappearance of birds with his doubts about the existence of God suggests that there are times for Thomas when the universe, as in relational cosmology, seems sufficient within itself without need to reference a fixed eternal framework.

In an interview, demonstrating his interest in the cosmic revelations of the contemporary physical sciences, Thomas admitted: 'I wouldn't say that I'm an orthodox Christian at all and the longer we live in the twentieth century the more fantastic discoveries are made, the more we hear what the universe is like I find it very difficult to be a kind of orthodox believer.'[60] Thomas's talk at the outset of this interview of 'fantastic discoveries' and the new, emergent vision of the universe have rarely been used by critics to discuss his poetry and his burgeoning interest in birds. In his poetry, a relational cosmology emerges in which every ecosystem, in which birds and animals occupy their own niche, merges, like the gases and water of the upper biosphere, into those adjoining it. They do so in ways that, through the birdwatcher's integrated 'spirituality' and 'materiality', define and redefine cosmology, theology, 'animality' and anthropomorphism: 'materialising from nothing, snow- / soft, but with claws of fire, / quartering the bare earth / for the prey that escapes it; / hovering over the incipient / scream.'[61]

ACTS OF DESECRATION

The extent to which Thomas's poetry addresses cosmological and theological concerns is rooted in his faith, but also in his sustained observation of bird life. This is an important difference between his poetry and Leslie Norris's prose for whom, as was noted earlier, the machine is also an emblem of human exceptionalism and the bird a representative of the interconnectedness of the universe. Although stimulated like Thomas by this binary, Norris, more specifically than Thomas, addressed the desecration of birds of which humans were capable.

It has often been overlooked that the post-Second World War rural life that runs through Norris's short fiction is generally conceived from the perspective of animals, at the centre of which is the intervention of humankind and our machines. As Waldau says of animal history, Norris's work offers examples of inspirational connections forged between ourselves and animals and the baffling cruelty of which we are capable.[62] This is certainly true of the short story 'The Mallard' which opens with the blades of a tractor driven by the narrator's neighbour, Old Normanton, 'cutting straight through a mallard duck'.[63] But this accidental, yet inevitable, act of post-war mechanical violence is immediately contrasted with Old Normanton rescuing the twelve eggs on which the bird had been sitting and giving them to one of his broody hens. However, this is soon followed by a further reminder of how the sense of interconnectivity of which we are capable of discovering can be devastatingly undermined by a single barbaric act. When the ducks hatch, Old Normanton clips the young birds' wings to keep them at the pond. As the narrator says of one of them: 'He could fly, but in a curious lopsided way, sideways to the face of the pond. Then, as he landed, he flicked his body somehow, so that he hit the water facedown, or stomach-down anyway.'[64] Old Normanton appears to exemplify the animal theorist Yi-Fu Tuan's notion that humans can find pleasure in subjugating animals in this way: 'Power over another being is demonstrably firm and perversely delicious when ... submission to it goes against the victim's own strong desires and nature.'[65] Old Normanton seems to find something gratifying in robbing the birds of their freedom and their primary mode of being.

At times, the voice of Simmonds, the narrator, too, emblematises human dominance over animals and indifference to their physical and psychological suffering. In describing how the mallard hen was killed and how the bird with clipped wings has been robbed of his capacity to fly properly, Simmonds is strangely neutral and matter-of-fact. Thinking of the youths who stoned his ducks, he curiously admits: 'this used to make me mad, but in a way I could understand it too.'[66] But Norris is interested in the contradictions within human attitudes toward birds and Simmonds is also capable of establishing close relationships with his ducks which break down the usual human–animal boundary: 'They are pretty intelligent, are ducks'; 'they'd gossip to me'; 'I knew them individually'; 'they are extraordinarily different'.[67] Simmonds observes that the duck that visits him has the 'loudest and most demanding voice I've ever heard' and he reveals that when he feeds her: 'she talks to me all the time she eats, chuckling and muttering.'[68]

However, also central to this story and to the history of other species, is the possibility of humans (as in R. S. Thomas's poetry) learning from nature. The popular scientist Steven Johnson observed, as noted in Chapter 2, what he called the 'adjacent possible': 'a kind of shadow future, hovering on the edges of the present state of things, a map of all the ways in which the present can reinvent itself.'[69] Simmonds's close connection with the ducks makes him realise that they have more human qualities than he had expected. This realisation brings about a change in himself which recognises the sense of being which birds and humans share. Whereas previously he had only thought of birds in terms of the flocks of which they were members, he now sees them as individuals and different from each other. Retrieving a duck, which has more than likely been killed by his neighbour, is part of his re-education: 'I picked her up. She was unbelievably light and her poor feathers were dry and harsh. Her eye was a blob of excrement.'[70] He is stunned by the fragility of the body beneath the covering of feathers and the fragility of an animal that has passed makes the life more precious.

Norris's short story 'Prey' offers the reader an alternative order of nature in which birds of prey adapt to human dominance over the planet. Hawks and kestrels hover over a motorway because they have learned that they will find road kill there, exacerbated by the way in which small animals like voles and rabbits are encouraged into the soft banks of earth heaped by diggers and earth-shifters. Humans are agents that objectify and devalue nonhuman animal life. Similes associate the hawk with human objects and inventions; it is described as 'still as porcelain' and 'hanging, a machine for looking and killing'.[71] This is in sharp contrast to how the bird appears through binoculars in nature's wider interconnectivity: 'his sudden little shifts as he changed his wing-tip hold on the wind, the swift flutter of tail and finger-ends as he adjusted his view of the upturned world.'[72]

The way in which the bird in Thomas's poetry and Norris's prose is revealed in, and through, nature's interconnectivity is part of a wider change in the way in which birds have been perceived. Despite the differences between Thomas's and Norris's work, but underlining their similar concerns, is their shared sense of what in animal studies has been called the 'adjacent possible'. The extent to which we can glimpse the future in the present and thereby reinvent the present is centrally important to both writers and to the spirituality which is embedded in their appreciation of bird life. As discussed in the next section, this newfound sense of the present is important to the way in which the bird itself has been reinvented in animal studies.

BIRD INTELLIGENCE AND INTERCONNECTEDNESS

As Ackerman points out, there has been a massive shift from the days when it was thought that 'birds had brains so diminutive they had to be devoted only to instinctual behavior'.[73] Contemporary animal studies, as she says, has a strong focus on 'what evolutionary forces have been at play in shaping bird intelligence' and within this framework the role of 'ecological problems … [birds] facing unforgiving or unpredictable environments' and pressures that have propelled the evolution of a flexible, intelligent mind: getting along with others, claiming and defending territory, dealing with pilferers and thieves, finding a mate, caring for offspring, sharing responsibilities.'[74]

Initially, the importance of the relational world entered avian studies through the role of birds as 'warning lights' and 'monitors of the environment', highlighting global threats from, for example, pollutants, such as oil, toxic chemicals, population growth, deforestation, pest control, 'force-feeding' of the land, hunting and trade in live birds.[75] But even among those accepting that 'we are all – animals, plants, humans – inextricably bound together on one beautiful but fragile planet',[76] the concept of a relational cosmology is still inclined to be argued in human-centric terms that might go unnoticed, such as 'birds are an essential part of the quality of our lives', 'saving the birds, in a very real sense, is saving ourselves', and 'what kind of world would it be if so much beauty and fascination were lost'.[77] It is something for which many animal theorists are constantly alert. As Waldau says: 'Discussions of broad-sounding topics like "sustainability" often remain so insistently human-centred that they amount to what can be thought of as "environmental speciesism", that is, a framing of environmental and conservation programs solely in favour of the human species.'[78] Despite the tenacity of human centricity, human exceptionalism has begun to change as far as avian studies is concerned. As Bateman, Diamond and Schreiber point out: 'In the last century, people enjoyed natural history by making collections of bird's eggs, butterflies or pressed flowers. Now we make lists, buy field guides, binoculars and cameras, and our hunting instincts are sublimated in photographic trophies rather than stuffed ones.'[79]

In Wales, the shift from a culture of 'collecting' and 'pressing' nature to recording birds in their habitats is indebted to Welsh-language children's magazines, such as *Cymru'r Plant* which contributed to stimulating young people's interest in the different species of birds, as well as keeping alive their Welsh-language names, through regular features, such as 'Adar Bach Y Wlad' (Small Birds of the Countryside).[80] Such continuous coverage of the diversity and extent of birds in Wales for children helped spawn a plethora of published field records, contributions to journals such as *Nature*, an annual 'Welsh Bird Report' in *Nature* and numerous ornithological books.[81]

The wider significance of publications such as *Cymru'r Plant* is made clear by the advocacy in contemporary animal studies for an education in which children are not 'removed from the more-than-human world' and are presented with an alternative to 'radical dismissals of nonhuman animals, challenging myopias and self-inflicted ignorance'.[82] Each piece in *Cymru'r Plant* admires the size, colour and appearance of its featured bird but also includes descriptions of their natural habitats, the effect of the seasons upon them, and, if applicable, their migration patterns. From these short articles, children, and in many cases adults in the household, were encouraged not only to seek out and identify specific species but imaginatively to engage with them and the wider environmental system which they and humans share. Another important children's magazine, *Cymru*, contributed to education in these areas with a regular feature, 'Byd Natur' (Natural World), which included briefings on flowers as well as birds, and occasional articles on farming.

Such writing about birds and their wider environments in these magazines resonates with a concern in animal studies for politics that recognises the relevance of animals to much of human life but does not give priority to human interests.[83] The naturalist Roger Lovegrove tellingly reveals in his book about the red kite in Wales (a conservation success story in that it has been brought back from the brink of extinction) that it 'is not solely about the bird itself; it is also about people': 'It is the story of a succession of dedicated men and women who have striven over the years to help maintain the kite as a British breeding bird.'[84] Lovegrove's book emblematises a cultural shift in the way in which animal history is approached; a movement from history that, as Waldau says, obscured the harm done to animals and led to 'depleting then destroying, entire populations, communities, and, eventually species'.[85]

In this respect, *The Kite's Tale* is an important work, not for the story of the red kite alone, but for the way in which it resonates with the emphasis in contemporary ecology on the need to think seriously about interconnectedness. Waldau points out that while extinction commands much attention, it is rivalled by the extent of the harm that animals suffer,[86] which is important also to Lovegrove who reminds us how the Game Laws of 1840 cost the lives of numerous animals and birds by the use of traps, poison and guns and how the red kite's history can be conceived in terms of periods of constructive and sympathetic attitudes toward wildlife alternating with human activities that made the bird's existence and well-being precarious.[87]

In effect, Lovegrove's *The Kite's Tale* impressively combines a tribute to the awakening of consciousness which brought the red kite back from near extinction; vivid accounts of the bird's beauty, subtle agility and power of flight; a comprehensive understanding of the red kite's habitat and the balance of forces supporting the preservation of natural environments; a fresh perspective on the history of Wales from an animal, and especially a red kite's, interests; and a much-needed acknowledgement of the contribution of research and animal science to sustaining the bird population in Wales. Throughout the book, the magnificence of the red kite as a living being in its own right is kept in the foreground and its story never allowed to slip into human-centred concerns:

> As it soars, the kite gives a perfect opportunity for appreciation of its grace. Because it is disproportionally light for its large size, it floats and drifts with a lazy ease and buoyancy which no other bird, not even a harrier, can match. It can check or hold on the wing or pivot and pirouette with the fairy delicacy of a ballerina. As it swings round, the light will suddenly catch its plumage and fire the russet red of the body and upper tail or highlight the translucent patches on the underwing and the white crescents above; at such a moment one never fails to catch one's breath or draw a gasp of appreciation.[88]

Of the many imaginative engagements with birds of prey in Welsh-language writing, one particularly deserving of attention is 'Dynwared' (Birdsong) by the Welsh-language poet Menna Elfyn. As if it were a contemporary 'llatai', it emphasises the beauty of birdsong – 'Buon yn telori fel adar heddiw' (Today we sang like the birds) and engages in a reverent naming of birds – 'Chwibanogl y mynydd, / y robin hy' a'r drudwns' (The mountain curlew, the bold robin, / and starlings) – and conjures up the hawk as a carrier of prayer.[89] But it is the depiction of the poet narrator and her companion making a hawk with their hands and watching its imaginary wings sweeping the sky which invokes a bird, like Lovegrove's the red kite, in tune with its environment and humans revelling in its powers of flight. Elfyn conjures up the hawk which, as with the birds in the work of Thomas and Norris, impressed the poet for their beauty and agility but also for the way in which they are attuned to their habitats and manifest the characteristics of their species.

ENCOUNTERING CONTEXTS/ CHALLENGING COSMOLOGIES

Whether an encounter with a bird opens on to a spiritually uplifting experience, as it does for Euros Bowen, or something that is ambivalent and difficult to unravel, much depends on the location in which it occurs and, as Derek Ryan says, how far our 'assumptions about the divide between humans and animals [have] been seriously challenged'.[90] From the perspective of animal studies, writing about encounters with birds, and how they change the human worldview, is important to the wider project in animal theory of deconstructing the human–animal model that 'neutralises and objectifies nonhuman life'.[91]

How animal studies and writing about birds can be seen as engaging with each other is interestingly demonstrated in Gillian Clarke's innovative version of a 'brief encounter' poem, 'Heron at Port Talbot' (originally published in *Letter from a Far Country*, 1982). The poem has two of the contexts to which animal theorists, like Ryan, have drawn our attention: the physical location of the encounter, in this case the motorway on which the poet narrator is driving, and the encounter with the bird in our thoughts.[92] The poet drives past former steel works – the ghosts of a once, industrial-rich society – which, like the machine in Thomas's and Norris's work, reflect a cosmology determined by human exceptionalism and the belief that we control the world. But the remnants of heavy industry are overshadowed now by hillsides and mountains reclaiming their old presence, symbols of a different kind of cosmology in which life is part of a wider natural order and not an industrial order based on what could be dug out of the earth. At one level, the heron (a bird with green conservation status and protected by the Wildlife and Countryside Act 1981) resonates with the recovery of the landscape, providing the sense of hope which Waldau suggests humans look for in birds.[93] But the near violence of the sudden encounter is a wake-up call: 'we almost touch, both breaking flight.'[94] While neither has the time to be cautious of the other, as in Williams Parry's 'Y Llwynog', the focus is again on the eye contact between them, an insight into the heron's mind and his beauty: 'I see his living eye, his change of mind, / feel pressure as we bank, the force / of his beauty.'[95]

The differently travelled paths of the human and nonhuman momentarily intersect, this time almost dangerously, and each seems to search for something in the other. The heron brings something new into the human world which is very old, a recognition of a deeper sense of being which humans and animals might share in a more enriching way. In this case, it is symbolised in the re-opening of the heron-roads which are themselves the product of a close relationship with nature and an understanding of the natural environment which has been lost and needs to be reclaimed. Recalling the way in which birds in the medieval period were seen as angels, mentioned earlier, the heron is described as an 'archangel' and, as such, invokes a spirituality which is embedded in the animal's beauty. Like all 'brief encounter' poems, 'Heron at Port Talbot' is based on different levels of interruption: of the poet's driving, of industrial society, of the exploitation of the mountains, of the destruction of nature, and of the failure of humans to see themselves as sharing the environment with other species.

There is a remarkably similar but potentially even more violent incident in Leslie Norris's short story 'Prey' and, once again, it is the motor vehicle that has changed the nature of the human and animal encounter: [A hawk] 'swooped almost into my windscreen as I drove under the downs. He came late out of his dive, wings and legs braced in front of the glass. I saw the open hook of his beak, his furious yellow eye.'[96] This may be contrasted with another of Norris's stories which is more along the lines of the traditional 'brief encounter' genre. Having left his car, symbolic of walking away from the modern, mechanised world, the narrator encounters a hawk and makes his way onto the beach near which there is 'a straggle of blackthorns', engaged in a 'constant struggle with salty seas': 'Above them stood a hawk, a yard or two above them, balancing in the wild gusts. As I looked, he cut through the wind like a winged blade, sweeping along the thicket, raking it, driving the little birds out before him.'[97] Watching the hawk brings the narrator close to a fellow species. As he stands in his own skin, as it were, in the gathering storm, he feels, with the bird, the spit and sting in the wind.

In Norris's story 'Prey', in Clarke's poem 'Heron at Port Talbot' and in Lovegrove's description of the red kite, the writer and the bird are brought closer together. It is as if the bird in perfect harmony with its environment, through its intelligence which in some respects transcends human sensibilities, and its presence within the wider 'mesh' of the universe, says something to the author that has needed to be said for some time. This is the subject of the next section, which focuses on what birds reawaken in us.

REAWAKENING A SENSE OF BEAUTY

Despite the long history of human interest in them, birds frequently appear in creative and nature writing as if they are being discovered for the first time. In his account of the rescue of a raven, Neil Ansell studies the bird in his hand as if he has never seen one before: 'I had always taken ravens to be jet black, but this close up the bird was two-tone, its plumage shone with a glossy metallic sheen in purple and green. It felt like an incredible honour to have such a beautiful wild creature in my hands.'[98] This focus upon the beauty and colour of a bird that he is seeing close-up for the first time is comparable to how the Shropshire nature diarist Hilda Murrell views a kestrel which lands on a power-line pole in front of her:

> It was a female, a rich brown all over – just not red enough to be called chestnut. Her back was barred horizontally with dark brown, also her wing-coverts, but the bars on these were much smaller and closer. Long black wing-quills and a broad black band near the end of her tail, and a narrow band of white at the tip. Her legs were conspicuously rich yellow with black talons, and her eyes were large, round and dark.[99]

Each of these texts exemplifies how birds can reawaken a sense of beauty in humans which has somehow become dulled. But, within this reawakening, the bird itself is re-enlivened. As Jennifer Ackerman points out: 'Birds have possibly the most advanced visual system of any vertebrate, with a highly developed ability to distinguish colours over a wide range of wavelengths.'[100] The kestrel's colourings and feathers, like those of Ansell's raven, provide a superlative example of natural patterning. But Murrell exemplifies how, in order to appreciate the colour and patterning of birds such as these, the human mind has to be open and susceptible to beauty. In fact, in both texts, the participant-observer moves from 'intellect', ascertaining the identity of the bird and its presence, to 'imagination' through which the writers are able to appreciate the respective bird's quintessential nature. The birds enable their observers to appreciate that colour, patterning and beauty are inseparable and as such bring the two writers into a world that is beyond their everyday understanding.

In effect, creative and nature writers distinguish colour and patterning as codes of identification (which is generally the approach in ornithological writing) from a transcendent sensitivity to the colour and pattern of birds which somehow provides insight into the mysterious power of creation. There are several notable examples of this insight in Norris's short fiction. In 'The Waxwings', for example, a seven-year-old boy is transfixed and excited by a flock of waxwings from northern Europe:

> Their heads held crests of chestnut, a black stripe ran dramatically through each eye, their bodies were tinged with pink, the incredible tails, short and thick, were tipped with a brand of yellow as bright as summer. But it was their wings, carrying them boldly through the trees as they ate like locusts, that the boy saw most clearly. Strongly barred with black and white, the secondary feathers looked dipped in vermilion sealing wax, as hard and shining as sealing wax. He thought they were like hundreds of candles sparkling through the trees.[101]

Although the boy is too young to understand or 'express the significance' of what he sees, the third-person narrator exclaims: 'their colours, oh, the colours.'[102] The colour and pattern of the birds as indicators of their essential presence and as a transcendent force, as it were, are encapsulated in the description of their impact on the boy. The birds are said to have 'blazed in his illuminated mind', a phrase which significantly points to the spiritual nature of the experience.[103]

How the Welsh countryside nurtures reverence for the diversity and the sophistication of bird life comes to the fore in Murrell's journals:

> On an oak tree on the far side there were a pair of Treecreepers working busily like little mice. They were almost circular except for the tails, brown with streaks above, with a light inverted V in the wing-quills – a very dark line through the eye – all silvery-white below. Their movements were mouse-like too – a quick dart, then the body still, but the head going lightning from side to side in the crevices of the bark. They started at ground level and worked up the trunk; when they came to branches they worked the underside, hanging upside-down.[104]

In this entry, there are many of the features that characterise human and animal encounters in creative writing: an observer transfixed, admiring the beauty and agility in the bird life in front of them; an alternation between stillness and movement; and animal bodies perfectly adapted to their environment. But the intensity of the bird life which she describes in her journals – in a few moments she sees a whitethroat, a swift, a long-tailed tit, a reed bunting and a yellow wagtail – brings to the fore not simply its diversity but the wonder of this diversity.[105]

However, perhaps the principal contribution of Murrell's work to animal studies is its focus on the importance of learning to develop a rapport with birds and animals. Suggesting that most of us hear far more than registers in our consciousness, Murrell anticipates the concern in animal studies that we have cut ourselves off from other living beings.[106] Her journals exhibit the need for what the Zoologist and broadcaster John Downer labels 'sound sense',[107] noted in Chapter 1, which is itself an important dimension of the sensibility of rural people among whom Murrell lived. The countryside memoir writer D. Parry-Jones, who regards a chorus of birds as one of the most emotional sounds of the countryside, remembers the preacher Dafydd Evans for the way 'he understood instinctively the language of the ants and the bees, indeed the language of all the living creatures around him'.[108]

Listening to wildlife immediately challenges controversial assumptions about human superiority over them. One of the most controversial assumptions of the major European philosophers – Descartes, Kant, Heidegger, Lacan and Levinas – which can be traced to Aristotle, is that we are superior to animals because we possess language. Murrell, like many nature writers and contemporary animal theorists, steps outside this binary, suggesting that we need to consider animal sounds, calls, codes and signals not in relation to human language but the mode of being of birds and animals. There are times when bird calls to Murrell's ears are so varied and intense that they are wonderfully overwhelming: 'There was a cuckoo in the wood, calling incessantly. Also a Green Woodpecker calling and drumming, and another loud repeated bird-call which I did not know ...'[109] Neil Ansell, too, describes a comparable experience of hearing a female owl in the mating season: 'Then she flew over on silent wings ... the whole time she kept on calling, a soft crooning call that I had not heard before and was audible from close by.'[110] Living in rural Wales, in close proximity to barn owls, Butler is excited by the revelation that 'they have many calls to indicate a wider range of emotions: everything from fear, hunger, marking out territories, discovering suitable nest sites, invitations to mate and aggression.'[111] Each writer disassembles humankind's belief in its own powers of communication which, as in the case of hearing, is inferior to that of many animals. In her diaries, Murrell stresses not only the wonder of bird song but of the being that creates it: 'This extraordinary diversity in powers of hearing is due to the different designs of ears in the natural world, and the amount of each animal's nervous system or brain which is devoted to receiving the sounds.'[112]

However, while many environmental and creative writers help open their readers' eyes to the beauty of nature, there are aspects of the animal world about which they find it difficult to write, at least without contradiction and ambivalence. This is a subject to which I now turn.

ENTERING GOD'S WILDNESS?

Chapter 5 discussed how, in contemporary animal studies, encounters with animals are important if they lead humans to question the divide between ourselves and nonhumans. There are no better examples of this, as far as birds are concerned, than those which bring us into contact not only with the beauty of nature but also the predatory violence which is at its heart. Coming to terms with the role of predator and prey in the order of nature informs a lot of writing about the natural world and the nature of animality.

Clarke's 'Peregrine Falcon', a dramatic revisioning of the 'brief encounter' poem, reveals a different face of nature from even 'Heron at Port Talbot'. As Butler, whose passion for birds of prey is matched by his knowledge of them, points out, peregrine falcons are 'at the very top of their particular food chain' and have several *modus operandi* when hunting: 'hard and fast level flight', 'a long-ranging shallow attack' and, as Clarke has witnessed, the 'most spectacular ... classic "stoop".'[113] Although the poet is aware of the falcon's presence and how the bird has turned the countryside into a 'scullery',[114] it still has the capacity to take her by surprise through the speed of its descent – as Butler says, using wind and thermals it can climb to hundreds and even thousands of feet[115] – and by its explosive impact with its prey. In what at one level is a shocking but realistic poem – Clarke is writing from inside of what Butler calls the bird's 'killing cone', 'an invisible shadow across the moorland or valley below which increases in size the higher the bird mounts'[116] – all that is left of the prey after the predator's attack is 'a rose-ringed foot / still warm'.[117] However, as in the many examples of humans witnessing animal prey being devoured by their predators, the encounter is not simply between humans and animals/ birds of prey but, as Quine says, between a human observer and 'the naturalistic process of life and death'.[118] The thoroughgoing understanding of the relational universe, for which Kurki argues,[119] involves animal studies engaging with the cycle of violence and consumption on which the natural world turns[120] and ourselves being clearer about what relationality means for our understanding of 'animality'.

Examining writers observing, sometimes struggling to come to terms with, the cycle of violence and consumption often involves rethinking how we conceive of 'animality'. The emphasis has shifted (and needs to) from the interrelation of beauty and violence, with which many writers have concerned themselves, to the extent to which, as Quine says in his study of R. S. Thomas's work, 'anthropocentric ideas about animals, nature and God complicate spiritual and material unity'.[121] This change in focus involves rethinking the cycle of violence and consumption and considering the extent to which it is problematic because of our own removal from the naturalistic process of life and death.

How far our assumptions about violence in nature have been determined, and distorted, by anthropocentric assumptions and insufficient closeness to nature is an important theme in another version of the brief encounter poem, 'Hill Country Rhythms', in which Hooker disturbs a hawk at his kill, which leaves him stunned: 'Sometimes I glimpse a rhythm / I am not part of, and those who are / could never see.'[122] In the poem, Hooker is an outsider on many levels. As a human he is separated from the rhythms of the animal world and, as the last lines make clear, he feels alienated from the farming community in which he lives. But, without the 'exclusivist notion of speciesism' which animal theorists like Waldau feel mitigates against meaningful interspecies relations,[123] Hooker is able to look through the natural processes in whose glare he is caught, and past the initial shocking otherness of the bird of prey, to wonder at the sophistication of the bird – which 'curves / away and with a sharp turn / follows the fence; and the fence / lining a rounded bank flies / smoothly downhill'[124] – and to revel in its autonomous self-expression. But, now closer to the animality of the hill country, he has to face, and reflect on, the fact that birds kill and this is part of its life rhythms: 'bodiless, / bloody wings spread' and 'wings / dismembered at my feet.'[125]

However, it is interesting to compare Hooker's disturbance of a hawk at its kill with Ansell's encounter with a merlin in its remote habitat:

> My first sighting of a merlin in these moors has never been equalled. I was deep in the hills, more than a day's walk from home, and was following the ridge line west ... I was approaching one [of the concrete marker posts] when a merlin slipped low across the hillside towards me and alighted on the post, ruffling up its feathers as it landed. It was a little male, barely bigger than a thrush, and sat only a few feet away. He was subtly coloured in delicate pastel reds and blues, except for his brilliant yellow legs with jet-black talons that made it look like he had been painting his nails. His miniscule hooked beak made me think of a parakeet or budgerigar rather than a bird of prey. I had frozen, and he seemed quite unconcerned by my proximity. We waited like this, both still and alert, until he finally took off.[126]

The bird's beautiful colouring and self-possession are noted in the same breath as his talons and hooked beak. Ansell cannot easily accommodate this ambivalence, downplaying the bird as a predator by comparing his talons to painted nails and his beak to that of a budgerigar. But in doing so, Ansell is drawing the reader into a conversation about the coexistence of beauty and violence in nature. This encounter recalls an incident in Norris's story 'Prey' in which the beauty and patterning of a female hawk, when viewed close-up, is similarly aligned with her essence as a bird that hunts and kills in order to feed:

> I saw the clear outline of her every feather. Rust brown, bracken brown, red where the light got to her, her back and her long slim tail were barred with strips of darker color. Her head turned down and her yellow eye blazed with her one purpose ...The sight of the hawk there, within feet of him, was for him a miracle; but I stood still, seeing her scaled legs and her unblinking eye, and said nothing.[127]

In many respects, the reader is given a choice as to whether they should focus their attention on the beauty of the colour and elaborate patterning of the bird or on its capacity as a killing 'machine'.

Such choices are at the heart of R. S. Thomas's engagement with birds. Those that feature in his poems, such as swifts, martens and owls, have been at the forefront of animal science's interest in how animals and birds have developed sensory worlds quite different from ours (as noted in Chapter1). Jonathan Balcombe points out how migrating birds use earth's magnetic field to orient themselves.[128] In 'The Place', Thomas, separating himself from scientists who study migratory birds, contemplates the martins as a birdwatcher and the owner of the house to which they return year after year. As a birdwatcher, Thomas's wonder is not only at the science – 'Watching them fly / Is my business' – but at the relationality of living beings: 'my method is so / To have them about myself / Through the hours of this brief / Season and to fill with their / Movement.'[129] In this regard, Thomas is interested, like contemporary animal studies, in the way in which the study of birds and animals, as Ryan says, 'opens up possibilities for other forms of meaning-making and world-making'.[130] In this relationality, the birds' cycle of migration and the inspiring 'animality' which emerges from them, Thomas finds confirmation of his confidence in the eternal process of creation: 'knowing the site / Inviolate through the outward changes.'[131]

However, in other poems about birds, Thomas offers one of the most forthright attempts in modern Welsh writing to resolve the apparent contradictions posed by the interconnection of beauty, violence and consumption in the natural order. As a birdwatcher, he understands, and has been led by his experience of birdwatching to understand, that he is part of the larger natural cycle of creation within a relational universe. Through what Quine describes as an 'embodied sense of-being-in-the-world',[132] to which the activity of birdwatching contributed substantially, Thomas apprehends a god who comes forth not as an anthropomorphic projection conjured out of human divorce from the naturalistic processes of life and death, but 'a wild otherness' in which the 'material' and 'spiritual' must be rethought. Through what Quine sees as Thomas's embedded experience of nature, Thomas's god is 'a god of extremes, the unknowable God that is the naturalistic processes of life and death'.[133]

In Thomas's 'Barn Owl', the bird is a carefully thought-through emblem of the cycle of creation – 'It repeats itself year / after year in its offspring'[134] – which through the bird's echolocation – 'hovering ... making both ends meet / on a scream'[135] – provides an image of the cycle of violence and consumption integrated with that of birth and new life. The owl is not something that may necessarily be discovered through intentional searching but 'happens / like white frost as / cruel and as silent'.[136] Despite its initial appearance – 'soft /

feathers camouflaging a machine'[137] – it has a starker presence than the birds that adorn the medieval 'llatai', and which only a poet who is also a priest and a birdwatcher will know is 'the voice / of God in the darkness cursing himself / fiercely for his lack of love'.[138]

The legacy of writing about birds in their natural habitats, which in Wales can be traced through nonconformist writing and children's magazines to the medieval 'llatai', accommodates the way in which humans have invested birds with religious, aesthetic and cultural significance. But it has also stressed the beauty, agility and autonomous self-expression of birds in their own right. Contemporary writers like Hooker, Norris, Ansell, Murrell, Clarke and R. S. Thomas reflect the developing awareness of the intelligence and emotional capacity of birds and see them as part of a relational cosmology. A later chapter will discuss the interplay of different cosmologies and their significance for how humans see themselves and their relationship with animals. But, for the moment, this chapter closes with the thought that while the works of the writers discussed can champion a relational cosmos, they also explore the coexistence of contradictory cosmologies. The recurring themes of their work are those of human–animal studies today: human exceptionalism, the disingenuous denial of other animals as sentient beings, self-exclusion from a wider animal world, and conundrums at the heart of the natural order such as the coexistence of beauty and violence.

7

Domestication and 'Domesecration'

The nature of 'domestication' is a major theme in contemporary animal studies.[1] The agricultural industry, companionable animals, 'pets', zoological gardens, animal circuses, animal shows and aquariums are now the subjects of careful, rigorous analysis, especially the extent to which animals experience domination, subjugation and even cruelty. Animal theorist and psychologist, Yi-Fu Tuan points out: 'Dog shows cater to the usual human vanity and competitiveness but they also provide the occasion and the excuse to demonstrate openly and to public applause the power to dominate and humble another being.'[2] The categories of 'companionable animal' or 'pet', as animal theorist Paul Waldau argues, has little to do with animals themselves. They are culturally constructed concepts in which different animals are grouped together because of inherent and amenable characteristics which humans have exploited while disregarding how other traits have been distorted or suppressed to serve human purposes.[3] As Derek Ryan points out, pet keeping is fraught with paradox. While pets, especially cats and dogs, mean much to their owners and occupy privileged positions in domestic households, they are also regarded, to employ Ryan's phrase, 'less-than-animal' and have lost the ability to think, act and fend for themselves.[4]

As a theme, the human domination of animals has become paramount in both introductory works to the discipline of animal studies and texts devoted to specific species.[5] The animal rights writer Gary Francione is particularly uncompromising in his criticism of human dominance over pets, whether specifically bred for the pet market or captured in the wild.[6] These discussions are often placed in contexts within which the inherent characteristics of particular species adopted as domesticated or companionable animals serve as a commentary upon human exceptionalism and human–animal power structures. In his history of the way in which animals have been exploited and abused in the expansion of human societies, the American sociologist David A. Nibert argues that migration and invasion was made possible by, and necessitated, the enslavement of large groups of domesticated animals such as cows, goats, horses and sheep.[7] It was the use of horses as instruments of war and vehicles of transportation, he maintains, which turned nomadic pastoralists into highly militaristic peoples, giving them the capacity to travel great distances, enabling them to make hit-and-run raids and allowing them to lay siege to cities.[8] But, as he points out, in this context, horses were not simply ridden: 'For long-distance raids, each warring pastoralist was accompanied by a string of captive horses, mostly females. The *milk*, blood, and flesh of horses were used as nourishment, and fermented horse *milk* was consumed as an alcoholic beverage.'[9]

Nibert has coined the term 'domesecration', from a fusion of 'domestication' and 'desecration', because he believes that the word 'domestication' reflects the delusional and hegemonic notion of 'domestication' as a 'benign partnership'.[10] He argues:

> In reality, the 'domestication' of highly social animals – which developed out of hunting them – was no partnership at all but, rather, a significant extension of systematic violence and exploitation. The emergence and continued practice of capturing, controlling, and generally manipulating other animals for human use violates the sanctity of life of the sentient beings involved, and their minds and bodies are desecrated to facilitate their exploitation: it can be said that they have been *domesecrated*. *Domesecration* is the systematic practice of violence in which social animals are enslaved and biologically manipulated, resulting in their objectification, subordination, and oppression.[11]

Although Tuan is not mentioned by name in Nibert's study, his concept of 'domesecration' can be seen as a development of Tuan's notion of degeneration among domesticated dogs where 'an animal may lose much of its natural vigor and still be serviceable as a pet'.[12] Nibert's notion that the minds and bodies of domesticated animals 'are desecrated to facilitate their exploitation' resonates with Tuan's contentions that 'it is even desirable that a pet not be endowed with too much vigor and initiative' and that 'the pet, if it is to find acceptance in a well-run household, must learn to be immobile – to be as unobtrusive as a piece of furniture'.[13]

While accepting, as we have said, that pets are less-than-animal, Ryan argues: 'To present a purely cynical view of human-pet relations would, however, be to ignore the very important everyday encounters with pets that prompt humans to think about nonhuman life.'[14] Donna Haraway, whose work is based on narratives of 'becoming with' animals and emphasises the singularity of animals in their situated roles in the world, takes the importance of everyday encounters with companionable animals further. Stressing their importance as a bond between humans and nonhumans, she avoids talk of dominance, subjugation and hierarchical relations in the domestication of animals, which she prefers to see, in Ryan's words, as an 'intimate material and conceptual entanglement'.[15]

In contemporary animal studies, as discussed in Chapters 1 and 4, 'captivity' is defined as a psychological, as well as a physical, confinement and involves what Nibert tries to summarise in his term 'domesecration': restrictions and loss of control, forced interspecies interaction, psychological suffering, and physical abuse.[16] While accepting that the impact of captivity on an animal depends on the captive situation, captivity in animal studies has acquired a greater emphasis on the responsibility of owners/captors to ensure that the captive animal experiences the best possible subjective life.[17]

Unlike Nibert, Tuan argues that, when set against a broad background, 'the making and maintenance of pets' might be a 'relatively innocuous occupation' and asks, not without incredulity, whether pet keeping and the demonstration of affection to companionable animals is really 'tainted by the urge to dominate'.[18] Like Ryan who argues that the power relationship between humans and animals evident in zoos has not even yet been fully deconstructed,[19] Tuan maintains: 'The breeding and training of animal pets, the establishment of zoos ... are closely parallel themes, and none can be truly understood outside the context of the others.'[20] Tuan offers a model in which 'power and domination are manifest in different ways: some are innocent, even benignant, others are savage, though perhaps most are both necessary and infrangible composites of good and evil'.[21]

While Nibert emphasises the role of violence in the domestication of animals, Tuan stresses the part played by affection, but, like Ryan, he places affection within a model of human and animal hierarchical structures: 'Affection mitigates domination, making it softer and more acceptable, but affection itself is possible only in relationships of inequality.'[22] Like Nibert, Tuan finds in the keeping and maintenance of animals as pets, the delusional and hegemonic notion of a 'benign partnership', pointing out: 'The word *care* so exudes humaneness that we tend to forget its almost inevitable tainting by patronage and condescension in our imperfect world.'[23]

Whether the word 'domesecration' is accepted or not as a more realistic alternative to 'domestication', it renders the concept and process of the 'domestication' of animals more controversial than has been commonly acknowledged. Alasdair Cochrane who, as observed in Chapter 1, finds talk of the inherent value of animal life too ethereal, takes a different approach from Nibert's conception of animal minds and bodies being 'desecrated to facilitate their exploitation'. Maintaining that there is nothing intrinsically harmful in the domestication of animals, his emphasis falls upon the obligation of pet owners, for example, to ensure that domesticated animals are not made to suffer or be killed. Arguing that animals who are kept as pets, especially if they come from a line bred for domestication and/or a specific role in human society, are not necessarily harmed, he concedes that some owners abuse their domesticated animals.[24] As he points out, in the United Kingdom alone, according to 2005 statistics, cruelty to pet animals reported to the RSPCA saw a 77 per cent increase over previous figures: of the 94,130 abused animals, 24,000 were dogs and 11,400 smaller domestic animals.[25]

Following an interest in animal studies in indirect as much as direct cruelty to animals, Cochrane links specific examples of indirect animal abuse to specific animal rights that support his case that pet ownership should be overhauled and better regulated: animals have the right not to be confined with insufficient space for them to move around, to be provided with sufficient stimuli to keep them from being bored and frustrated, and not to be allowed or encouraged to become morbidly obese (which makes them vulnerable to diabetes and heart, kidney and liver failure).[26] Pet keeping can, but not necessarily, violate the right of animals not to be killed because some pet owners take on pets with insufficient thought about what is involved, as happened in the COVID-19 pandemic. But even at other times, when the lives of pet owners change in circumstances that are inevitable and which really they should have anticipated – for example, starting a family or moving home – pets are often abandoned or placed in rescue homes where many are euthanised because they cannot be rehoused.[27]

A NONCONFORMIST PERSPECTIVE

The term 'domestication', which animal studies recognises can be a positive experience (albeit with limitations), and its anti-image 'domesecration', can touch the nerve endings of people with experience of, or empathy with, colonisation based on what is at the heart of the domestication of animals: control, enforcement and inducement. One of the country memoirs of D. Parry-Jones sees the Welsh cob as reflecting the long-standing rebellious spirit of south-west Wales which can be traced to the Rebecca Riots (1839–43): '"Welshman" among horses, impulsive quick in the uptake, spirited, impatient of the whip and the settled place.'[28] But in a pointed analogy to what was happening to the Welsh language and culture at the time when he was writing, Parry-Jones also remembers how the mares were mated with large Hackneys to produce a horse with the right carriage spirit. He notes how it was 'feared' that the Welsh cob would be 'hackneyed out of existence. His spirit ... diffused through many types on Carmarthenshire farms': 'For the sake of his gameness and endurance [the Welsh cob] has been crossed with larger and more lethargic strains, until, at one time, his admirers became alarmed that he would die out as a class of his own.'[29] Often the analogies, as here, are cryptic, but at other times they are explicit, as when a Welsh horse-dealer and trainer is confronted with an English Shire horse: 'Take them away. I don't understand them, I have no use for them. Take them away.'[30]

However, analogies to the anglicisation of Wales are not the only specific Welsh references that enter into the discussion of 'domestication' among animals in Welsh writing. The training and domestication of animals, and the joy which animals are alleged to experience once they accept their owner's control and discipline, were recurring themes in Welsh-language, nonconformist and evangelical writing about animals. From this perspective, the domestication of animals was perceived as analogous to humans welcoming Christ into their lives. This is exemplified in a post-1950 story, 'Tim', about the training of a young sheepdog, by the evangelical writer Mari Jones.[31] In learning to identify, and respond to, the shepherd's whistles and commands, the dog is drawn closer to the shepherd, like the Christian to his Lord, and finds a richer quality of life in obeying him and doing things for him.[32]

Tim is well-fed, he is not beaten nor even shouted at, and he is allowed plenty of time for his training with the opportunity to learn at his own pace. At one level, the way in which the dog learns his master's whistles and commands and how to control sheep is a source of wonder (which attracts people to sheepdog trials even today). But, at another level, he has been 'domesecrated' in so far as he has lost his freedom. He has been deprived of his capacity to join and run with other dogs and to do what he pleases. Like a slave, he is obliged to obey his dominant owner. From this perspective, it might be argued, as we noted in Chapter 1, that there is no more such thing as 'benign' domestication as there is 'benign' slavery. This view is controversial because, whatever truth it contains, it becomes extremely polarising. And Mari Jones's nonconformist perspective is equally polarised and polarising. In her writing, the skill, sophistication and intelligence of the dog is not as developed as his obedience to his master and the analogy to Christian obedience and trust in Christ.

Mari Jones's Christian, evangelical writings about animals are also controversial because they treat animals as manifestations of instinctual behaviours which humans have suppressed in supposedly becoming more-than-animal. Implied in this view are the two contrasting movements identified by the French philosopher and semiotician Roland Barthes: an ascendency from animal to humankind and a descendance from human to animal.[33] He sees the ascendancy of humankind as running in tangent 'to another, symmetrical movement: the domestication of animals'.[34] The controversy over the way in which evangelical writers throughout twentieth-century Wales thought in these terms lies in the polarised way in which they associated 'animality' with 'beast' or 'savage' and with negative traits such as aggression, violence, greed and the so-called impurities of the flesh. But Welsh writers, from areas such as nonconformist west Wales where, as the literary scholar M. Wynn Thomas says, there was 'a residual oral society',[35] also contemplated a shared animality among humans and nonhumans arising from a rejection of human superiority. From this perspective, the imaginative movement from human to animal is not necessarily a descent into savagery, or indeed a descent at all, but a journey into a state of being which is more sensitive to the wonder and awe in nature emblematised, for example, in R. Williams Parry's 'brief encounter' poem 'Y Llwynog', discussed in Chapter 5.

GWYN JONES'S 'THE BRUTE CREATION'

One of the most notable stories about the boundary between 'domestication' and 'domesecration', written from outside the nonconformist perspective of animality but still influenced by it, is Gwyn Jones's 'The Brute Creation'. Jones was part of a generation which, like R. Williams Parry, broke from nonconformity and some of his stories, like the early poems of R. S. Thomas, deliberately offer an anti-image to the way in which the more positive strands in nonconformist culture idealised the relationship between humans, animals and nature. The distance which Jones is able to place between himself and his animal protagonists creates a space in which he pursues dark themes that sometimes border on the grotesque.

'The Brute Creation' conjures up the Welsh hills in ways in which they were perceived by medieval Welsh writers as remote sites of secret practices which were the antithesis of what happened in semi-rural and urban Wales (as discussed in Chapter 2). In this particular story, the Welsh hill farms stand in contradistinction to the lowlands of south Wales where animals are more inclined to be accepted as sentient, intelligent beings. The hill farmer Red Head contrasts the challenges that he faces on the uplands with what he perceives as the more comfortable lives of the lowland farmers whom he dismisses as 'squat, basin-bellied, fat-legged'.[36] In the structure of the story, the lowlands are more obviously a site of 'domestication' based, as in Mari Jones's work, on allegedly comfortable relationships between humans and animals (if the psychological impact of captivity on animals is disregarded). But the more remote hill farms – associated with the nonconformist perception of a descent into animality and with 'domesecration', abuse and violence – are the anti-image of lowland Wales.

The interest in contemporary animal studies in the psychology of animal behaviour provides an appropriate framework within which to discuss this story. The initial description of sheepdog trials in 'The Brute Creation' is impressive for its understanding of how dogs, which have the capacity to apprehend and solve problems and are sensitive to 'alarm and irresolution' among the sheep,[37] can feel anxious themselves. At this point in the text, the conventional definitions of human and animal are brought into question by a deeper appreciation of the cognitive and psychological capacities of animals than in, for example, Mari Jones's 'Tim'. The tension and excitement of the trial, the anxiety of the shepherd, and the dog's desire to do her best are conveyed in the prose itself where the long, short, deep, relaxed, fierce, loud and quiet whistles are reflected in the rhythm and length of the sentences. This in itself suggests how, in farming culture, sheepdogs are emphatically perceived as sentient and intelligent beings that should be treated as such. The farmers and shepherds in 'The Brute Creation' clearly share this view, advising that Red Head's dog be treated gently and (like Mari Jones's Tim) allowed to learn in phases by being entered into the novelty class of the competition first.

At one level, 'The Brute Creation' emblematises how dogs involved in live, especially sporting, entertainments, as contemporary animal historians such as Susan McHugh have noted, become 'strictly breed-identified', in this case the Welsh sheepdog.[38] But the strong identification of particular skills with a specific breed can place too much expectation on a particular dog. In 'The Brute Creation', sheepdog trials bring out the emotional and cognitive capacities of Red Head's dog, together with the skills which she has learned. But the shepherd's behaviour, after the dog misunderstands and confuses his whistles, denies the dog's right to be protected from psychological and physical abuse. The depiction of Red Head's dog following him at a distance – frightened, shamed and slunking – as he seeks solace in spit-and-sawdust, backstreet establishments is an anti-image to the sheepdog trials, domestication in the benign sense and how humans should treat other animals: 'He had no need to threaten; her bones had softened inside her. He could wait for the reckoning; delay would add to the pleasure.'[39] Moreover, this is not cruelty caused by indifference, with which (as discussed in Chapter 3) many of the prosecutions brought by the RSPCA in Victorian and Edwardian Wales were concerned, but perverse sadism. It is that kind of cruelty which, as noted in Chapter 3, the late Victorian and Edwardian press condemned as the nation's vice.

The way in which Red Head treats the prostitute he picks up exemplifies how the cruelty which men show their animals can be transferred to women, as discussed in Chapter 1. Significantly, it is the prostitute, as a member of a subjugated gender and class, who shows sympathy for, and tries to feed, the starving dog left on the street below her window before she throws Red Head out of her room. However, the dog's decision to follow Red Head rather than the prostitute not only begs questions about the training of dogs and their acceptance of the limits and conditions imposed on them, but human domestic abuse to which it is analogous. The story encourages the reader to contemplate why people, and more often than not women (the dog in this story is significantly female), remain trapped in abusive relationships. The dog has been bullied and conditioned to the extent that she no longer knows her own mind or what is good for her. The primal need to be looked after, her misplaced loyalty and her fear determines her behaviour: 'She kept her distance, her haunches tight, her head hanging forward.'[40] In this 'domesecrated' state, which Gwyn Jones's story suggests is analogous to human 'domesecrated' relationships, the dog is as frightened of abusive language and threats as of physical violence itself.

We have already observed, in Chapter 1, that through 'play' animals challenge and confirm power relations and in the case of play between animal and owner this involves testing who really is in control. When Red Head reaches a pond in which he intends to drown his dog, his distortional way of looking at things, exaggerated by his heavy drinking, means he is actually looking at water running over pebbles. The dog confuses his owner's dying with playing and, following the instincts of a young dog, engages with him as a fellow animal: 'She wanted to join in the game. Emboldened now and dizzy with joy that the black of the day was behind her, she leapt for his arching back, and stood proudly with her two paws on his shoulders. She could feel him moving in muscle and lung, and she tried ecstatically to lick his face.'[41]

Once again, the narrative depicts the dog's need to engage with another sentient being in a positive relationship. Eventually, the dog realises that the drunken shepherd is dead and the story closes on a note of longing: 'She moaned in her throat before her long and lonely howl went tingling to the moon.'[42] Throughout the story, the dog undergoes a number of transformations and the final image of her howling to the moon suggests a wolf and a return to the wild. In offering an anti-image to the nonconformist, didactic story of shepherds, their dogs and their sheep, 'The Brute Creation' provides a critique of that genre and its approach to animality.

GWYN JONES'S 'TAKE US THE LITTLE FOXES'

Gwyn Jones's 'Take Us the Little Foxes' is structured around established taxonomies that determine that some animals are conceived of, and treated, differently from other animals to whom they may be similar in form and genetic make-up. Throughout the story, Dewi Lloyd, a roadman who is perceived as simple-minded, stands in contradistinction to more influential villagers, such as Davies, who behaves 'as though he owned all the pigs and people in Llanvihangel'.[43] When

Dewi overhears Davies talking about digging up three young foxes after their mother has been killed, it is clear that he does not see them as fellow beings with whom he shares the planet and he has no conscience about killing them. His way of speaking about them as 'little red fellas' reflects how white Anglo-Americans in American westerns of the period referred to native Americans, while his staccato language, declaring that he will 'stroy um', underscores his lack of empathy with them.

In contrast to Davies, when Dewi first sees the young foxes, he recognises them as fellow sentient beings: 'three wickedly-pretty heads a-cock at the scape of their boots'.[44] It comes as no surprise that he asks Davies if he might take one of them. Such a request is outside Davies's understanding of the countryside and, from his human exceptionalist perspective, he can only respond: 'You're daft, Dewi. What 'ud a man to do with a little fox, 'cept destroy him?'[45] While his response is uncompromising, the phrase 'a little fox' betrays a slight crack in his exceptionalism through which he has the potential to see them as young animals in need of care and affection, as Dewi does.

Davies perceives foxes in a way determined by the wider human community in which he tries to safeguard his role: 'I ain't like you, Dewi – I got a position to keep up, and I got my duty to do.'[46] Here there is a resonance with the countryside of the predominantly English gentry and the big houses (discussed in Chapter 2) in opposition to which Dewi presents an anti-image. But Davies is closer to Dewi (a representative of the rural Welsh heartland) than he cares to admit and, in the course of the story, he comes to appreciate that Dewi does not suppress his own animal side and to understand what animals and humans have in common. Dewi challenges Davies on an intellectual level, questioning the boundary which humans impose between foxes and dogs: '"Get a kennel," cried Dewi. "Keep him on a lead, like a good boy, see Mr Davies – lovely man!" With the last two words he dribbled visible respect and affection.'[47] The phrase like 'a good boy' suggests that the boundary between dogs and foxes in relation to humans is a porous one, an emergent theme in animal studies where the exposure to human activity is seen as setting the fox down the path of domestication and how urban foxes, like early dogs, are overcoming their fear of humans.[48]

Not willing to be put off by Davies, Dewi takes one of the foxes and before going to his home with him, he asks a friend, Myfanwy Price, if she would be willing to look after him. Through Myfanwy,

Jones pursues the themes of prejudice and the assimilation of negative cultural attitudes. Her response underlines the delusional way in which humans see themselves in relation to animals, labelling some acceptable and others unacceptable: '"What's it this time?" she scolded. "Weasels, hedgehogs, or is it a camel or a helephant from Hinja you want me to bother with?"'[49] Myfanwy's juxtaposition of animals that are seen as vermin with those perceived as exotic seems confusing but such definitions of animals are based upon people's distance from them, evident in Myfanway's mispronunciation of 'helephant' and 'Hinja'. At this point, the story contributes to our awareness of how animal suffering and cruelty at the hands of humans is based on human exceptionalism, anthropocentrism and colonial discourse and is more deconstructive of human–animal relations than the Victorian and Edwardian press tended to be despite its part in exposing animal cruelty.

In the relationship between Myfanwy and Dewi, and between Dewi and Mr Davies, Jones deconstructs how animals are ethically, metaphysically and philosophically interpreted and defined. When Dewi reveals that he has a fox, her response is typically determined by her ignorance of them, analogous to how specific peoples throughout history have been stereotyped and persecuted: 'Don't you bring no old fox in here, Dewi Lloyd. I'll screech the place down first.'[50] She retreats from him not only calling him formally by his full name – Dewi Lloyd – but placing the animal in a conventional taxonomy by referring to it as an 'old fox'. The story asks, which perspective is the more delusional, Dewi's or Myfanwy's or Davies's? In 'Take Us the Little Foxes', the community's assumptions about foxes are based on myth and hearsay, while Dewi's knowledge is based on real-time, physical contact with the animal: he 'peeped under his coat at his treasure. He was there all right. "There's a boy," he crooned, "little fox, look – llwynog bach!"'[51] The transition to Welsh intensifies the affection that Dewi feels for the fox but also suggests a richer possibility of human and animal relationships.

First rumour and then sightings of Dewi taking his fox for evening walks and to work on a leash blur the boundary between foxes and dogs, posing questions about the relationship between 'domesticated' and 'wild' or 'true' animality. But the absent presence here is the wolf, of which there are 4,000 dogs to every one, making it difficult, as Susan McHugh says, to compare the species.[52] Whereas the dog is integrated with human culture, and the wolf as a pack animal shuns human contact, the fox is a liminal figure, overcoming his fear of humans to feed on our trash.[53] Llwynog bach is caught nervously between the 'domesticating' of the 'wild' within him and the 'untamed' which remains deep in his animal genes: 'For the first couple of months llwynog bach was uneasy; he'd curl himself into his brush, but be up quivering at a cycle bell or distant bark, and if he heard a squawk or a duck go quack, tapes of spittle would hang from his chops to the ground.'[54]

The account of the relationship between the fox and Dewi during the training reinforces the fact that animals are sentient beings and have the capacity to feel fear and suffer anxiety. However, the story also casts doubt on Dewi's understanding of what he is doing to llwynog bach in trying to transform a wild animal into his pet. In pursuing the implicit comparison between a domesticated dog and a tame fox, the story moves to that critical moment in all training when the pet is let off the leash for the first time. When Dewi releases llwynog bach, he waits, fearful that the fox will make his escape. Llwynog bach's initial behaviour suggests that dogs that come from an ancestry of domestication will behave differently from a first-generation, tamed animal: 'In August he put all on one throw, and in the moonlight took away the lead from the fox's neck, who first scouted round, not exuberantly like a dog, but with a furtive, dubious joy, and then was lost in the shadows of the hedge.'[55]

Dewi's wait for llwynog bach's return is different from that for a domesticated animal. The prospect of his partially domesticated animal accepting the 'wild' within and not returning creates the highly charged moments of expectation as Dewi scans the woods in front of him. It is an experience which falconers know well and is described vividly by Daniel Butler:

> When flying, no falconer can think of anything other than his hawk for more than a few seconds ... On the one hand it was wonderful to see her revelling in her total freedom, rolling on the air currents and clearly knowing she was the mistress of her domain, but on the other hand the same realisation was simultaneously disquieting.[56]

Llwynog bach's enjoyment of his freedom takes place out of sight and the reader sees him revelling with Dewi on his return, which mirrors that of a domesticated dog coming back to its owner: 'a piece of shadow slipped forward on the right of him, and the next second he was rubbing the rakish head, kissing the cold nose.'[57] However, the imagery, 'a piece of shadow', suggests that although the fox has returned to Dewi, his undomesticated self – like that of Butler's hawk – remains in the countryside and outside their relationship forever. Ironically, Dewi rewards llwynog bach, as any dog trainer would do, but he does so with a rabbit, appealing to the wild within the fox. While llwynog bach allows part of himself to be tamed, Davies, secretly following and spying on them, retreats into, or reclaims, the animal within him.

When Davies accompanies Major Downing, the magistrate, to Dewi's cottage to shoot the fox after complaints have been received about missing food and animals, they cross the threshold into a new awareness of the human and animal. Llwynog bach has the capacity to understand the threat to him: he 'rose and slunk to the corner behind his master, into half-darkness, ears erect, muzzle forward, pulsing with terror.'[58] It is knowledge that comes through, and possesses, his whole body. In his apprehension as to what might happen, Dewi shares the fox's terror, 'chew[ing] spittle with fright'.[59] The tension in this part of the story is indebted to the way in which literature, ahead of animal theory, resisted the extent to which animals were represented, as Ryan says, 'on our own terms, mediated through human language and weighed down with cultural assumptions'[60] (as discussed in relation to T. Rowland Hughes's monkey in Chapter 4 in a scene comparable to this one). But this passage anticipates modern ethology and the current interest in animal studies, as we have seen, in an animal's capacity to feel, reason, communicate and be aware of their own death. Major Downing and Davies do not simply witness the fear shared by Dewi and llwynog bach but feel it, too, in their animal selves. Simultaneously, the prejudices and preconceptions they have had about foxes are displaced by new, richer possibilities in the relationship with them.

Davies's secretive observation of the affection between Dewi and the fox (which he has been persuaded to release into the hills as an alternative to being killed) depicts not simply a redefinition of the relationship between human and animal, but of what it means to be human:

> The brute ran forward, right into Dewi's embrace. Then he brought a paper package from his pocket and held it out to the fox, who carried it some feet away and settled down to eat, Dewi meantime talking to him

like a Dutch uncle ... he could make out Dewi lying on his back, waving his arms all shapes, while llwynog bach circled deliriously or mock-worried his ragged sleeves. The keeper's face split on an oath and a grin, but he was concerned lest the fox get wind of him, so he slid back, stood up, and started on the long walk home.[61]

'Brute' is Davies's word and betrays not simply the conventional, culturally determined attitude toward foxes but Davies's somewhat desperate attempt to hold onto it. The word 'embrace' is not one which he, nor many others, would have expected to use in describing that relationship. While the opening words in this passage – 'The brute' – are indicative of the distance Davies has always maintained from foxes, the scene that he witnesses breaks down this remoteness, signified in his closing grin. Dewi and the fox are communicating as animals, with a sense of fun and enjoyment in their shared animality. They remind us, but extend the scope of, Donna Haraway's reflection: 'Our kind of capacity for perception and sensual pleasure ties us to the lives of our primate kin.'[62]

Behind the contrasting assumptions of Davies and Dewi about animals, there are almost two cosmologies. Davies exemplifies a cosmology in which animals are objectified and devalued, but Dewi seems to belong to a different universe which is much closer to the relational cosmos of late-twentieth-century science in which, as Milja Kurki maintains, everything is interconnected through 'networks of relations'.[63]

Jones's portrayal of the fox and Dewi at play is remarkably close to how foxes are emerging as subjects of study in animal science. Although they hunt alone, the fox is now seen as a family-oriented animal. An adult pair will live with cubs in the spring and with juvenile foxes and other subordinate adults in the autumn. The latter, who are often grown-up cubs from the previous year, help with the rearing and grooming and play with the young cubs.[64] In reflecting on the play between llwynog bach and Dewi, we may recall Tuan's association of play with learning passivity but also how to 'dominate', which he suggests 'is a vital sign of life': 'Play, in these instances, ideally mixes dominance with affection, control with nurturing care.'[65]

Seeing animals outside conventional, cultural taxonomies is important to the majority of literary texts written about them but none more so than Glyn Jones's intriguing short story 'The Golden Pony', which is the subject of the next section.

INNER ANIMAL HOLD

As the literary scholar Tony Brown reminds us, Glyn Jones spent summer holidays on his uncle's Carmarthenshire farm, 'Y Lan' where his uncle bred horses. There, Jones encountered 'a magnificent golden pony' by which he was 'enchanted' and 'which would come to him when he called'.[66] 'The Golden Pony' betrays the influence of the Welsh storytelling tradition and, like the middle Welsh Mabinogi makes use of dream to move between fantasy and reality. When the reader is introduced to the golden pony, the story's protagonist, Rhodri, conjures it up from another dimension: 'Whenever he was completely absorbed, whenever his eyes, his ears or his heart were fuelled and satisfied, he seemed to have fallen beneath the spell of that gentle golden-coated creature to whose world he attributed all loveliness and joy.'[67] 'The Golden Pony' subtly invests the horse with a magical quality, redolent of traditional Welsh stories about animality: 'and the golden naked horse moved round in his mind in a glowing ring, casting upon it the radiance of its strange loveliness.'[68]

Jones's story expands his real-life, childhood encounters with the pony at 'Y Lan' into the story of a boy who, on the death of his parents, goes to live with his grandparents on an island, which he hates because of the bullying teacher, the other boys in his class who dislike him, the intimidating gaze of his grandfather and the violence of the island as a whole. He is able to survive by building himself a cave overlooking the sea in which he can hide and seek out possibilities within himself. Unlike his grandparents and the others on the island, he has a sense of responsibility to animals, refusing to light a fire near his cave because a robin has built a nest in the overhead boughs and her eggs have hatched.

On his arrival on the island, Rhodri is upset by the continual yelling of a chained-up dog 'in unremitted agony': 'it was an agony like a tearing of the flesh to hear the crying mount up again to a fresh climax of howls and yells.'[69] The dog's misery is contrasted with the extent to which the large ginger mare which works the traces has adjusted to her 'domesecration' (symbolised by her jingling chains and the sweat impressions of her harness). Her discovery of this inner possibility is encapsulated in the moments when she is most herself, standing only in her natural coat.

By contrast, the dog, initially, is so constrained, or 'domesecrated', that he cannot find a way of adjusting to his environment as he seems to appreciate the mare can: 'the dog heard the jingling and his crying increased in anguish.'[70] The dog has a sensitivity and intelligent awareness which Rhodri's grandfather lacks in his stooped, indifferent walking and eyes that neither see nor know. Rhodri, on the other hand, recognises needs and emotions which himself and the dog share and, as the story develops, Rhodri and his grandfather are each defined by the extent to which they allow themselves to become participants in their encounters with animals. Making his decision to free the dog from the former pigsty in which it is kept on a short chain, Rhodri frees himself as well as the dog from solitariness, indifference and cruelty.

Once released, the dog takes the boy through a series of phases in each of which the boundaries which human animals place between themselves and animals dissolve. The primary sense in this section is touch, the most intimate of the senses and the dog and the boy are taken back to the primal, the pre-symbolic and the experience of the mother. In this respect, a deep, instinctual and intuitive knowledge is shared by the animal and the human:

> He held the dog against his body to comfort him and the little creature leaned up against him, shivering and whimpering softly. His nose on the boy's cheek was cold and moist like the touch of a snail. In a few moments he began gently to lick the child's face with his rough tongue. Every time Rhodri moved, the dog seemed to cling to him and his crying began again, but now it was only soft and plaintive. The child unfastened the chain and took the dog into his bedroom. They both slept.[71]

When the story shifts to the golden pony, we lose sight of the dog and the bond that seems to be developing between him and Rhodri. It seems as if the dog's purpose in the text is to introduce us to the empathy which we are capable of establishing with animals, which in Rhodri's relationship with the pony becomes more complex and ambivalent.

In the boy's first glimpse of the foal, the primary sense once again becomes sight. The foal, like those born every May eve in the 'First branch of the Mabinogi', is of impressive handsomeness which transcends the immediately visible:

> Out of the stable a beautiful golden foal bounded into the sunlight. The child's eyes opened with wonder and delight at the sight of her. She was

the most beautiful thing he had ever seen and she was alive, she was moving and sunlit, and in his presence. Her coat was a pale limpid golden, a flamy honey-colour that seemed to flash off its fluid brilliance into the sunlight as she moved. Her mane and tail were already long and plentiful, to him they were as white as snow, but her muzzle had the dull smoky look of dark velvet. Her coming was a gap of ecstasy and pure silence. She trotted uncertainly into the middle of the yard, shying and prancing on her beautiful long legs, bewildered by the unsheltered brightness of the world.[72]

The relationship between the dog and Rhodri, despite the freedom that he finds through the boy, suggests that he will always be less-than-animal. However, the pony, from the time when she is first introduced into the story, is more-than-animal. Several elements of the encounter between the pony and Rhodri are redolent of the brief encounter poem 'Y Llwynog', discussed in Chapter 5: the focus on sunlight; the unworldly colour and beauty of the animal's coat; the combination of her fluidity and caution (fearful of the environment she has entered); the way in which the observer feels privileged to be in her presence; and how she brings something magical into the world. The repetition of the word 'golden', the reference to 'sunlight', the emphasis on brightness and on purity (her mane and her tail are 'as white as snow') suggest an animality that has not been compromised.

As the boy does everything for the pony and begins to ride her, in other words 'domesticate' her, the animal loses her uncompromised beauty and seems to struggle to retain the qualities that signified that she was more-than-animal:

The pony's coat was honey-yellow, and where the light fell upon her back it shone like a saddle of pure silver. She had been rolling and upon her shoulder was a pale grass-stain, like a green patch of the most delicate Verdigris. With her head drooped forward on her arched-out neck, a thick lock of mane hung between her ears on to her brow the colour of the froth of meadowsweet. Her muzzle had a dusty look as though it had been thrust into dark pollen. Her wavy tail broadened out and then tapered irregularly to a point that almost touched the grass.[73]

The compromise is suggested through subtle differences between the two passages: the pony's coat is no longer 'honey' but 'honey-yellow'; she is no longer 'sunlit' but has a patch of sunlight on her back; she is grass-stained; her muzzle is no longer 'dark velvet' but 'dusty'; her neck is 'arched-out' and her 'broadened out' tail also falls 'irregularly'. The references to flower and vegetation suggest that she is now much more a part of her environment and less a transcendent symbol. Here, the pony, who allows the boy to ride her, becomes attuned to forces that occasionally affect her behaviour. At the end of the story, Rhodri tries to escape the island and takes the pony with him to swim clear. But they become separated. While Rhodri swims so far out in his pursuit of freedom and independence that he almost drowns, his final image of the pony is of her being swum back to the island which, unexpectedly for him, she does not want to leave.

'The Golden Pony' has a number of loose ends. The reader does not know how the relationship between Rhodri and the pony will develop, if at all; the dog disappears from the narrative, leaving the reader to wonder what happens to it and whether it will be treated differently by the boy's grandfather in the future or whether he will rechain it. Unlike many of Gwyn Jones's stories about animals, there is no neat conclusion and it seems to present the reader with the openness, but also the unexpected turns, in relationships between animals and humans. In the final image of the pony being swum back to a life of domestication, or even 'domesecration', an animal that was once more-than-animal is now less-than-animal.

LESLIE NORRIS'S GREYHOUND

The Romans were the first to classify dogs – as *canis villatica* (house dog), *canis pastoralis* (shepherd's dog) and *canis venatici* (sporting dog) – and left this legacy to ancient Welsh laws. Sporting dogs enjoyed a more privileged position than, say, working dogs and, as Chapter 2 observed, the greyhound has benefited from this. It has a long ancestry as a hunting dog (which can be traced to Egypt, Greece and Rome) and by the Middle Ages the greyhound was highly prized by the nobility as a hunter. In tenth-century Wales, as Chapter 2 noted, it was protected by the laws of Hywel Dda but in twenty-first-century Wales greyhounds are deemed a major animal welfare problem. At the end of their racing lives some are rescued but many of them face the prospect of being abandoned – 140 greyhounds in Wales (2,800 in Britain) are abandoned every year – and/or euthanised.[74]

Leslie Norris's short story, 'The Highland Boy', anticipates and allows us to engage with contemporary animal theory around the domestication of sporting and working dogs. The outset of this chapter noted that, in contemporary animal studies, the domestication of animals is perceived as frequently involving violence, and, even where it involves affection, this is offered within a power relationship and a hierarchical human–animal structure. Not coincidentally, in a story in which Highland Boy is involved in power relations with his owners, violence is ever present in the background. His first owner, Uncle Cedric, and then Cedric's nephew, the narrator (who takes the greyhound off his hands), initially avoid violence. But, at the end of the story, Uncle Cedric fights with villagers who slander him and, inspired by that fight, the boy takes on the local bully who has always waited for him outside his uncle's sweet shop.

As in many of Norris's stories, humans are not always honest with each other and, in that respect, Highland Boy (who is suspicious, conceals his true intentions and slyly weighs up everyone and everything that comes before him) is analogous to the way in which humans in the story think and behave. Anticipating the interest in contemporary animal studies in psychological interplay between owner and domesticated (or 'domesecrated) animal, the narrator admits: '[Highland Boy's] expression was at once conciliatory and untrustworthy.'[75] The contradiction between 'conciliatory' and 'untrustworthy' encapsulates the two sides of 'domestication'. As observed earlier, although the domestication and captivity of animals can prove a positive experience, largely down to the type of domestication and what the animal is being rescued from, it can also involve depriving them of their characteristic traits and instincts, thus preventing them from thriving and achieving their best possible life. After killing Uncle Cedric's cat, and having tested the power relationship between himself and his owner, Highland Boy's eyes are described as 'mild and distant'.[76]

As animal historians have pointed out, the history of dogs is really a long narrative of 'canine adaptation to human cohabitation'.[77] But, in 'The Highland Boy', Norris explores the flipside of the relationship that animal theorists have stressed: 'domesticated dogs bear the double-bind of sharing many of the maladies as well as the joys of living the so-called good life.'[78] Highland Boy seems imprinted with the guile and cunning of the human community in which he lives. On the bus bringing everyone home from the dog race on which the villagers have lost money, one villager describes Cedric as a 'fly one': 'You won't find many as fly as Cedric. Have you ever known him to do an honest day's work? Never. All he does is sit in his shop, growing rich and planning the schemes and tricks by which he robs his friends of their money.'[79] The way in which the community turn against Cedric mirrors the way in which they turn against Highland Boy, for racing greyhounds soon fall out of favour if they fail those who see them only as 'pretexts for gambling'.[80]

Throughout the story, similes and metaphors are used to suggest that in many respects humans and nonhumans are interchangeable. Humans are compared to animals: the gang of boys who intimidate the narrator are 'perched like a row of twelve-year-old vultures'; the narrator, in trying to avoid the gang, is 'sprinting and jinking like a startled buck'; and uncle Cedric has a habit of standing which makes his elbows 'stick out like the stubby wings of a sparrow'.[81] Animals are compared with humans and with other animals: in one race, Highland Boy waits for the dog running second only to 'gambol along beside him, smiling and twisting in an ecstasy of friendship'; Cedric's new dog is 'silken-coated and sided like a Bream'; Highland Boy enters a trap like a 'gentleman' and is compared to 'a reformed scoundrel, wearing his drab colour with the proud humility and decency of a deacon'.[82] The moments that lift the story out of the guile, suspicion and silent (and sometimes not-so-silent) threats of the community are those which bring together animals, like Highland Boy's expression of friendship to another dog in a race, or humans and animals, as in the narrator's reaction to the smallness of his dog compared to the other greyhounds: 'I felt like crying.'[83]

The violence which erupts – involving Cedric and those who slander him, and, in a separate event, the narrator and the gang leader who habitually intimidates him – seems inevitable but also cathartic. However, these incidents have to be set beside the avoidance of violence, as in the narrator being advised to keep Highland Boy away from the track for a while and Cedric, after the quarrel on the bus, escaping to Cardiff to stay with his cousins until things calm down. The story ends with an image of peace which, characteristically of pacifist writing, transcends a pervading atmosphere of distrust and hostility when the narrator's father brings Highland Boy into the house and they both connect:

> He had a basket down by the fire, but most of the time he'd be leaning against my father's knees, fawning on my old man in the most shameless manner. It used to be sickening to see them together, watching them walk down the garden with leisurely dignity, or stand silently together while they contemplated some gentle problem.[84]

However, this conclusion introduces another level of irony into the story which encourages the reader to rethink what they have just read, and which draws attention to animal intelligence and the fact that Highland Boy is able to manipulate the context and the community in which he is captive to his own advantage. Not performing in a race in the way that is expected of him frees him from the nasty and brutish life of the racing greyhound (outlined in Chapter 2) and enables him to enjoy a much more peaceful and comfortable life as a domestic pet. In this regard, the story sees the greyhound as more controlling than his owners and more manipulatively intelligent than the humans, who are unable to read his mind, realise.

'Highland Boy', as a story featuring a dog that turns the tables on its owners and leaves the reader reflecting on the cognitive capacity of animals, is an appropriate text with which to conclude this chapter. 'Domestication' is one of the most questioned concepts in contemporary animal studies. In some literature about animals, such as children's stories (discussed in Chapter 8) and nonconformist-inspired writing, domestication is seen as a benign relationship between an animal and its owner, while companionable and even working animals are depicted as finding satisfaction in obedience and submission. However, in the light of growing awareness of the psychological abuse involved in domestication, it has become increasingly seen as depriving animals of their freedom and opportunity to live a full and satisfying life. Much of the animal and nature writing that offers critiques of domestication is structured around the cultural taxonomies in which animals are defined and, to a great extent, hidden; human exceptionalism; and the power structures in which animals are controlled. But the comparison of 'domestication' and 'domesecration' also involves, as was noted in Chapter 2, what Steven Johnson has described as the 'adjacent possible',[85] in which the condition of animals and the human–animal relationship that characterises the present can be reconfigured.[86] Thus, if we adopt his concept, it is possible to think that in 'domestication', and even 'domesecration', there are possibilities of satisfying human–animal relationships. The extent to which this is a theme in children's literature involving domesticated animals is the subject of the next chapter.

8

THE CHILDREN'S BOOK PET

Rachel Poliquin points out that the story book pet is not based on any biological or scientific classification but 'on the animal's proximity and expendability to humans'.[1] Central to this proximity, according to Poliquin, is 'domestication' but what she perceives as 'domestication' might be more accurately thought of as 'domesecration'. In thinking specifically of cats, she argues: 'Once they became household companions, their fond owners frequently oversentimentalized them into declawed, defanged prettiness devoid of all predatory nature.'[2] Poliquin does not mean this literally, of course, but is drawing attention to the way in which, as observed in Chapter 7, we seek to 're-educate' animals, suppress some of their natural traits and characteristics and check their predatory instincts in order for us to keep them as pets.

Yi-Fu Tuan emphasises the role of affection in human relationships with their pets, but like other animal theorists, such as David Nibert and Derek Ryan whose work was discussed in Chapter 1, he is also interested in how humans show affection to animals within power relationships and hierarchical structures. As he says: 'Affection mitigates domination, making it softer and more acceptable, but affection itself is possible only in relationships of inequality.'[3] And, as discussed in Chapter 7, Tuan, like Nibert, is wary of the hegemonic notion of a 'benign partnership' between humans and animals, pointing out: 'The word *care* so exudes humaneness that we tend to forget its almost inevitable tainting by patronage and condescension in our imperfect world.'[4]

The current interest in animal studies in the interplay of domination and affection in human relationships with their pets provides an appropriate framework within which to discuss domestication in children's literature. But, as Chapter 2 observed, religious nonconformity proved a significant cultural presence in Wales in the nineteenth and early twentieth centuries and this, too, is a significant context in which to consider Welsh children's literature from this period. Animals in nonconformist-inspired children's literature often reflected roles that they had in nonconformist (religious education) stories as well as traditional Welsh storytelling which included, as the literary scholar M. Wynn Thomas points out: 'lots of magical animals. People metamorphose into squirrels, powerful owls, talking cockerels and foxes, as well as garrulous parrots.'[5] This double-edged resonance, as it were, where animals in their relationship with children are analogous to a Christian upbringing but part of a more fantastical anti-image gave an edge to animality in late-nineteenth- and early-twentieth-century children's literature.

Welsh-language, didactic children's literature, employing a nonconformist religious framework, can be traced to Nel Wyn's *Hywel a'r Garth* (1899), which proved important to Welsh-language children's literature as it developed into the twentieth century. In a preface addressed 'at y Plant Da' (to the Good Child), Wyn expects the young reader to search for deeper meanings or truths: 'A wnewch chwi chwillio am y *Wers*?'[6] Among the deeper truths in *Hywel a'r Garth* are the benefits of a loving relationship with others, including animals – which partly anticipates the concept of a relational universe in late-twentieth- and early-twenty-first-century natural sciences – a lesson which Hywel learns from a visitation by an angel. But this interconnectivity between the human and animal world in Welsh children's literature in the late nineteenth and early twentieth centuries is associated with domesticated animality (analogous to Christianised humanity) rather than untamed animality (analogous to the savage and the beast in humankind). These two approaches to animality ran uneasily beside each other in nonconformity like the two aspects of nonconformist culture itself mentioned in Chapter 2: the 'joyless, grim, oppressive and fearsome' dimension, as M. Wynn Thomas describes it,[7] and a less fearsome strand promoting human and animal relationships alongside the Welsh language and Welsh culture.

The nonconformist insistence, epitomised by Nel Wyn, that writing for children should not simply be about adventure and escapism but education, inquiry and intellectual stimulation encouraged the search for deeper meanings and analogies in children's writing more generally. Interestingly, this is also the case in Christian inspired texts from outside Wales which were translated into Welsh around the same time, such as *Yr Hen Ddoctor* (originally published in English as *A Doctor of the Old Style*) by the Scottish Presbyterian minister Reverend John Watson (aka Ian MacLaren).[8] *Yr Hen Ddoctor* is realistic but also altruistic, focusing on Christian self-sacrifice and the mission to help others. Throughout the narrative, the emphasis is upon the needs of the patient and what the doctor is willing to sacrifice, despite his age. However, through this typically multifaceted, religiously inspired text, there is a darker undercurrent exposing what the horse has to endure. In *Yr Hen Ddoctor*, the self-sacrificing medical practitioner accepts animals as a means to an end. He relies on his horse to visit patients, either riding on his back or using him to pull a trap, often in difficult conditions like swollen rivers, which results, on one occasion, in injury to his horse and himself. Although the doctor's horse is never treated deliberately cruelly, what he has to endure might be seen as amounting to 'domesecration' and as an anti-image to the close, idealised partnership between humans and animals that nonconformist writing in Wales also promoted.

The declassifying imagination of the twentieth century after the First World War brought animals out of the scriptural taxonomies of religiously inspired writers and out of the cultural taxonomies which celebrated the role of animals in the military and in war. But this religious mode of writing for children was readily adapted in Welsh and non-Welsh writing following the world wars to provide them with some kind of solace. It goes without saying that, as a result of these wars, many children lost one or both their parents, other family members and their closest friends. Stories about the relationship between children and animals often served a subliminal purpose, providing those who had lost loved ones in their lives with an imaginary, loving partnership.

But simple as many of these stories appeared to be, even those for very young readers raised deeper concerns, and they often alluded to situations to which war and its aftermath had given rise. Bearing in mind the concentration of population in industrial belts, and their close-knit communities, it is not surprising that the blitz on the cities in Wales and England, especially London, in the Second World War was as psychologically as physically devastating.

In post-war Wales, there was need for stories in Welsh which provided children with comfort and helped them to cope with the social issues and problems of a nation that had to be rebuilt. This demand is reflected in the translation into Welsh of books catering even for very young children such as those by the well-known English children's author of the time E. R. Boyce. His story 'Tim' – published in 1953 in a translation of his *The Green Book* – exemplifies how such translations not only broadened the awareness of Welsh-language children regarding social issues but human relations with animals. 'Tim' features a cat who lives on the road without a home. The cat's situation is analogous to human homelessness during and after the Second World War, and, since Tim is a very old cat, the condition of senior citizens. Chapter 7 noted the developing interest in animal studies in domestication as involving a captive who is dependent upon a captor who in turn benefits from the relationship at the captive's expense. From the interplay of these psychological dimensions, domestication involves restraining and retraining an intelligent being capable of independent, intentional actions to meet human needs. Tim is torn between the freedom of the road (signifying his untamed animality), which can be difficult for an elderly animal, and the comfort of the house, which involves him accepting human control and modifying his behaviour accordingly. The two options are symbolised simply for young readers in the closed door that shuts out the cat and the open door which allows him access.

The two children in 'Tim' welcome the cat but the narrative, simple as it seems, implies that while he will be cared for and kept comfortable, he will lose something of his identity: 'Nid hen gath y ffordd wyt ti / Ein cath ni wyt ti / Cei fyw yn ein tŷ ni' (You are not an old cat of the road / You are our cat / You can live in our house).[9] The conclusion, reflecting the impact of the war, stresses possession and summarises what 'domestication' means for animals. The repetition of 'our' in the above quotation – 'ein cath' and 'ein tŷ' – conflates the possession of bricks and mortar with the ownership of a living being and signifies that the cat is giving up its freedom in what may be more 'domesecration' than 'domestication'.

DOMESTICATION AND ANIMAL AUTONOMY

The importance of translations of mid-twentieth-century children's literature in English into Welsh to developing awareness of domestication and animal welfare among young Welsh-language speakers cannot be overlooked. For example, the translation of Enid Blyton's

'Nature Books' into Welsh,[10] provided a focused appraisal of the tension between the expressive autonomy of animals and captivity. While the shortage of original Welsh-language books for children in post-Second World War Wales encouraged the translation of such English works, the reasons for this particular choice, apart from the popularity of Blyton with children, might well lie in the extent to which it resonates with indigenous Welsh-language literature. The 'Gair i'r Athro' ('word to the teacher') encapsulates the mood of children's authors in England and Wales in the 1950s. The stories are described as 'difyr a swynol' (jolly and magical) but their translator, Daisy Meirion Roberts advises: 'y mae mewn gwirionedd yn llawr iawn mwy na hynny' (there is much more to them than this).[11]

In the story, 'Y Robin Cyfeillgar' (The Friendly Robin), robins build their nest on the top of a cupboard in a children's bedroom as a result of the care shown by them which resonates with the wider interest in birds promoted, as discussed in Chapter 6, by Welsh magazines for younger readers. But the story suggests that they represent the attitude toward wildlife of a new generation as they are anxious to keep the nest secret from their parents. The bedroom windowsill, which the birds feel secure enough to cross, is analogous to the boundary between the domesticated and the undomesticated but also between humans and animals and, in the years after the war, between nationalities and races. In the kindness that the children show the birds, which emerges from their identification with the mother bird and their recognition of caring instincts within themselves, Blyton's text is redolent of pacifist writing. But in the difference between the children's and adults' attitude toward birds as sentient cohabitants of a shared world, the story introduces a dichotomy which is not readily found in interwar, Welsh-language children's magazines. At the conclusion of the story – when the young are hatched – the children have no wish to keep them as 'domesecrated' pets.

The conflict between retaining an animal as a pet or releasing it to the wild is a recurring theme in contemporary writing for children. In Gillian Clarke's poem for young readers 'The Osprey',[12] in which a bird has broken its migration from Lapland to Africa in Wales, those who feed the bird want to keep it, deluding themselves: 'You could tell it was happy.'[13] Typical of Clarke's writing for children, this seemingly simple line is more complex than it appears, begging the question (which is central to the poem) as to whether this seemingly innocuous observation is an anthropomorphic projection and an attempt to justify their ambition to keep an exotic pet. Later in the poem, those who feed the bird command it to 'Stay!'[14] as if they were training a more familiar type of pet such as a dog and emphasising that however kindly meant, they are seducing, restricting and confining a sentient being. This is contrasted with the sense of wonder at the way in which birds are able to migrate across continents and the sophistication of their intuition which acts as their compass, reflecting the approach to migrating birds in Welsh children's magazines like *Cymru'r Plant* and the developing interest in the intelligence of birds in contemporary animal studies.[15] The true wonder is not as much in the Osprey *per se* but, at the end of the poem, in her lifting off and turning south.

Clarke's poem makes an interesting comparison with Hilary Llewellyn-Williams's 'Feeding the Bat'. Bats constitute a quarter of the mammal population on earth and have been on the planet for about 50 million years. Now an endangered species,[16] the bat has been 'desecrated' in literature, which often associates it with vampirism, the undead and the uncanny; and, together with the way in which its face has been seen as a gargoyle, this has led to it being viewed (to reintroduce a discussion from Chapter 5) as a 'strange stranger'.

But current perception of humans and animals as cohabiting in a relational universe enables the bat to be seen in contemporary nature books for children as an animal in its own right within this network of interconnectivity.[17] Freed from the cultural taxonomy which has imposed bizarre connotations upon it, the bat is being slowly restored to its place as an important component of the wider ecosystem.[18] As insect eaters, bats are destroyers of pests, help pollinate flowering plants and disperse seeds from trees and plants. Moreover, animal science has enabled us to realise that the bat's tightened and twisted face (which humans have perceived of as hideous) is part of a wondrous and sophisticated system that enables the bat to navigate in total darkness through echolocation, sending out ultrasound beams in many directions, and receiving and decoding echoes, even possessing a strangeness filter which ensures that it is not misled by rogue pulses.

Llewellyn-Williams's poem revolves around the discovery of a bat that initially appears to be dead. But the fact that the bat is an endangered species on account of its declining population and seeming fragility – 'a small cold palmful / a hunched and sorry scrap'[19] – makes it all the more precious. In the course of the poem, the bat, which was suspended between life and death, as it is looked after becomes caught, like Clarke's osprey, between wild, independent animality and domestication:

> So we found
>
> a box, and a place by the stove, and scrounged
> a spoonful of dogfood from the corner shop
> and waited. When the scratching started
>
> we crowded round to listen: it was alive![20]

Chapter 1 noted the concern in contemporary animal studies that, as humans trying to empathise with another species, we often make mistakes, as exemplified here where the poet-participant feeds dog food to an animal that in the UK lives wholly on insects. However, the real discovery, on which the poem is based, is the realisation of the bat's beauty and subtlety, and its sophisticated echolocation system, supplanting the cultural mythologies:

> It moved
> its clever head from side to side, gave
>
> delicate soundings. Two eyes, dark points of light
> gleamed, not at all blind, and long questioning
> fingers gripped mine.[21]

Throughout this book, I have made repeated reference to the debate in contemporary animal studies over whether domestication can ever be a truly benign relationship between humans and animals or whether it is inevitably cruel because it imposes a condition of powerlessness on an independent thinking being capable of self-motivation and prevents them from expressing the characteristic nature of their species. This debate provides an interesting framework within which to discuss Llewellyn-Williams's poem. At one level, the bat appears to want a relationship with a human: 'it consented / to be fed from the end of a stick.'[22] But, as noted at the beginning of this chapter, the human display of affection toward a nonhuman animal generally alternates between affection and dominance within a power relationship and hierarchical structure. In showing the bat affection, the poet-participant infantilises the bat – 'Laughing, we squeezed / waterdrops onto its nose, to hear it sneeze / minute bat sneezes'[23] – and in the apparent 'play' between them, we are reminded of the importance of play among animals in which they challenge and confirm power relations and test who really is in control (discussed in Chapter 7).

Inevitably, in animal studies anthropomorphism is perceived as an ever-present, potential bias in how we perceive and think about animals and Llewellyn-Williams's poem has to be read with this in mind. The way in which the bat's apparent responsiveness is interpreted betrays a human-centred perspective: 'After the second day / it arched its back to be stroked, and played / a biting game, neck stretched impossibly / backwards / slyly grinning.'[24] The tension in the poem between the poet-participant's potential anthropomorphism and her desire to discover the bat's own expressive autonomy emblematises, once again, our need to be attentive to both the similarities and differences between ourselves, our situation and the animal with whom we are seeking to empathise.[25] This is evident in the ambivalence of some of the language that tries to capture the bat's difference but, at another level, maintains its 'alien' presence: the humans watch 'the supple greedy / slip of a tongue flick the droplets down'[26] and how it turns 'its goblin face to the window'.[27] However, the tension is not simply in the language but in the narrator-participant's attitude itself to the bat, particularly her developing anxieties over what she may be imprinting on it. The poem closes, like Clarke's 'Osprey', with an image of the bat in flight, significantly free of human imprinting – 'my ears tuned to its music, swooping, flitting about'[28] – so that what remains is the wonder of the small mammal in its own right.

The three texts discussed in this section introduce children to the dilemmas of domestication through the discovery of wildlife. The emphasis in each work is on the extent to which humans need to think through the implications of captivity for the animal. But the next section turns to animals that have been bred for domestication even though they retain something of the 'wild' within them.

THE CALL OF THE WILD

The translation of *Tosca's Christmas* by Matthew Sturgis and Anne Mortimer into Welsh as *Nadolig Tosca* (1990) offers an interesting example, within an established lineage of translations of children's literature concerned with animals and animality, of how such translations in the second half of the twentieth century extended understanding of the complexities of domestication.[29] Both *Nadolig Tosca* and the 1950s story *Tim* (albeit intended for a younger readership than *Nadolig Tosca*) are concerned with the domestication of cats, pose questions about animal capacity for feelings and are analogous to wider issues of the time.

As the sociologist Adrian Franklin points out, pets play a significant role in the construction of self-identity within a family, but there have been relatively few sociological studies of them.[30] Pets are an integral part of a family, bound up with its social orientation and more generally human and nonhuman lifecycles, especially in relation to age and ageing.[31] But the redefinitions of domestication and captivity in contemporary animal studies (discussed in Chapter 7) as psychological as well as physical states of being provide a more complex picture of even animals bred in, and for, domestication kept as pets. Thus, in *Nadolig Tosca*, the cat, adopted by humans, retains some of the independence and self-motivation which domesticated animals are often perceived of as losing. As such, he is both within and outside the family.

As the key character in the story, Tosca provides Mortimer with an opportunity to examine the tensions between his inner self as subject (he wants to sleep and eat as he pleases) and the boundaries which confine him (which come crashing down when he pulls the Christmas tree over). In doing so, the story resonates, once again, with the developing interest in animal studies in the differences as much as the similarities between ourselves and others with whom we empathise.[32]

Tosca's regular disappointment at Christmas, that he does not have a gift of his own, distinguishes him from the rest of the family but is analogous to his other unfulfilled needs. This condition structures the story, which initially focuses on his unhappiness in the house; then depicts his misery in being shut out in the cold; and concludes with the resolution brought about by the intervention of the magical Siôn Corn. The scene in which the cat, in the outside cold, taps on the window but is ignored because the humans are too busy to notice him, depicts how, as an animal, he has emotions comparable to humans and suggests that shutting him out of the warmth of the home and family is an example of indifferent cruelty toward him. But this incident is also resonant of the condition of the homeless at Christmas, how their emotions and needs at this time of year are overlooked, and the wider indifference of those who are well-off toward those who have fallen on hard times.

While he is shut out of the house, and before the arrival of Siôn Corn, Tosca wants to be allowed back in and is in a condition similar to that of Tim in the 1950s story. He is caught between the 'domestic' as signified by the warmth and potential care of humans inside the house (who in keeping him as their domestic cat have reaffirmed rather than disassembled the boundary between human and animal) and the 'undomesticated' life where freedom from 'domesecration' allows him to be his untamed self (but without the care and comfort that domestication brings and leaving him at the mercy of humans who are indifferent to animals, symbolised by the cold, steely snowman). In accidentally pulling down the Christmas tree, signifying the social structures within the house, Tosca opens the reader's eyes to the tension between confinement and independence within the condition of domestication from both the animal's and the owner's point of view. But, at the end of the story, Tosca's assertion of his being and his temporary exclusion from the family suggests how this tension might be resolved. The solution lies in re-signifying the 'pet', which is suggested by the fact that for the first time he has his own stocking on the mantel piece. Although it has been provided by Siôn Corn (who is outside the family and a magical, imaginary presence), it is analogous to the change in Tosca's status within the house (involving recognition of his needs and desires more generally) that is necessary to resolve the animal–human conflict and create a more equal and meaningful relationship.

An interesting later work of translation than *Nadolig Tosca* from the perspective of animal studies, *Yr Arch Anifeiliaid Bach: Y Gath Fach Fusneslyd* (The Animal Arc: The Small Meddlesome Cat) (2012), is again a seemingly simple story but with more depth of meaning than at first appears.[33] Like 'Tim' and *Nadolig Tosca*, it is concerned with the domestication of small animals and the tension between the human home and the call of the wild. As a text originally written in English, its Welsh translation once again expands what is available to young Welsh-language readers examining the boundaries between 'domestication' and 'domesecration'. The book prompts young people to think about the impact of domesticity on animals by reminding them at the outset that the cat, Emerallt (Emerald) looks like a tiger: one of the child characters, Mali, is fascinated with the species and searches for countries in which tigers are found in jungles. Significantly, she does not associate tigers with zoos. The control of animals is central to the narrative in which Emerallt is taken to a vet (Mali's father) in order to have a chip inserted in his neck, which will enable his owners to have him returned to them should he become lost. This is an example of how domestication, as pointed out in Chapter 2, is dependent upon veterinary care which actually enables it. It also raises the issue as to whether we mean 'lost' from a human perspective (implying that Emerallt is a possession) or from the cat's perspective where 'lost' means a bid for freedom which Emerallt attempts every time he is placed in his cat cage.

The fact that Emerallt now has a name emphasises his enforced adoption by the family. Naming of domestic animals is important as part of the process, as the Welsh writer Angharad Price says, 'gwneud creadigaethau'r dychymyg yn gyfarwyd ...'[34] (of making imaginary creatures familiar). In Welsh literature, as Price argues, it involves 'trawsnewid y preifat, neu'r personnol, a'i wneud yn gyhoeddus' (transforming the private or the personal and making it public).[35] In this novel, the choice of name is based on the colour of Emerallt's eyes which, like the description of his striped appearance, suggests how he has become an object of the human gaze. But his name is significant on a number of levels. An emerald is a variety of the mineral 'beryl' as Emerallt is part of the cat family. There is a difference between the emerald which the owners had in mind in giving their pet this name and the emerald in its natural state. The emerald stone which is sold as jewellery is 'treated' to enhance its colour and its irregularities removed, which is analogous to the training and domestication of a cat that is taught to accept human control and behaviours and become as its owners wish. It suggests that although Emerallt occupies a privileged position, he is less-than-animal and more associated with culture than nature, perhaps, as Derek Ryan says, like all pets.[36]

The way in which so-called domestic animals are haunted by the wildness which domestication tries to train out of them is approached differently from these stories in Gillian Clarke's poem, 'Jac the Cat' (in her collection of poems for young readers, *The Animal Wall and Other Poems*). The cat is said to have 'gone wild', which means he is reclaiming the wildness within his domesticated self. While Emerallt's eyes are green as emerald, suggesting he has become a desirable possession to humans, Jac's eyes, described as green fire, signify the desires within him and his deep-rooted urge for independence which have been 'desecrated'. Throughout the poem, Jac is disturbed by the storm, but Clarke eschews focusing on the noise, on thunder or lightning as many children's texts do, and emphasises what is awakened within him (his true, untamed self, his true animality) by the wildness of the storm. The storm is not seen by Jac as a threat but as a point of origin with which he wishes to be reunited. Unable to sleep, or lie down, he has 'got the wind / on his mind'.[37]

The concept of 'domestication' as 'domesecration' is the absent referent in another of Clarke's poems for young people, 'Breaking the Horse', concerned with an initial encounter between a young woman and her horse, which, like the cats in the texts discussed, was bred for domestication. While the primary sense in the other texts that have been discussed in this chapter has been sight, in this poem it is touch.[38] As noted in Chapter 1, in her study of the horse, Elaine Walker emphasises: 'Ways of training horses have changed over the years, often reflecting changes in humans' understanding of themselves, rather than horses.'[39] The young woman in Clarke's poem knows how to 'domesticate' her horse as humanely as possible and her approach is based on a profound understanding of a different, embodied knowledge from the cognitive knowledge by which most people live. She waits in the grass for the horse to come over to her so that she may break him in with gentleness. She feels, and makes contact with the horse, through bringing their bodies together, through the sharing of their respective breaths (symbolic of their common animality) and through the breaking down of the boundaries between sight, feeling and touch, so that she can 'feel' the physical animality of the horse with her eyes as they travel over him.

In appreciating the different parts of the horse – body, hoof, fetlock, shoulder, head, vertebrae and ribcage – through his physical and metaphysical presence, the young horse 'breaker' reverses the way in which large animals intended for slaughter and butchery are imagined as carcasses on which a taxonomy of different cuts of meat (as discussed in Chapter 2) is imprinted. Trainer and horse respect each other's essential presence as living beings and there is a strong sense of gentleness on the young woman's part as an expression of wonder at an animal. This is exemplified when she kneels before the horse, losing her human dominance over him and, on her knees, offers up an apple. It is also an image of asking for forgiveness, for all the pain and suffering which humans have caused horses. The title of the poem, 'Breaking the Horse', can be read as 'breaking' the usual approach to, and method of, breaking a horse (that might be suggested by the word 'bronco', which connotes a 'rough' and masculine attitude to them) and as 'breaking' the emotional distance between human and horse.

This chapter is not an exhaustive study of the pet in children's literature, but an introduction drawing attention to the tension in much children's writing, including much overlooked translations of animal stories by English writers into Welsh, between 'domestication' and 'domesecration'. It has suggested that, throughout texts for children about pets, the animal may not be as content as it seems and that although it may not be physically abused, it might suffer psychological trauma. But these works rarely present the relationship between the owner and their pets in totally negative terms, often suggesting the possibility that in the domestication of animals, there are always numerous, unthought possibilities.

9

CONFLICTING COSMOLOGIES: THREE STORIES BY GWYN JONES

We have seen that according to animal scholars, such as Paul Waldau, human and animal relations are often characterised by the assumption that animals are mere commodities and can be treated accordingly, by the exclusivity of speciesism, by our short-sightedness and ignorance and by our denial of animal sentience and intelligence.[1] But, as discussed in Chapter 8, a counterpoint to this argument is the empathy that we are capable of establishing with animals through a better understanding of the similarities and differences between us.

The conflict between these two approaches to animal–human relations constitutes the structure of much of Gwyn Jones's short fiction, which reflects his sustained interest in animals and animality but also his fundamental rethinking of the cosmological assumptions that define not only our role and status but the collaborations and ethical commitments we build with others, especially animals. The difficulty of addressing animals as literal, sentient beings (without consciously or unconsciously turning away from them as analogies to exclusively, human issues) provides Jones with a creative challenge. But the analogous dimension of his work is offset by his strong sense of a shared animality between humans and animals and of interspecies relations.

'THE PIT'

As a writer, Jones is especially interested in characters who, because of their cosmological assumptions, display human and/or gender exceptionalism and in animals, sometimes those on the periphery of society, who become part of a human awakening to a more relational and interconnective universe. The short story 'The Pit' examines the contention from evangelical Christianity, based on human exceptionalism, that animals emblematise negative traits (for example, unbridled sexuality, 'bestiality' and aggression) and the equally controversial linking of animality outside Christian thinking with a kind of metaphysical ascent rather than, in evangelical thinking, a spiritual descent (as discussed in Chapter 7). The story juxtaposes several brief encounters: between the central protagonist, Akeman, and Jane Bendle, in whose house he is temporarily lodging; between Akeman and Jane's husband; and between Akeman and a rat. The plot hinges on Akeman's lust for Jane; they kiss in her kitchen and the reader suspects, as do they, that they have been seen by Jane's husband. A man who enjoys caving, Akeman tells her husband of his intention to explore the disused pits, into one of which he descends the following day, ignoring warnings of the danger in doing so. The rope holding him gives way in a landslide and Akeman finds himself trapped. He suspects, as does the reader, that Bendle, having seen the attempt to seduce his wife, has undone the rope.

The story begins by trying to disentangle the literal presence of animals from their analogous and metaphorical associations. But in the animal world above ground where anecdotes of sheep and a dog having fallen over the mountain edge have entered local folklore, the screaming of jackdaws, startling a sheep with her lambs, is both 'real' and an analogy that is crucial to the narrative. While the birds can be seen as an emblem of order in the way in which they wheel and return, they are also a symbol of disorder in their 'raggedly' and 'uneven flight'.[2] The metaphorical nature of the birds is further developed through the conception of one of them as 'a reprobate with a hanging feather',[3] which later proves analogous to Akeman himself and the threat that he poses to the Bendles's marriage. But this anti-image of the jackdaw as reprobate applies not only to Akeman but to Jane Bendle who comes close to betraying her husband and suggests, without going all the way with Akeman on this occasion, that she might be willing to prostitute herself.

However, the central image in the story is not the jackdaw but the rat. In choosing to focus on a rat, Jones introduces one of the animals whose negative presence is most fixed and defined through the cultural taxonomies with which it has been imprinted. As Waldau says, the rat is one of the urban nonhumans that 'provide connections to other-than-human dimensions of life on earth'.[4] Developing this point, Karen Sayer points out that rats carry with them 'many layers of meaning within the borderlands of animal-human relations' and 'have long been treated in art and literature, politics and satire, print and broadcast media as capable of taking on the most deplorable human characteristics'.[5] It is also one of those animals, as Jones realises, that in writings about it seems to slip in and out of its cultural and literal manifestations. Although quintessentially a peripheral animal on the margins of society, rats have pushed back against human settlements to make their own spaces: consuming stores of food, carrying disease to humans, and causing damage to goods and property.[6]

In 'The Pit', the rat becomes, to employ Waldau's words, a part of the 'fascination with natural places and wild, free-living animals', a recurring theme in contemporary geographies of animal life.[7] Jones's evident fascination with the rat as an independent, free-living being in a hidden setting is based on its capacity, which has generally gone unnoticed, to assess and become familiar with the threats posed by particular locations and to achieve a deep knowledge of their environments. In this regard, Jones's portrayal of the rat anticipates the way in which it is approached in contemporary animal studies. Not as a plague carrier that comes from ethereal dark places, but an intelligent, sentient being that, as Jonathan Burt says, is able to 'adapt with humans to the ever more complicated structures and networks that are produced by modernisation'.[8] Jonathan Balcombe points out that animal science has discovered strong parallels between rats' use of whiskers and humans' use of fingertips to explore their surroundings.[9] Because of its capacity to adapt to widely different environments, animal historians, like Burt, argue that rats have been highly 'successful in their competition with other species' and even believe that the rat 'promises greater attainment than that of humans'.[10]

Through Akeman's brief encounter with the rat, Jones lifts the animal out of its cultural associations with plague, disease and evil[11] and allows it to stand more fully revealed as a living being in its own right. In doing so, he complements the sociological approach with a psychological perspective, but he does pursue the familiar, cultural construction of the rat as the inverse mirror of humankind, associated with human failings and disasters such as war and with dark, out-of-the-way places. The depth of the pit in which Akeman encounters the rat is analogous to the rat's innermost being to which we often pay too little regard. He depicts the way rats are perceived as living in a kind of parallel universe to humans, reflecting back to them the inner reaches of their psyches.[12]

Trapped under ground, cut off from the world above, Akeman, echoing the more negative nonconformist perception of animals, descends not only into the pit but into animality, seeing himself as trapped: '"Like a rat," he sobbed, "like a rat".'[13] But, as he becomes more like a trapped animal, he achieves a closer integration with the environment so that 'the sounds he made were now part of the mine'.[14] In trying to calculate his bearings and how he is going to escape, Akeman arrives at a better understanding of the animal within himself and the animality around him. He realises how animality is a combination of instinct, reasoning, patience and calculation. This is encapsulated in the animal he sees: 'two tiny green points of light. They moved, and he came to know it was a rat watching him.'[15] As the watcher becomes the watched, Akeman recognises that the animal's green staring eyes have a steadiness which he must discover within himself in order to survive his ordeal. When he eventually escapes, he drags himself with 'animal patience' and only emerges because he has become 'half human'.[16]

However, in the way in which it revolves around animal imagery and the nature of animality, the conclusion of the story is somewhat enigmatic. When Akeman encounters Jane, with her husband, on a journey he knew she would undertake, she has a 'face grey and rat-like',[17] which causes us to wonder whether it refers to the rat's history in striking back against human society or the rat's capacity to assess situations and survive. Akeman and the reader rethink her role in the story and are encouraged to speculate as to whether she has the scheming and the qualities necessary to have played a part with her husband in his accident or even to have acted alone.

'THE GREEN ISLAND'

'The Pit' stands comparison with Jones's longer story 'The Green Island' which is similarly concerned with emotional and sexual conflict, extramarital sexual involvements, the nature of 'animality' and 'humanity', and, in Christian evangelical terms, the ascent from, and descent into, animality. A young couple, the Merrills, are staying with a Mr and Mrs Absalom on the remote Welsh coast from which it is possible to see and reach an island by boat. As in much writing about animals, and redolent of the secret countryside of Welsh medieval poetry (discussed in Chapter 2), it is a place that inspires sexual instincts, desires and secret affiliations.

The story opens with Merrill lying down and trying to place himself at the centre of nature, 'till the wild things had grown used to him'.[18] The animals and birds he watches are watching each other and, like the rat in the earlier story, himself. They are depicted in their literal capacity, devoid of human anthropomorphic or psychoanalytic projections: a hawk hovers above a hare, 'his long dark ears still as pitcher handles, his eyes an unlidden jewel.'[19] The stillness and beauty of the hare are appreciated by Merrill who is very close to it. But for the hawk, which is 'black and distant', it is prey. The hawk, like the relationship between, and within, the two couples, becomes a manifestation rather than simply a textual symbol of the 'compressed and savage energy of nature'.[20]

The opening animal triangle corresponds to the human quadrangle in which Merrill watches Dafydd Absalom's wife expectantly and cautiously, with an eye on her husband. As Akeman wants to take Mrs Bendle into the woods in 'The Pit', Merrill wants to take Mrs Absalom (who, too, has a 'two-fold sensuality of mind and body'[21]) to the Green Island. When her husband and Mrs Merrill are away for the day, she reticently surrenders to Merrill's persistence. But, on the island, having sex with her, Merrill realises that they are not driven by an instinct that is analogous to animality, for animals in their own 'reality' follow different urges: 'For we are not, he thought, like those marvellous magpies riding the sky because love and procreation whirl them to their natural joys; this was at once more sluggish and more febrile; and furtive.'[22] This difference between the human couple and animal pairing reflects the way in which humans have become divorced from the animal within themselves and have lost contact with other species. This argument is pursued through the person of the Wise Man, Joseph Jones, who with real, and sometimes assumed, knowledge of traditional remedies is part folk-healer and part charlatan. His remedies for humans and animals, which are sometimes successful, are based on animal properties such as an 'old forgotten shepherd's maggot-cure' for rotten bones; mutton-fat as a treatment for shingles, which was successful in Dafydd Absalom's case when he was a child; and a slice of home-cured fat bacon as an application to a bad cut.[23]

Together on the island, as the boat drifts out of their reach, Merrill and Mrs Absalom become marooned as Akeman is trapped by the landfall in the pit. In 'The Pit', the reader is led to suspect that Mrs Bendle may have had a hand in the accident. In 'The Green Island', the suspicion is that Dafydd Absalom, realising that Merrill and his wife were stranded on the island in a storm, deliberately delayed rescuing them for several days. Abandoned, Merrill and Mrs Absalom turn deeper into their animal selves (as did Akeman while stranded underground), especially in 'their need for companionship and comfort'.[24] Their entrapment on the island becomes a vehicle whereby Jones, once again, examines the permeability of the boundary between the human and the animal and explores what the breaking down of this barrier reveals about 'humanity' and 'animality'. The tension between Merrill and Mrs Absalom vacillates between blame and forgiveness, conflict and peace, and distance and intimacy. Trapped on the island, they find themselves in a bubble of animality. But the animals and the animality that they encounter there, as in 'The Pit', open them up to a different, relational cosmology in which human and animal are interconnected. Merrill watches the rabbit that they snare fight and escape: 'Like an animal, he went on repeating; like an animal. He touched the long hot scratches [left by Mrs Absalom] on his cheek. Like an animal.'[25] While he sees cruelty and violence in Mrs Absalom – 'But she sat up violently, thrusting at him … Everything that was cruel in her rushed to her tongue'[26] – it is a while before he realises that in her, as in himself and in the other animals on the island, there is the same instinct for survival. Gradually, the animal within them takes them over as the animal came to dominate Akeman: 'He licked his lips as an animal licks its hurts.'[27] The island becomes a snare in which they are both caught.

When they are rescued, almost like Akeman in his escape from the pit, Merrill feels the force of the animal within him: 'he felt safety, as an animal feels it which breaks from the trap and turns to its lair and scents the well-loved pungencies'.[28] Reminding us of Mrs Absalom fondling the head of the pregnant dog, his rescuer, the Wise Man, 'patted him as he would an animal he was tending, and Merrill felt suddenly eased as those animals did'.[29] This brings to mind the spider which Merrill and Mrs Absalom saw on the Green Island, untouched by the storm and the quarrelling couple, which in its quiet animality provided an image of survival and permanence:

> A pin-head spider clawed his way down an invisible line, then up, then down, unperturbed by these colossi who shut him from the sun,

exhausting and renewing their loves in a rhythm nature now imposed on them and they not at all on nature.[30]

'SHEPHERD'S HEY'

Like 'The Pit' and 'The Green Island', 'Shepherd's Hey' pursues the theme of human exceptionalism but places more emphasis on the cosmology which has given rise to it. Set in a remote sheep farm in the Welsh hills, 'Shepherd's Hey' is structured around different cosmologies from which humans derive contradictory and conflicting assumptions about their status and their roles. Much of the first part of the story is devoted to a life lived according to a relational cosmology from which the shepherd Craddock obtains his view of himself and his animals as part of a wider interconnectivity as is evident in the way in which a ewe and her lamb are depicted at the beginning of the text:

> He had come like a little red diver, curled and sticky, into the March morning. The ewe was struggling to her feet; she stared at this undreamt-of-visitant with surprise and alarm, and when his tail made its first feeble flip she scuffled backwards as though from danger. But soon she came forward again, the drag of all the world's time upon her, sniffed cautiously, and nervously licked at him. Her eyes began to roll, puzzled but possessive; she licked a second time, and from that moment he was completely if incredibly her own.[31]

The emphasis in this passage on disbelief, caution and uncertainty and the transition between the senses – staring, sniffing and licking – blurs the distinction between human and animal. The remoteness of the farm and the hills (which in medieval Welsh poetry was an anti-image to cultural life) brings the shepherd closer to animality (what it is and what it says about the human) and into a close working relationship with his dog, each understanding their different tasks. Consistently, Craddock feels privileged to be working with animals, marvelling at the stoicism of the sheep in the fierce wind, 'half drifted over with snow'.[32] As a shepherd, his sense of a wider interconnectivity extends beyond individual sheep to the flock as a whole, recognising their longer-term, collective needs. This role, as the 'farm's stay', defines him in relation to the animals at the centre of his life. In bringing lambs to home fields, the barn and into his own cottage, the distinction between the domestic and the outside world is collapsed.

Craddock's life is disrupted by the arrival of Salome Trent who is seeking shelter and whose sense of herself and her role in the world is derived from a different kind of world in which humans interact with nonhuman others as objects against an empty background. It is not simply Craddock's working routine that is interrupted, it is the love and faithfulness which he finds in his relationship with his sheepdog, his contact with nature and his sense of isolation from other humans. Shown into Craddock's small house, the first thing Salome witnesses is Craddock cutting the skin off a dead lamb and placing it over an orphaned one to persuade the ewe to accept it as her own. Once again, the detail in which this is described conveys Craddock's understanding of animality as part of the traditional knowledge that he has acquired:

> For the second time that day the ewe pondered the unfamiliar scrap before her. She was sure this was not her lamb, and yet there was her own smell all over it. She sniffed disbelievingly and turned her head away, but was drawn despite herself to sniff and scent again.[33]

But this successful piece of animal husbandry serves as a central image in the story in other ways too. In its emphasis upon deceit, self-deceit, suspicion and instinct conspiring against judgement, the text turns subtly from animal to human concerns as the literal sheep and lamb become analogous to the relationship between Craddock and Salome. But although the story slips into their human needs, it doesn't entirely supplant the focus on the reality of animal lives. Among the subjects that now preoccupy animal studies that Salome introduces into the text is what Waldau calls the 'disingenuous, self-serving denials of other animals' sentience and complexities'.[34]

The relationship between Craddock and Salome – vying between primal needs, physical appetites, intellectual joisting, trickery and judgement – has to be read within the wider context of the animal needs and animality that is all around, as well as within, them. With Salome's presence, the agenda which drives Craddock's daily life, based on the needs and demands of the farm, is shifted to new preoccupations. It starts to revolve, like those of the ewe faced with the orphaned lamb, around suspicion, deceit and the awakening of long suppressed desires. The merger of the house, barn and fields in meeting the needs of the flock is now further redefined as Salome occupies his small bedroom and he sleeps in the barn. The objects that she discovers under his bed – potatoes, rusty mole traps and nailed boots – confirm how he has no clear definition of the different spaces and how the conventional classifications based on domestication become less applicable in the remote countryside. In Salome's mind, they underscore the remote Welsh hills as an anti-image to urban society but also suggest how her sense of agency is rooted in a coherent, intra-action among objects.

As in many of Jones's stories, the understanding of animals that comes from contact with them is contrasted with the ignorance of those distanced from them. Salome compares her husband to a toad or a crocodile, significantly admitting, as one remote from animals, that 'she wasn't sure what a crocodile was, save that it was slimy and yet hard and very unpleasant'.[35] Nevertheless, unlike her husband, she has the potential to be drawn into a closer interconnectivity with animals, for example, in the way in which she looks after the dog when Craddock retreats for the night to the barn and her marvelling at how the ewe is duped to accept the orphan lamb.

Although Craddock works hard and endlessly, there is an inner freedom, depth of meaning and spirituality in his life. But Salome, as his anti-image, is caught in a snare of materiality evidenced in her wanting to 'touch' (dupe) him, in her searching for his money and in the real diamond earrings that she wears. When Craddock sits and talks with Salome, he finds it satisfying at a deep, primal level, as does she: 'She heard it tolerantly, for she liked the feeling of company his words gave her, and the novelty of his ideas flattered her with a sense of her understanding.'[36] When Craddock responds to her invitation to swill her hair, the relationship between them becomes physical and implicitly sexual. The primary sense in which their relationship is described shifts from sight to touch. But when Salome suddenly appears naked in the bedroom doorway, the primary sense in the narrative, once again, becomes sight and the frame of reference becomes not the material universe but biblical and mythical human history:

> The firelight glowed upon her in crimson and shadow, blazoning the long lean legs, the snake-supple torso and shoulders. Red fire struck from the pendants in her ears, and on her uplifted right arm glowed a broad copper-hued bangle. Her hair was a dark crown.[37]

The jewellery brings to Craddock's mind some of the women of the Bible: the 'daughter of Baal or maiden of Ashtaroth?' or, as she reminds him, Salome.[38] The comparison of her body to that of a snake does not connect the human and animal in the way they have been linked in the story until this point but associates her with the serpent in the Garden of Eden and with Eve. The focus shifts from animal instinct to human passion as culturally and historically constructed: 'This vision of barbaric splendour, in the accents of a fair-ground.'[39] In turn, the jewellery and the fair-ground, once again, emphasise the way in which Salome's life has been defined in a crude kind of way by objects and by deception whereas Craddock's life has been determined by his proximity to nature and to animals.

When Salome's dishonest husband suddenly enters the narrative, the animal imagery in the story changes from that generated by actual contact with actual animals to simile and metaphor dependent upon cultural and mythical conceptions of them. Recalling, once again, the Garden of Eden, Harry describes his wife as 'supple as a snake', referring to her mind and manipulative talents as much as her body. He is seen as an 'out-of-hole rodent' with 'rat-eyes [that] showed malice' and 'rat-like persistent evil'.[40] Harry and his wife emblematise how, as Waldau reminds us, we are 'regularly surrounded by diverse likenesses, words, and phrases that call to mind other-than-human animals' in images that 'imply debasement, disdain, dismissal, and the like'.[41] His speech is full of what is described as 'gabble', centred on his trickery and deceit, around which 'threats, wheedling, insinuation and sweet reason' fall endlessly,[42] whereas, in talking to Salome about his life, Craddock employs only 'bold, uncunning words'.[43] Ironically, Harry suggests to Salome: 'If we can't take the human line, where are we?'[44] The 'human', in his eyes, is defined by objects such as the red-hot poker and the 'great trap thing on the wall',[45] instruments of pain and torture that further reflect how human exceptionalism distances humans not only from other humans but from animals.

As the animal theorist and literary scholar Derek Ryan suggested, speciesism (which pervades Harry's language and behaviour) is most effectively examined when it is placed in context with wider human abuse and cruelty.[46] Through the relationship between Harry and Salome, and their attitude toward the animals and toward Craddock, the text emblematises a burgeoning argument in contemporary animal studies, summarised by Waldau: 'Just as social constructions have reduced women to merely men's property [which is how Harry sees Salome] and thereby created myriad injustices and much suffering, so, too, social constructions that demean nonhuman animals foster one problem after another.'⁴⁷ However, the final image of the story is of the order with which it opened, within which the human and animal coexist in a wider interconnectivity: 'Followed by the dog, he set briskly off with one backward glance at the flickering tail of the lamb. He was the farm's stay, he had only one pair of hands, and there was blessedly much to do before mid-morning.'⁴⁸

In much literature about animals, writers are challenged by tension between the literal and metaphorical representations of animals. Where animals are turned into analogies to extreme manifestations of human exceptionalism, the animal as a living sentient being sometimes slips from the text. Jones's short fiction frequently emphasises how human communities engage in the subjugation of others including animals. But it also challenges the way in which animals are perceived as commodities and assigns this way of thinking about them to specific sensibilities and, in turn, to particular cosmologies. In his work, the deployment of animals as analogies to human behaviour is supplanted by an examination of the challenges of empathising with them and how this might be achieved in a relational world.

10

ENTANGLED EMPATHIES: GILLIAN CLARKE AND KEITH BOWEN

This chapter concludes the book with further discussion of the concept of 'entangled empathy' because of its importance, as I have tried to show throughout, to understanding interconnections between humans and animals, and among animals, in a relational universe.[1] It compares how the work of a poet and an artist, who influenced her poetry about sheep farming in the Welsh uplands, may be read through this lens and how far their work provides a focus with which to engage with this concept. As noted throughout this book, 'entangled empathy' recognises, as Gruen says, both the similarities and differences between ourselves and our own situation and that of our fellow animals.[2] And in the works, based on sheep farming, discussed in this chapter, the focus is on our obligation to be aware of, and above all responsive to, another's needs, interests, desires, vulnerabilities and sensitivities and how this has the potential to revise human and animal relations in a complex, and in the case of Clarke's poem sequence, psychobiological context.

Concluding this introduction to animal studies in Welsh writing with a chapter devoted to sheep reflects the fact that they are the farm animal people catch sight of most often in Wales. The number of sheep in Wales today is almost twice the four million just after the Second World War, in 1947, and as the naturalist Roger Lovegrove points out, not least because of the levels of grant aid available to 'reclaim' moorland and increase stocking capacity.[3]

The early-twentieth-century American writer and political commentator Walter Lippmann famously said: 'We define first and then see.'[4] How culture has determined the way in which we see our relationship with animals is one of the most important, and perhaps one of the most controversial, areas of animal studies. As previous chapters have noted, cultural taxonomies constructed to make sense of the vast array of living beings in the world are largely unstable, constantly changing and controversial.

Sheep are one of the most maligned animals in Western culture. As the New Zealand animal theorist and literary scholar Philip Armstrong maintains, in Judaeo-Christian Culture, they are depicted as the archetypal sacrificial victim (Abel, the son of Adam and Eve, offers God the 'firstlings of his flock'); the incarnation of passive surrender (the Passover lamb's blood protected the Israelites from the death of their first born); and as the first scapegoat (God provides Abraham with 'a ram caught in a thicket' as an alternative to his son Isaac).[5] He observes that the 'overwhelming Western association of sheepishness with self-abnegating passivity ... is so deeply engrained that it remains in force well beyond its religious origins.'[6] However, a wider intercultural perspective suggests that, in other cultures, sheep have been seen differently and more positively. In Hopi and Navajo culture, for example, they are associated with 'sharpness of sight and hearing, and with power over nature and the body'.[7] And the native American view of sheep has been confirmed by the latest scientific research, which has found that sheep possess extensive spatial memories, the capacity to learn from experience and the ability, comparable to that of humans, to recognise faces, even after a long period of separation.[8]

Even within cultures which by and large have adopted the Judaeo-Christian anti-image of sheep, it is possible to find strong images that undermine it. This is especially the case in countries whose economies are dependent upon sheep, such as New Zealand and Wales. For example, the picture on the New Zealand two-dollar stamp commemorating the Year of the Sheep, 2015, suggests nothing of the passive, self-abnegating animal victim of the Judaeo-Christian tradition. In the foreground, a large ewe watches over her two small lambs. Standing full square, she appears determined and strong in her maternal role and her head is positioned so as to give her as full a view as possible of the surrounding countryside from which predators might emerge. In Wales, a sheep was featured on bank notes issued by the Aberystwyth and Tregaron Bank and in farming textbooks, and on a Player's cigarette card in 1915, sheep were featured in poses that exuded power, dominance, confidence and self-assurance.[9]

Sheep have been part of our existence for over 1,000 years: they were first domesticated, for milk rather than meat or wool, about 9,000 BCE in north-eastern Iraq and about 7000 BCE in Greece. Domestication did not happen overnight but through a long period in which they were slowly acclimatised to pasture and the ways of *Homo Sapiens*. For writers and artists, this process of 'imprinting' may have a profound resonance with the long process of the colonisation and 'domestication' of Wales as part of England, culturally and linguistically. However, in countries like Wales and New Zealand where the economy is dependent upon sheep, there is a paradox. As Philip Armstrong has observed: although sheep are everywhere, 'they are nevertheless for most of us, most of the time out of the way.'[10]

A YEAR IN THE LIFE OF A SHEEP FARM ON YR WYDDFA

Gillian Clarke's poem sequence 'One Year', like the photojournalist Keith Bowen's *Snowdon Shepherd: Four Seasons on the Hill Farms of North Wales* (1997) which appears to have helped inspire it, is set in the heartland of Welsh hill farming.[11] But 'One Year' approaches twelve months on a Welsh hill farm according to a number of the key themes in contemporary animal studies which we have already encountered, including animal intelligence and psychology and the interconnectivity among humans and animals in sharing this planet.

Bowen stresses the mothering ability of the Hardy Welsh Mountain ewe from the perspective of a sheep breeder: 'Her natural thrift and milkiness make her give all she has to her lamb.'[12] But Clarke, anticipating the focus in 'entangled empathy' on our responsibility to be responsive to another's needs, interests and vulnerabilities, pursues this perspective within a broader, psychobiological understanding of the ewe as a sentient being. But another context in which 'One Year' should be read is the recent development of landscape art and photography, to which Bowen's *Snowdon Shepherd* makes a substantial contribution, in which our view of sheep themselves and of our relationship with them are revised. In his *Sheep Sketchbook*, Henry Moore, whose drawings of sheep began with his exhibition in Florence in 1972, admits: 'At first I saw them as rather shapeless balls of wool with a head and four legs. Then I began to realize that underneath all that wool was a body, which moved in its own way, and that each sheep had its individual character.'[13] This transformation in the way Moore sees and understands sheep, communicated through his sequence of drawings, is very similar to the one which informs Clarke's poetry. In both works, the boundary between the human and animal species is crossed. Kenneth Clark is impressed that Moore's 'drawings express a feeling of real affection for their subject. It is no exaggeration to say that many of his sheep are drawn with love.'[14] This is also true of Bowen's drawings and Gillian Clarke's poetry. But in writing of Moore's work, Kenneth Clark makes an important point that is applicable to art and writing about animals more generally: 'We have a preconceived notion about sheep, based not only on their appearance, but on an association of ideas. This sketchbook shows that, as formal material, sheep can provide an astonishing range and variety.'[15] He suggests that the drawings in Henry Moore's *Sheep Sketchbook* are successful because, at home, 'he lives surrounded by fields full of sheep' and that they 'provide his most frequent visual experience'.[16] This, once again, can be applied to Bowen and Clarke, for their most striking work is rooted in their experience of working with sheep, or witnessing others doing so, or from sustained observation of them in the countryside.

Like Bowen's *Snowdon Shepherd*, 'One Year' might almost be read as a guide to Welsh hill farming. Both texts reflect the integration of hill farming and the seasons within a 'managed' life cycle for the sheep which can be traced to before the First World War. C. Bryner Jones, the Agricultural Commissioner for Wales at that time, described how Welsh mountain sheep, as a rule, are not 'put to the ram' until two years old to avoid interfering with their growth and constitution; they are bred from for two or three years as members of the flock; and in their fourth or fifth year drafted and sold off to the lowlands to breed and cross-breed fat lambs for one or more seasons and, eventually, sent to market.[17] Clarke and Bowen exemplify how such thinking, always responding to the latest technology and the vacillating sheep market, permeates the management of Welsh hill farms even today. But Clarke's work especially, contrasts the practicalities of hill farming with a shepherd's intuitive awareness of the rhythms of the landscape.

However, while there are parallels between Clarke's 'One Year' and Bowen's *Snowdon Shepherd* in their characteristically hill shepherd's approach to sheep farming, Clarke's poem-sequence focuses more on the experience of individual sheep, which enables her to bring the human and the animal closer together. In her poem sequence, the changes in the seasons, in the environment and in animality (emblematising the ongoing natural cycle) are extended to humans who are also participants in it. Humans and animals with long experience of the Welsh uplands are depicted as sharing an intuitive awareness of the hill country rhythms and the tensions between these embodied sensitivities and the more remote practicalities of managed farming. While external observation of nature and the animal world is important to Clarke's and Bowen's sequences, 'One Year' captures the internal experience of them on the part of animals and the capacity of shepherds to intuitively share in this.

DIFFERENT WORLDS

Ultimately, Clarke's 'One Year' is about different types of cosmology, providing different assumptions about how we see ourselves in relation to the wider, interconnective universe, and different kinds of knowledge: cognitive knowledge and the physical, intuitive sensibility of the animal body. The poems in the sequence prioritise animal, intuitive and embodied knowledge over cognitive awareness, examining the mountains and hill farms as something 'deep in [the] animal brain' and in the *cynefin* through 'their bones, nerves and blood'.[18] In her notes to the poem, 'Cynefin', Clarke suggests that *hiraeth* or 'longing' is the equivalent of *cynefin* but perhaps in regard to 'A Year at Hafod Y Llan', 'familiar habitat' is the closest English translation.[19] In *Snowdon Shepherd*, the *cynefin* is the boundary outside which the sheep, through what is passed from one generation to another, will not stray. Clarke's traditional Welsh word and concept suggest that the relationship of the sheep to the land is linked to hereditary practice but, also, to their intuitive capacity and how animals can inherit embodied knowledge through the generations. This is confirmed by the contemporary, environmental writer Daniel Butler also. He points out that the concept dates to a period when animals were left free to roam on the open hills: 'There was nothing to stop them wandering for many miles, they felt secure in familiar surroundings. They knew every fold of the land ... This was something they had learnt from their parents: knowledge passed down the generations.'[20]

The embodied awareness of the uplands in 'A Year at Hafod Y Llan' (which is one dimension of the experience of hill farming) is evident in the poem's empathy with the sheep's experience of it (sheltering, turning from the wind, gathering in the lee of fallen trees) and with the hill shepherd's appreciation of the mountain as being in the sheep and in people who work them. The streams, underground rivers and the wind in the mines lend the uplands a sense of power and energy which those who live in them come to know intuitively. To the human outsider, the seasons are something to be observed, but the animal brain is attuned to them at a much deeper psychobiological level. 'One Year' approaches them not through the calendar but as in 'February' (Y mis bach, the little month) from the impact of the gradual changes in the seasons, in this case, the lengthening of the day and the extra grazing time for pregnant sheep.

Clarke's interest in embodied knowledge and bodily intuition develops some of the perspectives of Bowen's *Snowdon Shepherd*. For example, in reflecting on winter among the hill farms, he focuses on a particular ewe racked by hunger, obvious in her hoofing the frozen ground and in her scraping for grass. But in Clarke's poem, a pregnant ewe in this situation is seen to have an inner life in another sense which is revealed in the poem like a Russian doll: the snow forms an outer fleece beneath which is the ewe's fleece, beneath which is her body, deep inside of which is a womb and inside of which is a foetus. The poem takes the reader from the macroenvironment, in which snow falls over the hills, to the blood-dark, microenvironment of the rocked cradle, safe from the cold.

There is a similar attempt at understanding the sheep's life cycle from a psychobiological perspective in 'Scan'. The poem begins with human intervention through technology in the natural life cycle. The sheep are driven by dogs from the hills to a scanning machine, an example of the way in which farming has become 'modernised'. But in keeping with time-aged practice, the sheep that are carrying a single foetus are sent to winter in valley pastures where the monitoring of their pregnancy with technology stands in contradistinction to the natural process whereby new life unfolds within them. This modern ritual of scanning, and the anxiety on the part of the sheep who are ignorant of what is happening to them, is seen through the eyes of a mother who would herself have undergone scans. But it brings together, through a psychobiological perspective, several rhythms which are observed but also felt intuitively through the sheep's body: the rhythm of the year, of the farm calendar, of the body itself and of the life cycle. How far Clarke develops psychobiological knowledge in 'One Year' is especially evident in 'Black', concerning the corralling of sheep that are no longer able to carry lambs.

The additional perspective which we find in Clarke's poem compared to Bowen's *Snowdon Shepherd* becomes obvious if the two texts are read alongside each other. Bowen describes: 'The first batch of ewes to be put on the mountain for the summer are the barren and those that have aborted lambs.'[21] Clarke's poem might be seen as a deconstruction of the shepherd's matter-of-fact, but also rather heartless choice of words quoted by Bowen: 'You see, there's nothing in 'em.'[22] In 'Black', there is much more emotional empathy with the ewe and with the psychological impact of biological change upon her, almost drawing out the desolation of the moment: 'They are barren, empty / without foetus, without future.'[23] But while individual human lives can be channelled to adoption or an alternative but meaningful life, the situation for sheep within the farming industry is much bleaker, 'the end of the line'.[24]

From a psychobiological perspective, Clarke's 'Stillborn' is as heart-rending as 'Black'. Nevertheless, there is a sense of wonder as well as tragedy in the poem. The confusion of the ewe faced with a stillborn lamb that should not be dead to her mind/body, and the obsessive repetition of instinctual behaviour in her endless licking, distinguishes this poem from others concerned with stillborn sheep. Unlike in 'Black', this is not 'the end of the line' for the ewe, and the poem can be read in conjunction with 'Mothering', which is juxtaposed with it in the sequence. Both poems concern an event which is included in Gwyn Jones's short story 'Shepherd's Hey', discussed in Chapter 9, and also in Bowen's *Snowdon Shepherd*: 'When a ewe loses a lamb she naturally becomes a potential adoptive mother, and another lamb is quickly sought as a replacement.'[25] But, once again, Clarke takes a different approach. 'Mothering' brings together two types of knowledge. The first is human knowledge passed down through generations of shepherds which involves removing the flesh of the dead lamb, quickly and out of sight of the ewe, and placing it over an orphaned lamb. As Bowen says: 'The shepherd works quickly to skin the dead lamb, and puts its coat on the foster lamb so that to the mother it smells like her own.'[26] But Clarke's poem more effectively enters the sheep's consciousness, proposing that there is a second type of knowledge that is important here: the sheep's intuitive recognition, through taste and smell, that this is her lamb whose stillness initially confused her, allowing her and the orphan to bond through the shared experience of suckling and hunger (which is beautifully captured in Bowen's painting of a lamb's first suckle with its mother[27]).

The bonding of ewe and lamb is a motif which runs throughout Henry Moore's *Sheep Sketchbook*:

> The lambing season had begun, and there in front of me was the mother-and-child theme. This is one of the favourite themes in my work: the large form related to the small form and protecting it, or the complete dependence of the small form on the large form. I tried to express the way the lambs suckled with real energy and violence.[28]

As in Clarke's poems, Moore's drawings bring a 'mothering' perception to bear on the sheep but not with the same depth as Clarke whose poems enhance the appreciation of shared experience between humans and animals through its psychobiological perspectives.

A discussion of the sensibilities within 'One Year' would be incomplete without including Clarke's companion poems, 'Labour' and 'Birth', which, too, bring together the embodied knowledge of the lamb-carrying ewe and the rhythms of the mountain felt in the sheep's body and grasped in the animal brain. The focus on one ewe enables the poem to examine her interconnection with her environment, deepening our understanding of her animality, *Umwelt*, intelligence and emotional capacity. The poems interweave the womb's upheavals with the movement of underground streams and the drumming of water within the mountain with the pounding of the ewe's heart. The emphasis in these poems is on how the animal feels and how her capacity for suffering is communicated through the depiction of her movements, in this case, once again, her ceaseless turning and hoofing the ground. In their account of the intensity of the sheep's emotion and suffering, they reflect but expand on the account of labour in Bowen's *Snowdon Shepherd*. 'Labour' provides details which any of us must imaginatively grasp: the turning and hoofing like human twisting and struggling; the long, low groans redolent of a human mother gasping and screaming; the pulling of grass for relief like gasps of oxygen; and, in both human and animal birthing, the last great muscular heave. In the last stanza of 'Birth', the focus is on need, instinct, impulse and pain. This is developed into the animal experience of delivery of the new life and its first ever cry 'at being alive'.[29]

'Last Gather', from 'One Year', ostensibly approaches the post-summer collecting of sheep and ewes from the point of view once again of the hill farmer. It is seen as part of the farm calendar but also of the natural, albeit managed, rhythm of the upland year. At one level, the sheep are perceived as objects of human action, 'penned / separated, driven apart', analogous, perhaps, to the migration and movement of peoples in times of natural disaster, invasion and the evacuation of refugees.[30] But the poem focuses on the separation of lamb from ewe from a psychobiological perspective which enables it to cross the boundary between species and gives depth to both nonhuman animal and human experience: 'They will cry all night, / lamb-grief and mother-grief.'[31] The contribution of Clarke's approach to animal studies is evident when her poem is compared with the way in which this event in the farming year is described by Bowen, drawing on his experience of working the Welsh hills as a shepherd but writing more from a managed farming perspective: 'The lambs must now be weaned off the ewes, so that they have time to come into season by next year. The ewes are sent up to the poorer pasture higher up the mountain, while the lambs are kept down to fatten on the better.'[32]

In 'To the Mountain', Clarke's psychobiological perspective focuses on the way in which the young cling to their parents, especially their mothers, and brings an appreciation of this to bear on the commotion and panic of a sheep drive. The poem takes the reader beyond the apparent chaos and the incessant noise to appreciate the capacity of young lambs to fear separation from their mothers and how ewes are able to feel this. In the poem, the flock gradually quietens as a type of knowledge, discussed earlier in relation to the *cynefin*, enters the animal brain. The ewes are perceived as recalling the mountain which has been such a part of their existence, as much in their bodies as in their minds. The lambs become aware of something which they have never previously experienced and which enters them through the blood of their mothers and their bonding with the flock. In this regard, the poem sequence contributes to the interest in contemporary animal studies in how intelligence, as we have seen throughout this book, is too often perceived in only human terms. The sequence brings to the fore not only the developing intimacy between sheep and ewes but a type of physical knowledge, passed through generations, which is felt in the innermost parts of an animal's being and suggests that animals such as sheep have a deeper and more sophisticated sense of being than has been realised.

In 'The Wethers Leave the Mountain' (wethers are castrated lambs sold for slaughter), Clarke once again brings a psychobiological perspective to the separation of ewes from their lambs. The gathering of the ewes at the end of summer is an important part of farming as a market-driven, economic process, in which farmers have been forced to distance themselves in deciding which animals they are taking and which they are leaving. Bowen reminds us: 'The ewe recognises the lamb by its smell and the lamb recognises the mother by her call.'[33] But Clarke's psychobiological approach expands on this point, describing how the bleats and cries that held ewe and lamb together throughout the summer, in the autumn becomes a grief-ridden cry of loss, pain and confusion. As throughout the poem sequence, the poet is stressing the importance of this kind of recognition to disassembling the barrier between humans and nonhumans and opening opportunities for a richer relationship between humans and other species.

'One Year' is an appropriate text with which to conclude this book, not only because of the importance of sheep to the Welsh economy and their strong presence in the Welsh countryside, but because the poem sequence depicts the coexistence of different types of knowledge, intelligence and sensibilities which sheep, in keeping with other animals, have developed to live and thrive within their environments. In his study of sheep, which combines animal studies and ecocriticism, William Welstead argues that animal studies challenges 'the false binaries that flow from human exceptionalism' and calls 'into question binary distinctions between humans and other animals, between the human-imposed categories of wild and domestic, nature and culture'.[34] He comes to the conclusion: 'We need to think about our values, about our relationship with human and non-human others and let our imagination adapt if we are to survive this new world.'[35] Clarke's work takes ideas and insights which resonate with contemporary animal studies further, frees sheep from the cultural taxonomies in which they have been misrepresented and overly reflects the relationality of the cosmology which the new natural and physical sciences have unveiled.

Afterword

The texts discussed in this book deconstruct the binary, hierarchical conceptualisation of 'animal' and 'human'. Reading them through animal theory provides frameworks which bring their radical, and sometimes controversial, subjects and themes to the fore, including human 'exceptionalism', the nature of 'animality' and 'humanity', 'speciesism' and how animals have developed other-than-human sensibilities, intelligences and emotional capacities. Their insights make it impossible for us not to rethink 'intelligence', 'cognition' and 'knowledge', which we have tended to see hitherto only from human perspectives.

The texts in this study were selected to reflect the breadth and diversity of writing about animals in modern Welsh literature but also as examples of the numerous and varied contexts in which we live with, use and encounter animals. As in animal studies more generally, these works provide us with opportunities of rethinking our notions of animality with reference to animals with which we have companionable and/or working relationships, such as dogs, cats, horses and sheep, but also those deemed at the margins of human settlement such as foxes, rats, moles and bats. As we have seen, it is unsurprising that birds feature in many of these texts because we encounter them briefly but most frequently. The chapter devoted to them revealed not only how, over time, different birds have been invested with different religious, symbolic and cultural meanings but how we now have more interest in, and a better understanding of, their sophistication and communicative capacities.

Many of the contemporary texts discussed resonate with the burgeoning interest in history from the perspectives of animals (exemplified in numerous studies devoted to particular species), which inevitably make inspiring but also uncomfortable reading, including shocking accounts of the way in which animals have been adopted, abused, objectified and devalued. This has brought about doubts over the domestication of animals which many of the texts examined, including literature for children, are inclined to see, controversially, as 'domesecration', a process by which their minds and bodies are desecrated to facilitate their exploitation by humans. This concept brings together fiction and non-fiction based on pets and companionable animals, with scholarship and press coverage of zoos, zoological museums, circuses and animals in street entertainment around new ways of seeing the confinement of animals as psychological as well as physical. Many of these institutions have a legacy of displaying exotic animals for entertainment which can be traced to the eighteenth century and well beyond to ancient societies centred on Athens and Rome. But the Victorian interest in the captivity and display of exotic animals was based on conceiving of them as signifiers of the imperial project and as the 'Other' at the limits of what was perceived of as Western 'civilisation' and of the human imagination. The way in which the 'zoological gaze' has changed over the years has led to more focus in contemporary zoos on animal welfare, conservation and education. But in animal studies, these new developments, especially as far as smaller zoos and aquariums are concerned, are still subjects of controversy and debate.

Although animal history brings hidden truths to the fore, it also suggests new ways of thinking about animals, including their more harmonious coexistence with people. As argued throughout the book, animal-based agendas are an important link between animal studies, animal theory and creative writing. The texts discussed examine the extent to which our assumptions about, and attitudes toward, animals may be based on outmoded cosmological conceptions, scientific discourses and sociocultural modelling which have been discredited and/ or surpassed. They challenge the ways in which animals have too often been conceived as part of a world of things against a background on which we project images of ourselves as special, intelligent and superior to other life on the planet.

Psychoanalytic approaches to animal studies have proved especially revealing in this respect, highlighting themes such as the psychological and emotive capacities of animals, the psychoanalytical pleasure humans derive from hunting and subjugating animals, hierarchical power-relations among animals and between humans and animals, and the significance of play. The texts discussed resonate with the interest in contemporary animal studies in captivity, in pet keeping, and in the rights of animals beyond thinking only about their protection but as having a right to a subjective life that enables them to fulfil their natural traits and characteristics as animals.

Contemporary texts about animals and animality, like those included in this book, often critique our cosmological, scientific and sociocultural assumptions and open up a wider understanding of the planet from an animal's agenda and *Umwelt*. The texts discussed reflect the way in which contemporary animal studies is embedded in the new way of perceiving the universe in relational terms – that all living forms are bound together through networks of relations – brought about by the natural and physical sciences. Through this more creative thinking, concepts such as 'animality', 'humanity' and 'cosmology' have become increasingly problematic and as needing to be deconstructed rather than constructed upon.

Such concepts have been raised in this book in the hope that further writing and scholarship will continue to challenge them, develop their deconstruction and extend the literary frame of reference in which they are addressed. More needs to be said about the prevailing dominance of ideologically loaded descriptors, even in animal studies itself, especially when set against the increasing subtle discussions of species, habitat, predation and types of nourishment entering environmental writing. Living, as we do, within a relational universe, the limits and the dangerous implausibility of continuing to treat 'nature/animal' as qualitatively different from 'culture/human' warrants further creative thought and study. In writing about animals and in animal studies, we are only just seeing the beginnings of a sustained focus on animals as social beings, on the ways in which they form societies of their own and the relevance to animals of, for example, social organisation, culture, psychology, power arrangements and geography.

Similarly, gene-culture coevolution – the extent to which identity arises with culture and remains independent of genetics – warrants more investigation in writing and scholarship about animals. Future projects might pursue the impact of the evolutionary dynamic in interactions between animal genes and culture over extended periods, examine the role played by culture in the development of animal behaviour or further research the extent to which the genes of a particular species have the ability to affect, and the capacity to be affected by, corresponding cultures.

Apart from bringing a new perspective to writing about history from the point of view of animals, gene-culture coevolution is an area of animal studies that has the potential to contribute to one of the most controversial environmental concepts affecting Wales in the twenty-first century, 'rewilding'. Aimed at increasing biodiversity and restoring endangered species and habitats clinging on for existence, rewilding has aroused opposition from farmers who fear that it threatens farming culture, agricultural sustainability and food self-sufficiency. The concept is perceived as requiring a flexibility of approach and, overlapping with gene-culture coevolution, long-term thinking about the impact on the *Umwelt* of animals as well as sustainable/conservation farming more generally.

These are but a few examples of areas which writing about animals and animal studies might further develop in the future. However, they demonstrate the extent to which animal studies in creative work and scholarship is likely to continue to be shaped by the concept of a relational universe that living and non-living forms share.

NOTES

1 Animals and Animality in a Relational Universe

1. Lee Smolin describes the core principles of relational cosmology in a number of texts: *The Life of the Cosmos* (London: Phoenix, 1997); *Three Roads to Quantum Gravity* (London: Phoenix, 2000); *The Trouble with Physics: The Rise of String Theory, The Fall of a Science and What Comes Next* (London: Penguin, 2008) and *Time Reborn: From the Crisis in Physics to the Future of the Universe* (Boston: Mariner Books, 2014). The salient work on natural philosophy from which the principles of a relational universe and the thinking in much contemporary animal studies becomes clear is Roberto Mangabeira Unger and Lee Smolin, *Singular Universe and the Reality of Time* (Cambridge: Cambridge University Press, 2015).
2. See, for example, Margo DeMello, *Animals and Society: An Introduction to Human-Animal Studies* (2012; rev. New York: Columbia University Press, 2nd edn, 2021); Lori Gruen (ed.), *Critical Terms for Animal Studies* (Chicago and London: The University of Chicago Press, 2018); Lynn Turner, Undine Sellbach and Ron Broglio (eds), *The Edinburgh Companion to Animal Studies* (Edinburgh: Edinburgh University Press, 2018); Derek Ryan, *Animal Theory: A Critical Introduction* (Edinburgh: Edinburgh University Press, 2015); and Paul Waldau, *Animal Studies: An Introduction* (Oxford: Oxford University Press, 2013).
3. Audra Mitchell, *International Intervention in a Secular Age: Re-enchanting Humanity* (Abingdon: Routledge, 2014), p. 10.
4. Milja Kurki, *International Relations in a Relational Universe* (Oxford: Oxford University Press, 2020), p. 68. For a discussion of the impact of this new cosmology, see, for example, Smolin, *Three Roads to Quantum Gravity* and, for the need to see humans within the context of a wider non-hierarchical universe, see, Smolin, *The Life of the Cosmos*.
5. Marc Bekoff and Jessica Pierce, *The Animals' Agenda: Freedom, Compassion, and Coexistence in the Human Age* (Boston: Beacon Press, 2017), p. 177.

6. Bruce Boehrer and Molly Hand, 'Introduction: Beasts in the Republic of Letters', in Bruce Boehrer, Molly Hand and Brian Massumi (eds), *Animals and Animality in Literature* (Cambridge: Cambridge University Press, 2018), p. 22 [pp. 1–26].
7. Kurki, *International Relations in a Relational Universe*, p. 3.
8. Kurki, *International Relations in a Relational Universe*, p. 59.
9. Ryan, *Animal Theory*, p. 77. See, also, J. M. Coetzee, *The Lives of Animals*, ed. Amy Gutmann (Princeton: Princeton University Press, 1999), p. 332.
10. See, Ryan, *Animal Theory*, pp. 103–6; Giorgio Agamben, *The Open: Man and Animal* (Stanford: Stanford University Press, 2004), p. 39; Brett Buchanan, *Onto-Ethologies: The Animal Environments of Uexküll, Heidegger, Marleau Ponty and Deleuze* (Albany: State University Press of New York, 2008); and Jakob von Uexküll, *A Foray into the Worlds of Animals and Humans with a Theory of Meaning*, trans. Joseph D. O'Neil (Minneapolis: University of Minnesota Press, 2010), pp. 69–70.
11. See, for example, Ryan, *Animal Theory*, p. 105.
12. See, for example, Jennifer Ackerman, *The Genius of Birds* (2016; rpt. London: Corsair, 2017); Jonathan Balcombe, *Second Nature: The Inner Lives of Animals* (Basingstoke: Palgrave Macmillan, 2010); Bekoff and Pierce, *The Animals' Agenda*; and Roger A. Caras, *A Perfect Harmony: The Intertwining Lives of Animals and Humans throughout History* (New York: Simon & Schuster, 1996).
13. Smolin, *The Life of the Cosmos*, p. 194.
14. Smolin, *The Life of the Cosmos*, p. 200.
15. Waldau, *Animal Studies*, p. 188.
16. Ryan, *Animal Theory*, p. 76.
17. See, for example, David Wood, 'Homo Sapiens', in Turner, Selbach and Broglio (eds), *The Edinburgh Companion to Animal Studies*, p. 296 [pp. 292–306]; Waldau, *Animal Studies*, pp. 16–17; and Ryan, *Animal Theory*, pp. 15–16.
18. Jacques Derrida, *The Animal That Therefore I Am*, trans. David Wills (New York: Fordham University Press, 2008), p. 48.
19. Derrida, *The Animal That Therefore I Am*, p. 48.
20. Derrida, *The Animal That Therefore I Am*, p. 48.
21. Derrida, *The Animal That Therefore I Am*, p. 49.
22. DeMello, *Animals and Society*, p. 48. Recent studies of particular animals have examined how Greek and Judaeo-Christian, as well as Eastern, cosmologies have shaped our understanding of them at different periods. See, for example, Dan Wylie, *Elephant* (London: Reaktion Books, 2008); Elaine Walker, *Horse* (2008; rpt. London: Reaktion Books, 2013); Jonathan Burt, *Rat* (London: Reaktion Books, 2006); Desmond Morris, *Monkey* (London: Reaktion Books, 2013); and Philip Armstrong, *Sheep* (2016; rpt. London: Reaktion Books, 2017).
23. For discussion of the concept of 'exceptionalism', see, for example, Waldau, *Animal Studies*, pp. 6–9 and 154–7; DeMello, *Animals and Society*, pp. 17 and 43; and Wood, 'Homo Sapiens', p. 295.
24. John Downer, *Supersense: Perception in the Animal World* (London: BBC Books), p. 8.

NOTES

25 Ryan, *Animal Theory*, p. 66.
26 Donna Haraway, *When Species Meet* (Minneapolis: University of Minnesota Press, 2008), p. 106.
27 Kurki, *International Relations in a Relational Universe*, p. 120.
28 Bekoff and Pierce, *The Animals' Agenda*, p. 179.
29 For recognition of nonhuman-based concepts of intelligence, see, for example, Ryan, *Animal Theory*, pp. 32–3 and Waldau, *Animal Studies*, pp. 141–2. Fuller, accessible discussions of the rethinking of intelligence across species of birds and animals are to be found in Ackerman, *The Genius of Birds* and Balcombe, *Second Nature*.
30 Waldau, *Animal Studies*, p. 90. See, also, Marc Bekoff, *The Emotional Lives of Animals: A Leading Scientist Explores Animal Joy, Sorrow and Empathy and Why They Matter* (Novato, CA: New World Library, 2007). For a succinct summary of key problems in this area of study, see Waldau, *Animal Studies*, pp. 187–9.
31 DeMello, *Animals and Society*, p. 423.
32 Daphne Sheldrick, 'The Rearing and Rehabilitation of Orphaned African Elephant Calves in Kenya', in Debra L. Forthman, Lisa F. Kane, David Hancocks and Paul F. Waldau (eds), *An Elephant in the Room: The Science and Well-Being of Elephants in Captivity* (North Grafton, MA: Center for Animals and Public Policy, 2008), p. 208 [pp. 208–12].
33 Bekoff and Pierce, *The Animals' Agenda*, p. 11.
34 Bekoff and Pierce, *The Animals' Agenda*, p. 11.
35 Downer, *Supersense*, pp. 67–94.
36 Bill Thomas, *Talking with Animals: How to Communicate with Wildlife* (London: W. H. Allen, 1986), p. 137.
37 See, for example, 'Red fox – People's Trust for Endangered Species'. Online. Available at *https://ptes.org/get-informed/facts-figures/red-fox/* (accessed 27 March 2021).
38 Ackerman, *The Genius of Birds*, p. 164. See pp. 159–96.
39 Susan McHugh, *Dog* (London: Reaktion Books, 2004), p. 22.
40 Ryan, *Animal Theory*, p. 34. Ryan is quoting Jacques Lacan, 'The Function and Field of Speech and Language in Psychoanalysis', in *Écrits*, trans. Bruce Fink (New York: W. W. Norton & Company, 2006), p. 245 [pp. 197–268]. The 'wagging dance' is usually called 'waggle dance' in English.
41 Ryan, *Animal Theory*, p. 34.
42 Noah Wilson-Rich, *The Bee: A Natural History* (Princeton and Oxford: Princeton University Press, 2018), p. 32.
43 Downer, *Supersense*, p. 8.
44 Lori Gruen, 'Empathy', in Gruen (ed.), *Critical Terms for Animal Studies* p. 148 [pp. 141–53].
45 Alexandra Horowitz, 'Behavior', in Gruen (ed.), *Critical Terms for Animal Studies*, p. 75 [pp. 64–78].
46 Ackerman, *The Genius of Birds*, pp. 223–5; Balcombe, *Second Nature*, p. 23.
47 Horowitz, 'Behavior', p. 75.
48 Gruen, 'Empathy', p. 148.
49 Gruen, 'Empathy', p. 148.

50 Amanda Boetzkes, 'Art', in Turner, Sellbach and Broglio (eds), *The Edinburgh Companion to Animal Studies*, p. 65 [pp. 65–79].
51 Kurki, *International Relations in a Relational Universe*, p. 125.
52 Boetzkes, 'Art', p. 65.
53 Boetzkes, 'Art', p. 65.
54 Ryan, *Animal Theory*, p. 12.
55 Waldau, *Animal Studies*, p. 12.
56 Walker, *Horse*, pp. 13 and 17.
57 Walker, *Horse*, p. 17.
58 Walker, *Horse*, p. 118.
59 Walker, *Horse*, p. 119.
60 Walker, *Horse,* p. 119.
61 Ryan, *Animal Theory*, p. 30.
62 Walker, *Horse*, p. 17.
63 Yi-Fu Tuan, *Dominance and Affection: The Making of Pets* (New Haven and London: Yale University Press, 1984), p. 4.
64 Tuan, *Dominance and Affection*, p. 4.
65 Tuan, *Dominance and Affection*, pp. 174–5.
66 Ryan, *Animal Theory*, p. 88.
67 Ryan, *Animal Theory*, p. 88.
68 Walker, *Horse*, pp. 15–16.
69 Armstrong, *Sheep*, pp. 38–40.
70 Bekoff and Pierce, *The Animals' Agenda*, p. 13.
71 Walker, *Horse*, p. 19.
72 McHugh, *Dog*, p. 198.
73 Walker, *Horse*, p. 19.
74 Tuan, *Dominance and Affection*, p. 89.
75 Tuan, *Dominance and Affection*, p. 89.
76 Tuan, *Dominance and Affection*, p. 95.
77 Tuan, *Dominance and Affection*, p. 89.
78 Tuan, *Dominance and Affection*, p. 89. See, also, Bekoff and Pierce, *The Animals' Agenda*, pp. 141–3.
79 Tuan, *Dominance and Affection*, p. 95.
80 Tuan, *Dominance and Affection*, p. 95.
81 Tuan, *Dominance and Affection*, p. 95.
82 D. J. Williams, *The Old Farmhouse*, trans. Waldo Williams (London: George G. Harrap & Co. Ltd, 1961), p. 161.
83 Daniel Butler, *The Owl House* (Bridgend: Seren, 2020), p. 191.
84 Butler, *The Owl House*, pp. 190–1.
85 Graham Downing, 'A Beautiful Story', *Shooting Times & Country Magazine* (28 April 2021), 15 [14–15].
86 Downing, 'A Beautiful Story', p. 14.
87 Downing, 'A Beautiful Story', p. 14.
88 See, for example, Balcombe, *Second Nature*, pp. 143–6.
89 Gruen, *Critical Terms for Animal Studies*, p. 2.
90 Among the more controversial areas are the concepts of 'subjectivity' on which animal rights might be based and how animal rights might be integrated with existing legal frameworks. See, for example, Waldau, *Animal Studies*,

p. 117; Ryan, *Animal Theory*, pp. 79–80, 120–1, 123–6 and 132; and Nicole Anderson, 'Ethics', in Turner, Sellbach and Broglio (eds), *The Edinburgh Companion to Animal Studies*, pp. 140–59.
91 Waldau, *Animal Studies*, pp. 117–19.
92 David A. Nibert, *Animal Oppression and Human Violence; Domesecration, Capitalism, and Global Conflict* (New York: Columbia University Press, 2013), p. 2.
93 Waldau, *Animal Studies*, pp. 119–20.
94 Tom Regan, *The Case for Animal Rights* (London: Routledge and Kegan Paul, 1983), p. 329.
95 Alasdair Cochrane, *Animal Rights Without Liberation: Applied Ethics and Human Obligations* (New York: Columbia University Press, 2012), p. 41. See, also, Mark Rowlands, *Animal Rights: Moral Theory and Practice* (Basingstoke: Palgrave Macmillan, 2009), pp. 86–9.
96 Cochrane, *Animal Rights Without Liberation*, p. 50.
97 Cochrane, *Animal Rights Without Liberation*, p. 43.
98 Cochrane, *Animal Rights Without Liberation*, p. 210.
99 Ryan, *Animal Theory*, p. 9.
100 Smolin, *The Life of the* Cosmos, p. 373.
101 Waldau, *Animal Studies*, p. 68.
102 Lori Marino, 'Captivity', in Gruen (ed.), *Critical Terms for Animal Studies*, p. 99 [pp. 99–111].
103 Lisa Rivera, 'Coercion and Captivity' in Lori Gruen (ed.), *The Ethics of Captivity* (New York and Oxford: Oxford University Press, 2014), p. 249.
104 Rivera, 'Coercion and Captivity', p. 249.
105 Marino, 'Captivity', p. 101.
106 Marino, 'Captivity', p. 101.
107 Cited Jane Jones, 'Mandatory CCTV in Welsh slaughterhouses to improve animal welfare', *Nation.Cymru* (6 November 2021). Online. Available at https://nation.cymru/news/mandatory-cctv-in-welsh-slaughterhouses-to-improve-animal-welfare/ (accessed 6 November 2021).
108 Marino, 'Captivity', p. 101.
109 Cochrane, *Animal Rights Without Liberation*, p. 152.
110 Cochrane, *Animal Rights Without Liberation*, p. 146.
111 Paul Sears, 'Ecology – a Subversive Subject', *BioScience*, 14/7 (1964), 11–13.
112 Waldau, *Animal Studies*, p. 93.
113 Waldau, *Animal Studies*, p. 93.
114 Timothy Morton, *The Ecological Thought* (Boston: Harvard University Press, 2010), p. 7. For a discussion of Morton's work, see Kurki, *International Relations in a Relational Universe*, pp. 118–19.
115 Kurki, *International Relations in a Relational Universe*, p. 115.
116 Kurki, *International Relations in a Relational Universe*, p.116.
117 Kurki, *International Relations in a Relational Universe*, p. 119. See, Morton, *The Ecological Thought*, p. 30.
118 Waldau, *Animal Studies*, pp. 93–4.
119 Waldau, *Animal Studies*, p. 94.
120 Bekoff and Pierce, *The Animals' Agenda*, pp. 171–7 [pp. 173 and 176].

2 Rethinking Animal Contexts: Rural and Industrial Wales

1. Derek Ryan, *Animal Theory: A Critical Introduction* (Edinburgh: Edinburgh University Press, 2015), p.117.
2. Anthony Conran, 'Introduction', Anthony Conran (ed. and trans.), in association with J. E. Caerwyn Williams, *The Penguin Book of Welsh Verse* (Harmondsworth: Penguin, 1967), p. 47.
3. Llywelyn Goch ap Meurig Hen, 'The Tit', in Conran, *The Penguin Book of Welsh Verse*, p. 151. Dafydd ap Gwilym, 'Y Ceiliog Bronfraith' (The Song Thrush), in Rachel Bromwich (ed. and trans.), *Selected Poems of Dafydd ap Gwilym* (Harmondsworth: Penguin Books, 1985), pp. 70–1.
4. D. Parry-Jones, *Welsh Country Upbringing* (1948; rpt. London and New York: B. T. Batsford Ltd, 1949, p. 39.
5. D. Parry-Jones, *Welsh Country Characters*, with illustrations by Lynton Lamb (London and New York: B. T. Batsford Ltd, 1952), pp. 167–8.
6. Parry-Jones, *Welsh Country Characters*, p. 84.
7. Parry-Jones, *Welsh Country Upbringing*, p. 132.
8. Roger Lovegrove, *The Kite's Tale: The Story of the Red Kite in Wales* (Sandy, Bedfordshire: Royal Society for the Protection of Birds, 1990), p. 5.
9. M. Wynn Thomas, *In the Shadow of the Pulpit: Literature and Nonconformist Wales* (Cardiff: University of Wales Press, 2010), p. 45.
10. Thomas, *In the Shadow of the Pulpit*, p. 39.
11. Linden Peach, *Pacifism, Peace and Modern Welsh Writing* (Cardiff: University of Wales Press, 2019).
12. Mari Jones, *Trwy Lygad y Bugail* (1970; rev. Llansawel: Mudiad Efengylaidd Cymru, Gwasg y Dderwen, 1973).
13. Thomas, *In the Shadow of the Pulpit*, p. 211.
14. Parry-Jones, *Welsh Country Upbringing*, pp. 30–1.
15. Thomas, *In the Shadow of the Pulpit*, pp. 214 and 208.
16. Thomas, *In the Shadow of the Pulpit*, p. 211.
17. Parry-Jones, *Welsh Country Characters*, p. 70.
18. Parry-Jones, *Welsh Country Characters*, p. 71.
19. Edward Armstrong, *The Farming Sector in Wales* (Cardiff: National Assembly of Wales, Research Studies, 2016), p. 2.
20. J. Geraint Jenkins, 'Life and Traditions in Rural Wales', Paper given to the World Conference on Records, 1980. Online. Available at *www.familysearch.org* (accessed 12 February 2021).
21. This aspect of animal farming is discussed more extensively in, for example, David A. Nibert, *Animal Oppression and Human Violence: Domesecration, Capitalism, and Global Conflict* (New York: Columbia University Press, 2013), p. 6.
22. Richard Moore-Colyer, *Farming in Wales 1936–2011*, ed. Tony O'Regan (Talybont, Ceredigion: Y Lolfa, 2011), pp. 75–6.
23. Moore-Colyer, *Farming in Wales*, p. 75.
24. James Law, *Meddyg y Fferm* (Edinburgh: Thomas C. Jack, Grange Publishing Works; Bangor: Evan Ingram, 1881), pp. v, ix–xxv.
25. *Llyfr Coginio* (Wrexham: Hughes and Son, n.d.), p. vi.
26. *Llyfr Cognio*, pp. 84–9.

[27] Deborah Denenholz Morse, 'Animal Subjectivities: Gendered Literary Representation of Animal Minds in Anna Sewell's *Black Beauty*', in Bruce Boehrer, Molly Hand and Brian Massumi (eds), *Animals, Animality and Literature* (Cambridge: Cambridge University Press, 2018), p. 190 [pp. 180–96].
[28] Carol J. Adams, *The Sexual Politics of Meat: A Feminist-Vegetarian Critical Theory* (1990; rpt. London: Bloomsbury, 2010), p. 37.
[29] Adams, *The Sexual Politics of Meat*, pp. 67 and 71. See also Ryan, *Animal Theory*, pp. 137–42.
[30] Jean Earle, 'Jugged Hare', in Meic Stephens (ed.), *Poetry 1900–2000* (Cardigan: Parthian, Library of Wales, 2016), pp. 126–7.
[31] M. W. Thomas, *Internal Difference; Literature in Twentieth-century Wales* (Cardiff: University of Wales Press, 1992), p. 111.
[32] Paul Waldau, *Animal Studies: An Introduction* (Oxford: Oxford University Press, 2013), pp. 34 and 35.
[33] See, for example, Adrian Franklin, *Animals and Modern Cultures: A Sociology of Human–Animal Relations in Modernity* (London: Sage Publications Ltd, 1999), p. 126.
[34] David Williams, *A History of Modern Wales* (1950; rpt. London: John Murray, 1969), p. 181.
[35] Jenkins, 'Life and Traditions in Rural Wales'. Online.
[36] Moore-Colyer, *Farming in Wales*, p. 62.
[37] Williams, *A History of Modern Wales*, p. 181.
[38] Available at *https://www.blackwelshmountain.org.uk* (accessed 17 August 2020).
[39] Roscoe Howells, *Farming in Wales* (Llandyssul: Gomerian Press, 1965), pp. 44 and 46.
[40] Nibert, *Animal Oppression and Human Violence*, p. 5.
[41] Moore-Colyer, *Farming in Wales*, p. 68.
[42] Moore-Colyer, *Farming in Wales*, p. 69.
[43] Moore-Colyer, *Farming in Wales*, p. 69.
[44] Moore-Colyer, *Farming in Wales*, p. 70.
[45] *Farming, the Environment and the Welsh Uplands* (an evidence review produced by Cynidr Consulting for RSPB Cymru), March 2019. For discussion of this report, see, also, Arfon Williams, 'The Future of Farming and Nature in Wales', Institute of Welsh Affairs. Online. Available at *https://www.iwa.wales* (accessed 24 March 2021).
[46] Williams, 'The Future of Farming and Nature in Wales'. Online.
[47] Williams, 'The Future of Farming and Nature in Wales'. Online.
[48] Paul Sears, 'Ecology – a Subversive Subject', *BioScience*, 14/7 (1964), 11–13.
[49] Waldau, *Animal Studies*, pp. 32–3.
[50] Milja Kurki, *International Relations in a Relational Universe* (Oxford: Oxford University Press, 2020), p. 59.
[51] Waldau, *Animal Studies*, p. 188.
[52] Nibert, *Animal Oppression and Human Violence*, p. 12.
[53] Ryan, *Animal Theory*, p. 18.
[54] *Results of the 2018 FSA Survey into Slaughter Methods in England and Wales* (Cardiff: Animal Welfare and Framework Branch, Welsh Government, 2019), p. 6.

55 *Results of the 2018 FSA Survey into Slaughter Methods in England and Wales*, p. 6.
56 Jane Jones, 'Mandatory CCTV in Welsh slaughterhouses to improve animal welfare', Nation.Cymru (6 November 2021). Online. Available at *https://nation.cymru/news/mandatory-cctv-in-welsh-slaughterhouses-to-improve-animal-welfare/* (accessed 6 November 2021).
57 Jones, 'Mandatory CCTV in Welsh slaughterhouses to improve animal welfare'. Online.
58 Jones, 'Mandatory CCTV in Welsh slaughterhouses to improve animal welfare'. Online.
59 Jones, 'Mandatory CCTV in Welsh slaughterhouses to improve animal welfare'. Online.
60 Frances Williams, 'At the Butcher's', *Flotsam* (Bridgend: Poetry Wales Press, 1987), p. 23.
61 Williams, 'At the Butcher's', p. 23.
62 Williams, 'At the Butcher's', p. 23.
63 J. M. Jones, W. J. Price and T. M. Thomas, *Gwewrsi i'r Safonau* (Cardiff and Wrexham: The Educational Publishing Company, n.d.), pp. 44 and 45.
64 Adams, *The Sexual Politics of Meat*, pp. 114–15.
65 Kurki, *International Relations in a Relational Universe*, p. 192.
66 Cynan Jones, *Everything I Found on the Beach* (Cardigan: Parthian, 2011).
67 Kurki, *International Relations in a Relational Universe*, p. 193.
68 Kurki, *International Relations in a Relational Universe*, p. 191.
69 E. Humphreys, 'Bullocks', *Collected Poems* (Cardiff: University of Wales Press, 1999), p. 60.
70 Humphreys, 'Bullocks', p. 61.
71 Humphreys, 'Bullocks', p. 61.
72 Humphreys, 'Bullocks', p. 60.
73 Humphreys, 'Bullocks', p. 60.
74 Peter Kulchyski, 'Bush/Animals', in Boehrer, Hand and Massumi (eds), *Animals, Animality and Literature*, p. 321 [pp. 319–33].
75 Humphreys, 'Bullocks', p. 61.
76 Kurki, *International Relations in a Relational Universe*, p. 194.
77 Donna J. Haraway, *Staying with the Trouble: Making Kin in the Chthulucene* (Durham, NC: Duke University Press, 2016), p. 1.
78 Gillian Clarke, *Roots Home: Essays and a Journal* (Manchester: Carcanet, 2021), p. 26.
79 Clarke, 'The Field Mouse', *Roots Home*, p. 27.
80 Gillian Clarke, 'Journal', *Roots Home*, p. 171.
81 E. Humphreys, 'Turkeys in Wales', *Collected Poems*, p. 66.
82 Humphreys, 'Turkeys in Wales', p. 67.
83 Humphreys, 'Turkeys in Wales', p. 66.
84 E. Humphreys, 'Dream for a Soldier', *Collected Poems*, p. 84.
85 Humphreys, 'Dream for a Soldier', p. 85.
86 Humphreys, 'Dream for a Soldier', p. 84.
87 Alasdair Cochrane, *Animal Rights Without Liberation: Applied Ethics and Human Obligations* (New York: Columbia University Press, 2012), pp. 93–102.
88 Cochrane, *Animal Rights Without Liberation*, p. 101.

89 Cochrane, *Animal Rights Without Liberation*, p. 101.
90 'Welsh farmers raise concerns over rise in veganism', BBC News (23 October 2017). Online. Available at *https://www.bbc.co.uk/news/uk* (accessed 13 November 2021).
91 *The Western Mail* (3 April 1884), 4.
92 *The Flintshire Observer Mining Journal and General Advertiser* (16 October 1884), 3.
93 *The Flintshire Observer Mining Journal and General Advertiser* (16 October 1884), 3.
94 See, for example, Lizzie Collingham, *The Hungry Empire: How Britain's Quest for Food Shaped the Modern World* (2017: rpt. London: Vintage, 2018), p. 232.
95 See, for example, Colin Spencer, *Vegetarianism: A History* (2016; rpt. London: Grub Street, 2017), p.275.
96 Cit. in John Burnett, *Plenty and Want* (London and New York: Routledge, 1989) and in Colin Spencer, *Vegetarianism*, p. 277.
97 *South Wales Echo* (September 1898), 2.
98 *South Wales Daily News* (19 October 1898), 3.
99 *Evening Express* (26 November 1903), 3.
100 *Prestatyn Weekly* (15 February 1908), 4.
101 *Prestatyn Weekly* (15 February 1908), 4.
102 Edward Maitland, *Anna Kingsford: Her Life, Letters, Diary and Work*, vol. 1 (London: Redway, 1896), p. 28.
103 Agnes Ryan, 'The Heart to Sing', unpublished autobiography, pp. 314–15. Cit. Adams, *The Sexual Politics of Meat*, p. 112.
104 'Welsh farmers raise concerns over rise in veganism'. Online.
105 *The Aberdare Times* (26 May 1888), 3.
106 *The Carmarthen Weekly Reporter* (20 October 1899), 1.
107 'Welsh farmers raise concerns over rise in veganism'. Online.
108 'Welsh farmers raise concerns over rise in veganism'. Online.
109 Spencer, *Vegetarianism*, p. 276.
110 See, Moore-Colyer, *Farming in Wales*, p. 69.
111 Anna Lewis, 'The full horrifying scale of the 2001 foot and mouth outbreak told by Welsh farmers in the middle of it', *Wales Online* (12 April 2020). Available at *https://www.walesonline.co.uk/news/wales-news/foot-mouth* (accessed 24 April 2020).
112 Lewis, 'The full horrifying scale of the 2001 foot and mouth outbreak'. Online.
113 Robin Turner, 'Foot and mouth: 2001 wounds reopened', *Wales Online* (29 March 2013). Available at *https://www.walesonline.co.uk/news/wales-news/foot-and-mouth-2001* (accessed 24 April 2020).
114 Gillian Clarke, 'Virus', in Gillian Clarke, *Making the Beds for the Dead* (Manchester: Carcanet, 2004), p. 56.
115 Clarke, 'Marsh Fritillary', *Making the Beds for the Dead*, p. 62.
116 Clarke, 'On the Move, February 2001' and 'Virus', *Making the Beds for the Dead*, pp. 58 and 56.
117 Clarke, 'First Lamb, 12th March 2001', *Making the Beds for the Dead*, p. 59.
118 Clarke, 'The Vet', 'Silence, February 2001', 'Woolmark' and 'Plague, Spring 2001', *Making the Beds for the Dead*, pp. 66, 57, 67 and 61.
119 Clarke, 'Pigs, summer 2001', *Making the Beds for the Dead*, p. 65.

120 Clarke, 'Wethers', *Making the Beds for the Dead*, p. 53.
121 Ceri Thompson, *Harnessed: Colliery Horses in Wales* (Cardiff: Amgueddfa Cymru [National Museum of Wales], 2008), p. 65.
122 Thompson, *Harnessed*, p. 14.
123 Rosemary Preece, *Coal Mining and the Camera* (Overton: National Coal Mining Museum for England Publications, 1998), p. 37.
124 Preece, *Coal Mining and the Camera*, p. 21.
125 Cit. Thompson, *Harnessed*, p. 41.
126 Thompson, *Harnessed*, p. 17.
127 Cit. Thompson, *Harnessed*, p. 54.
128 Thompson, *Harnessed*, p. 54.
129 Thompson, *Harnessed*, pp. 55–8.
130 Thompson, *Harnessed*, p. 58.
131 Martin Johnes, 'Pigeon Racing and Working-Class Culture in Britain, c. 1870–1950', *Cultural and Social History*, 4/ 3 (2007), 369–71.
132 Johnes, 'Pigeon Racing and Working-Class Culture', 361–2.
133 Johnes, 'Pigeon Racing and Working-Class Culture', 371.
134 Menna Elfyn, 'Perfect Blemish'/'Perffaith Nam', *New and Selected Poems 1995–2007/Dau Ddeholiad and Cherddi Newydd 1995–2007* (Tarset, Northumberland: Bloodaxe Books, 2007), p. 66.
135 Elfyn, 'Perfect Blemish'/'Perffaith Nam', p. 67.
136 'The Sully Coursing Meeting', *Weekly Mail* (22 October 1887), 5.
137 'Coursing', *Evening Express* (24 December 1901), 4.
138 'Pontnewynydd', *Pontypool Free Press and Herald of the Hills* (6 February 1891), 5.
139 See, for example, the report of results devoted to greyhounds: 'Caerwys', *Flintshire Observer Mining Journal and General Advertiser for the Counties of Flint Denbigh* (6 September 1888), 8 and 'Prize winners at Llanidloes Show', *South Wales Daily News* (18 August 1900), 6.
140 'Sale of Greyhounds', *South Wales Daily News* (21 April 1884), 4.
141 'Greyhounds Not Sporting Dogs', *Evening Express* (3 December 1900), 4.
142 Daryl Leeworthy, 'A Diversion from the New Leisure: Greyhound Racing, Working-Class Culture, and the Politics of Unemployment in Inter-war South Wales', *Sport in History*, 32/1 (2012). Online. Available at *https://doi.org/ 10.1080/17460263.2012.658965* (accessed 17 February 2020). See, also, Keith Laybourn, *Going to the Dogs: A History of Greyhound Racing in Britain, 1926–2017* (Manchester: Manchester University Press, 2019).
143 The League Against Cruel Sports, 'The State of Greyhound Racing in Great Britain: A Mandate for Change', in conjunction with GREY2KUSA worldwide. Online. Available at *www.league.org.uk* (accessed 17 February 2020).
144 Cynlluniad Cenediaethol Cymru, *The fate of racing greyhounds and working lurchers in Wales* (2003), p. 6.
145 See, for example, Rebecca Astill, 'Political leaders throw their support behind Hope Rescue's campaign against greyhound racing', *Wales Online* (20 October 2021). Available at *https://www.walesonline.co.uk* (accessed 15 November 2021). Rebecca Astill, 'Devastating pictures show why rescue centre wants to end greyhound racing', *Wales Online* (17 September 2021). Available at *https://www.walesonline.co.uk* (accessed 15 November 2021).

[146] *Atlantic Monthly* (June, 2015), cit. Marc Bekoff and Jessica Pierce, *The Animals' Agenda: Freedom, Compassion, and Coexistence in the Human Age* (Boston: Beacon Press, 2017), p. 179.
[147] Bekoff and Pierce, *The Animals' Agenda*, p. 179.
[148] Steven Johnson, 'The Genius of the Tinkerer', *Wall Street Journal* (25 September 2010), cit. Bekoff and Pierce, *The Animals' Agenda*, p. 179.

3 Emerging Animalities in the Victorian and Edwardian Welsh Press

[1] Paul Waldau, *Animal Studies: An Introduction* (Oxford: Oxford University Press, 2013), p. 188.
[2] Derek Ryan, *Animal Theory: A Critical Introduction* (Edinburgh: Edinburgh University Press, 2015), p. 76.
[3] *South Wales Daily News* (5 December 1891), 4.
[4] M. Wynn Thomas, *In the Shadow of the Pulpit: Literature and Nonconformist Wales* (Cardiff: University of Wales Press, 2010), p. 211.
[5] *Weekly Mail* (3 August 1907), 9.
[6] C. Bryner Jones (ed.), *Live Stock of the Farm*, vol. iv (London: The Gresham Publishing Company Ltd, n.d.), pp. 93–4. The content of the book suggests that it was published shortly before the First World War.
[7] *Cambria Daily Leader* (30 October 1914), 8.
[8] *Pembrokeshire Herald and General Advertiser* (12 February 1909), 2.
[9] *Weekly Mail* (4 June 1910), 4.
[10] Moira Ferguson, *Animal Advocacy and Englishwomen, 1780–1900: Patriots, Nation and Empire* (Ann Arbor: The University of Michigan Press, 1998) p. 44–5. See, also, Robyn S. Metcalfe, *Meat, Commerce and the City: The London Food Market, 1800–1855* (London: Pickering and Chatto, 2012) and Ted Geier, *Meat Markets: The Cultural History of Bloody London* (Edinburgh: Edinburgh University Press, 2017), pp. 77–118.
[11] *Pembrokeshire Herald and General Advertiser* (12 February 1909), 2.
[12] *South Wales Echo* (12 March 1896), 2.
[13] *Weekly Mail* (26 November 1904), 2.
[14] *Weekly Mail* (26 November 1904), 2.
[15] *Weekly Mail* (26 November 1904), 2.
[16] *The Chester Courant and Advertiser for North Wales* (8 May 1901), 3.
[17] *The Chester Courant and Advertiser for North Wales* (8 May 1901), 3.
[18] Elaine Williams, *Horse* (2008; rpt. London: Reaktion Books, 2013), p. 89.
[19] Williams, *Horse*, p. 89.
[20] Williams, *Horse*, p. 89.
[21] The novel has an interesting place also within twentieth-century Welsh pacifism through its translation after the Second World War: John Eilian (trans.), *Du Del* (Glasgow: Collins Clear-Type Press, 1954). John Eilian was the bardic name of the pacifist writer John Tudor Jones. For a discussion of this translation and its significance for Welsh pacifism, see Linden Peach, *Pacifism, Peace and Modern Welsh Writing* (Cardiff: University of Wales Press, 2019), pp. 177–84.

22 D. Parry-Jones, *Welsh Country Upbringing* (1948; rpt. London: B. T. Batsford Ltd., 1949), pp. 122 and 123.
23 Parry-Jones, *Welsh Country Upbringing*, p. 42.
24 Ceri Thompson, *Harnessed: Colliery Horses in Wales* (Cardiff: Amgueddfa Cymru [National Museum of Wales], 2008), p. 65.
25 Thompson, *Harnessed*, p. 39.
26 The 'Pit Ponies Charter' included requirements that all horses be examined annually by a veterinary surgeon; that any horse certified as unfit to work should be brought to the surface as soon as practicable; that a horse unfit for work should not be sold to a horse dealer but humanely destroyed, sent to a home of rest or be looked after by a responsible person; that each horse be housed in a single stall with a manger; that each horse be supplied with clean straw and its stables cleaned daily; and that each stable be of adequate size and adequately lit and ventilated.
27 *The Amman Valley Chronicle and East Carmarthen News* (23 November 1916), 1.
28 *Baner ac Amserau* (20 July 1910), 12.
29 *Baner ac Amserau* (20 July 1910), 12.
30 *The Rhos Herald* (23 July 1910), 8.
31 Cited Jane Jones, 'Mandatory CCTV in Welsh slaughterhouses to improve animal welfare', *Nation. Cymru* (6 November 2021). Online. Available at *https://nation.cymru/news/mandatory-cctv-in-welsh-slaughterhouses-to-improve-animal-welfare/* (accessed 6 November 2021).
32 *The Merthyr Express* (17 September 1910), 12.
33 *The Cambrian* (20 August 1909), 6.
34 See, for example, Peter Godfrey-Smith, *Other Minds: The Octopus and the Evolution of Intelligent Life* (London: William Collins, 2017); Carl Safina, *Beyond Words: What Animals Think and Feel* (New York: Henry Holt and Company, 2015); Barbara J. King, *How Animals Grieve* (Chicago and London: University of Chicago Press, 2013); Marc Bekoff, *The Emotional Lives of Animals: A Leading Scientist Explores Animal Joy, Sorrow and Empathy and Why They Matter* (Novato, CA: New World Library, 2007); and Marc Bekoff, *Minding Animals: Awareness, Emotions and Heart* (Oxford: Oxford University Press, 2002).
35 *County Observer and Monmouth Central Advertiser, Abergavenny and Raglan Herald, Usk and Pontypool Messenger and Chepstow Argus* (21 May 1904), 8.
36 D. Parry-Jones, *Welsh Country Characters* (London and New York: B. T. Batsford Ltd, 1952), p. 57.
37 Parry-Jones, *Welsh Country Characters*, p. 57.
38 Parry-Jones, *Welsh Country Upbringing*, p. 43.
39 See, for example, King, *How Animals Grieve*; Bekoff, *The Emotional Lives of Animals*; and Bekoff, *Minding Animals*.

4 Exotic Pets and Spectacular Entertainments

1 Yi-Fu Tuan, *Dominance and Affection: The Making of Pets* (New Haven and London: Yale University Press, 1984), p. 69.
2 Derek Ryan, *Animal Theory: A Critical Introduction* (Edinburgh: Edinburgh University Press, 2015), p. 36.

NOTES 205

3 Luce Irigaray, 'Animal Compassion', in Peter Atterton and Matthew Calarco (eds), *Animal Philosophy: Ethics and Identity* (London: Continuum, 2004), p. 195 [pp. 195–201].
4 *Barry Herald* (23 September 1898), 7.
5 *Barry Herald* (23 September 1898), 7.
6 *Welsh Gazette and West Wales Advertiser* (22 December 1910), 5.
7 *Welsh Gazette and West Wales Advertiser* (22 December 1910), 5.
8 *County Observer and Monmouthshire Central Advertiser, Abergavenny and Raglan Herald, Usk and Pontypool Messenger and Chepstow Argus* (27 February 1904), 5.
9 *Weekly Mail* (6 January 1894), 11.
10 Paul Waldau, *Animal Studies: An Introduction* (Oxford: Oxford University Press, 2013), p. 194.
11 *Denbighshire Free Press* (9 December 1905), 7.
12 See, for example, Caroline Grigson, *Menagerie: The History of Exotic Animals in England* (Oxford: Oxford University Press, 2016), Helen Cowie, *Exhibiting Animals in Nineteenth-century Britain: Empathy, Education, Entertainment* (Basingstoke: Palgrave Macmillan, 2014) and John Miller, *Empire and the Animal Body: Violence, Identity and Ecology in Victorian Adventure Fiction* (London: Anthem Press, 2012).
13 Rachel Poliquin, *The Breathless Zoo: Taxidermy and the Cultures of Longing* (Pennsylvania: The Pennsylvania State University Press, 2012), p. 87.
14 Desmond Morris, *Monkey* (London: Reaktion Books, 2013), pp. 44, 10, 18, 49 and 55.
15 Morris, *Monkey*, pp. 74 and 62.
16 Tuan, *Dominance and Affection*, p. 82.
17 T. Rowland Hughes, *William Jones*, trans. Richard Ruck (Aberystwyth: Gwasg Aberystwyth, 1953), p. 263.
18 Hughes, *William Jones*, p. 263.
19 Margo DeMello, *Animals and Society: An Introduction to Human–Animal Studies* (2012; rev. New York: Columbia University Press, 2nd edn, 2021), pp. 423–4. See, also, Peter Godfrey-Smith, *Other Minds: The Octopus and the Evolution of Intelligent Life* (London: William Collins, 2017); Carl Safina, *Beyond Words: What Animals Think and Feel* (New York: Henry Holt and Company, 2015); Barbara J. King, *How Animals Grieve* (Chicago and London: University of Chicago Press, 2013); Marc Bekoff, *The Emotional Lives of Animals* (Novato, CA: New World Library, 2007); and Marc Bekoff, *Minding Animals: Awareness, Emotions and Heart* (Oxford: Oxford University Press, 2002).
20 Lori Marino, 'Captivity', in Lori Gruen (ed.), *Critical Terms for Animal Studies* (Chicago and London: The University of Chicago Press, 2018), p. 99 [pp. 99–111].
21 Morris, *Monkey*, pp. 10, 74 and 78.
22 Derek Ryan, 'Literature', in Lynn Turner, Undine Sellbach and Ron Broglio (eds), *The Edinburgh Companion to Animal Studies* (Edinburgh: Edinburgh University Press, 2018), p. 332 [pp. 321–36].
23 *The Pontypridd Chronicle and Workman's News* (18 September 1891), 8.
24 *The Aberystwyth Observer* (31 May 1894), 6.
25 *The Aberystwyth Observer* (31 May 1894), 6.

26 *The Aberystwyth Observer* (31 May 1894), 6.
27 *The Aberystwyth Observer* (31 May 1894), 6.
28 *The Aberystwyth Observer* (31 May 1894), 6.
29 *South Wales Daily News* (5 June 1894), 6.
30 *South Wales Daily News* (5 June 1894), 6.
31 *South Wales Daily News* (5 June 1894), 6.
32 *Evening Express* (6 February 1909), 3.
33 *Evening Express* (6 February 1909), 3.
34 *Evening Express* (6 February 1909), 3.
35 *Cardiff and Merthyr Guardian, Glamorgan, Monmouth and Brecon Gazette* (6 February 1869), 3.
36 *Cardiff and Merthyr Guardian, Glamorgan, Monmouth and Brecon Gazette* (6 February 1869), 3.
37 *Evening Express* (11 May 1909), 4.
38 *Llangollen Advertiser, Denbighshire, Merionethshire and North Wales Journal* (24 July 1914), 5.
39 *The Aberystwyth Observer* (7 January 1872), 3.
40 *The Aberystwyth Observer* (7 January 1872), 3.
41 *Evening Express* (23 December 1909), 2.
42 *Evening Express* (28 November 1898), 3.
43 Mary-Ann Constantine, 'The Elephant at Tregaron', *The Breathing* (Aberystwyth: Planet, 2008), p. 34 [pp. 33–42].
44 'Tregaron Elephant Project'. Online. Available at *https://www.uwtsd.ac.uk/research/environment-archaeology-history-and-anthropology/tregaron-elephant-project/* (accessed 23 April 2020).
45 'Llansawel Elephant'. Online. Available at *www.llansawel.org.uk* (accessed 23 April 2020).
46 For a discussion of the history of the elephant from the animal's point of view, see Dan Wylie, *Elephant* (London: Reaktion Books, 2008).
47 Ryan, *Animal Theory*, p. 144.
48 See, for example, Tuan, *Dominance and Affection*, p. 69.
49 Constantine, 'The Elephant at Tregaron', p. 41.
50 Constantine, 'The Elephant at Tregaron', p. 41.
51 Constantine, 'The Elephant at Tregaron', p. 42.
52 Ryan, *Animal Theory*, pp. 1–2.
53 See, for example, Milja Kurki, *International Relations in a Relational Universe* (Oxford: Oxford University Press, 2020), pp. 42–6.
54 Poliquin, *The Breathless Zoo*, p. 87.
55 Tuan, *Dominance and Affection*, p. 70.
56 Tuan, *Dominance and Affection*, p. 70.
57 Adrian Franklin, *Animals and Modern Cultures: A Sociology of Human–Animal Relations to Modernity* (London: Sage Publications Ltd, 1999), pp. 75–6.
58 Available at *https://www.welshmountainzoo.org/about/about-us* (accessed 30 September 2020).
59 Available at *https://www.welshmountainzoo.org/conservation/introduction* (accessed 30 September 2020).
60 Ryan, *Animal Theory*, p. 3.

NOTES   207

61 Ryan, *Animal Theory*, p. 3.
62 Available at *https://www.welshmountainzoo.org/conservation/introduction* (accessed 30 September 2020).
63 Available at *https://www.welshmountainzoo.org/conservation/introduction* (accessed 30 September 2020).
64 An article posted on Nation.Cymru reported that the Welsh Mountain Zoo had been criticised in a report, 'Zoos: Financing Conservation or Funding Captivity?', by the animal welfare charity Born Free urging charitable zoos to spend more on conservation instead of new animal exhibits. According to Nation.Cymru, the report suggests that £1 million spent on a snow leopard enclosure might have been redirected 'in vital support for in situ conservation'. 'Welsh Mountain Zoo criticised in report urging more spend on animal conservation efforts', *Nation.Cymru* (22 July 2021). Online. Available at *https://nation.cymru/news/welsh-mountain-zoo-criticised-in-report...* (accessed 23 July 2021).
65 Hannah Lawrence, 'Wales lynx escape: Zoo "outraged" over killing of escaped big cat', *Independent* (11 November 2017). Online. Available at *https://www.independent.co.uk/news/uk/home-news/escaped-lynx-killed-borth-zoo-lilleth-humanely-destroyed-ceredigion-wales-a8049401.html* (accessed 18 August 2020).
66 Lawrence, 'Wales lynx escape'. Online.
67 'Council blames Borth zoo for escaped lynx shooting', BBC Wales (15 November 2017). Online. Available at *https://www.bbc.co.uk/news/uk-wales-mid-wales-41996377* (accessed 18 August 2020).
68 Gillian Clarke, 'The Company of Bones', *Zoology* (Manchester: Carcanet Press Ltd, 2017), p. 28.
69 Poliquin, *The Breathless Zoo*, p. 78.
70 See, for example, John Miller's discussion of Victorian adventure stories in Miller, *Empire and the Animal Body*.
71 William Griffith, *Anturiaethau Cymro yn Affrica* (Swyddfa Cymru: Cwmni y Cyhoeddwyr Gymreig, 1912), p. 61.
72 Griffith, *Anturiaethau Cymro yn Affrica*, pp. 60 and 59.
73 Griffith, *Anturiaethau Cymro yn Affrica*, p. 59.
74 Griffith, *Anturiaethau Cymro yn Affrica*, p. 59.
75 Griffith, *Anturiaethau Cymro yn Affrica*, p.59.
76 Griffith, *Anturiaethau Cymro yn Affrica*, p. 61.
77 Griffith, *Anturiaethau Cymro yn Affrica*, p. 62.

5 Brief Encounters

1 Derek Ryan, *Animal Theory: A Critical Introduction* (Edinburgh: Edinburgh University Press, 2015), p. 117.
2 Milja Kurki, *International Relations in a Relational Universe* (Oxford: Oxford University Press, 2020), p. 2.
3 Kurki, *International Relations in a Relational Universe*, p. 4. See, for example, Philip Armstrong, *Sheep* (2016; rpt. London: Reaction Books, 2017); Elaine Walker, *Horse* (2008; rpt. London: Reaktion Books, 2013); Susan McHugh,

    Dog (London: Reaktion Books, 2004); and Desmond Morris, *Monkey* (London: Reaktion Books, 2013).
4   Ryan, *Animal Theory*, p. 58.
5   Ryan, *Animal Theory*, p. 59.
6   Paul Waldau, *Animal Studies: An Introduction* (Oxford: Oxford University Press, 2013), p. 208.
7   Richard Gwyn, 'The Indifferent Gaze', *Welsh Arts Review* (17 April, 2021). Online. Available at *https://www.walesartsreview.org/the-indifferent-gaze-by-richard-gwyn* (accessed 16 April 2021).
8   Gwyn, 'The Indifferent Gaze'. Online.
9   Gwyn, 'The Indifferent Gaze'. Online.
10 Gwyn, 'The Indifferent Gaze'. Online.
11 Neil Ansell, *Deep Country: Five Years in the Welsh Hills* (London: Hamish Hamilton, an imprint of Penguin Books, 2011), p. 51.
12 H. Idris Bell, 'The Twentieth Century', appendix to Thomas Parry, *A History of Welsh Literature*, trans. Idris Bell (Oxford: Clarendon Press, 1955), p. 398.
13 Lori Gruen, 'Empathy', in Lori Gruen (ed.), *Critical Terms for Animal Studies* (Chicago and London: The University of Chicago Press, 2018), p. 148 [pp. 141–53].
14 Bell, 'The Twentieth Century', p. 398.
15 Maurice Merleau-Ponty, *The Visible and The Invisible*, trans. Alphonso Lingis (Evanston, IL: Northwestern University Press, 1968), p. 117.
16 R. Williams Parry, 'The Fox', in *The Penguin Book of Welsh Verse*, trans. Anthony Conran, in association with J. E. Caerwyn Williams (Harmondsworth: Penguin Books Ltd, 1967), p. 240; R. Williams Parry, 'Y Llwynog', in R. Williams Parry, '*Rhyfeddod Prin*' (Llanrwst: Gwasg Carreg Gwalch, Pigion, 2000), p. 20.
17 Williams Parry, 'The Fox', p. 240; Williams Parry, 'Y Llwynog', p. 20.
18 Gilles Deleuze and Claire Parnet, 'A Is for Animal', in *Gilles Deleuze from A to Z*, dir. Pierre-Andre Boutane, trans. Charles J. Stivale (Cambridge: Semiotext(e)/Foreign Agents at the MIT Press, 2011). Film.
19 Williams Parry, 'The Fox', p. 240; Williams Parry, 'Y Llwynog', p. 20.
20 Ted Hughes, 'Thought-Fox', originally published in *The Hawk in the Rain* (London: Faber, 1957).
21 Daniel Butler, *The Owl House* (Bridgend: Seren, 2020), pp. 42–3.
22 Kurki, *International Relations in a Relational Universe*, p. 119.
23 Kurki, *International Relations in a Relational Universe*, p. 120.
24 Kurki, *International Relations in a Relational Universe*, p. 120.
25 Kurki, *International Relations in a Relational Universe*, p. 120.
26 Gwynn ap Gwilym, 'The Badger', trans. Grahame Davies, in Menna Elfyn and John Rowlands (eds), *The Bloodaxe Book of Modern Welsh Poetry: 20th-century Welsh-language Poetry in Translation* (Tarset, Northumberland: Bloodaxe Books Ltd, 2003), p. 307 [pp. 307–8].
27 Ap Gwilym, 'The Badger', p. 307.
28 Ap Gwilym, 'The Badger', p. 307.
29 Ansell, *Deep Country*, p. 92.
30 Ansell, *Deep Country*, p. 92.

31 Gillian Clarke, 'The Presence', *Zoology* (Manchester: Carcanet Press Ltd, 2017), p. 13.
32 Waldau, *Animal Studies*, p. 243.
33 'The Presence' as a Welsh text recalls St Melangell, the Welsh patron saint of animals, who is specifically associated with hares. The myth concerning her, as recorded by Thomas Pennant (1726–1798), tells the story that as the daughter of an Irish monarch she fled to Wales where she lived as a hermit rather than marry a nobleman at court. One day while deep in her devotional prayers, she was disturbed by the Prince of Powys, Brochwel Ysgithrog, who, with his hounds, was in pursuit of a hare. Almost as if recognising a profound connection with Melangell, the animal took shelter beneath her robes and she outfaced the growling dogs who retreated. Impressed by her beauty and her courage, Brochwel gave her the land as a sanctuary and there Melangell became the abbess of a community of women.
34 Clarke, 'The Presence', p. 13.
35 Clarke, 'The Presence', p. 13.
36 Clarke, 'The Presence', p. 13.
37 Hilary Llewellyn-Williams, 'Mole', *The Tree Calendar* (Bridgend: Poetry Wales Press, 1987), p. 7.
38 See, for example, the website of the mammal society. Available at www.mammal.org.uk (accessed 5 June 2021).
39 Llewellyn-Williams, 'Mole', p. 7.
40 Noah Wilson-Rich, *The Bee: A Natural History* (Princeton and Oxford: Princeton University Press, 2018), p. 14.
41 Wilson-Rich, *The Bee*, p. 15.
42 Hilary Llewellyn-Williams, 'The Bee-Flight', *Book of Shadows* (Bridgend: Seren Books, 1990), p. 38.
43 Wilson-Rich, *The Bee*, p. 31.
44 Wilson-Rich, *The Bee*, p. 31.
45 Llewellyn-Williams, 'The Bee-Flight', p. 38.

6 Birds over Wales

1 F. Burns et al, *The State of the UK's Birds 2020* (Sandy, Bedfordshire: Royal Society for the Protection of Birds, 2021). Online. Available at www.rspb.org.uk (accessed 18 May 2021).
2 *The State of the UK's Birds, 2020*. Online [pp. 42–3].
3 *The State of the UK's Birds, 2020*. Online [pp. 44–5].
4 Robert Bateman, Antony W. Diamond and Rudolf L. Schreiber, *Save the Birds* (1987; rev. St John's, Newfoundland: Breakwater Books, 1989), p. 296.
5 Bateman, Diamond and Schreiber, *Save the Birds*, pp. 36 and 297.
6 Bateman, Diamond and Schreiber, *Save the Birds*, pp. 296–7.
7 Paul Waldau, *Animal Studies: A Critical Introduction* (Oxford: Oxford University Press, 2013), p. 243.
8 Rachel Bromwich, 'Introduction', in Rachel Bromwich (ed. and trans.), *Selected Poems of Dafydd ap Gwilym: A New Edition* (1982; rev. Harmondsworth: Penguin Books, 1985), p. xxiii.

9. Bromwich, 'Introduction', *Selected Poems of Dafydd ap Gwilym*, p. xxiii.
10. Yi-Fu Tuan, *Dominance and Affection: The Making of Pets* (New Haven and London: Yale University Press, 1984), p. 84.
11. Tuan, *Dominance and Affection*, p. 84.
12. Dafydd ap Gwilym, 'Y Ceiliog Bronfraith' (The Song Thrush), in Bromwich, *Selected Poems of Dafydd ap Gwilym*, pp. 70–1.
13. Dafydd ap Gwilym, 'Y Ceiliog Bronfraith' (The Mistle Thrush), 'Yr Wylan' (The Seagull) and 'Yr Ehedydd' (The Skylark), in Bromwich, *Selected Poems of Dafydd ap Gwilym*, pp. 70–3, 74–5 and 74–9.
14. Dafydd ap Gwilym, 'Y Ceiliog Bronfraith' (The Song Thrush) and 'Yr Wylan' (The Seagull), in Bromwich, *Selected Poems of Dafydd ap Gwilym*, pp. 70–1 and 74–5.
15. D. M. Lloyd-Jones, 'Rhagair', in Mari Jones, *Trwy Lygad y Bugail* (Llansawel: Mudiad Efengylaidd Cymru, Gwasg y Dderwen, 1970, rev. 1973), p. 4.
16. Waldau, *Animal Studies*, p. 32.
17. Neil Shaw, 'Ducks and swans are starving because of lockdown', *Wales Online* (21 May 2020). Online. Available at *wales.co.uk* (accessed 25 March 2021). An amber conservation status is unfavourable and is applied to species whose population is declining moderately.
18. 'Information-mute-swan-1'. Online. Available at *https://www.rspb.org.uk/birds-and-wildlife/wildlife-guides/bird-a-z/mute-swan/* (accessed 25 March 2021).
19. Euros Bowen, 'The Swan', in *The Penguin Book of Welsh Verse*, trans. Anthony Conran, in association with J. E. Caerwyn Williams (Harmondsworth: Penguin Books Ltd, 1967), p. 256.
20. Bowen, 'The Swan', p. 256.
21. Bowen, 'The Swan', p. 256.
22. Bowen, 'The Swan', p. 256.
23. Jeremy Hooker, 'Curlew', *A View from the Source: Selected Poems* (Manchester: Carcanet New Press, 1982), p. 88 [pp. 88–9]. The poem is also available in Meic Stephens (ed.), *Poetry 1900–2000* (Cardigan: Parthian, Library of Wales, 2016), p. 521 [pp. 521–2].
24. Milja Kurki, *International Relations in a Relational Universe* (Oxford: Oxford University Press, 2020), p. 167.
25. Jeremy Hooker, 'Curlews'. Online. Available at *https://poetryarchive.org/poem/curlew/* (accessed 28 December 2020).
26. Hooker, 'Curlew', p. 89.
27. For the science here, I am indebted to Bateman, Diamond and Schreiber, *Save the Birds*, p. 31.
28. Hooker, 'Curlew', p. 89.
29. Daniel Butler, *The Owl House* (Bridgend: Seren, 2020), pp. 38–9.
30. T. E. Nicholas, '*Llygad y Drws: Sonedau'r Carchar* (1940; rpt. Dinbycb: Gwasg Gee, 1941). Originally published in Welsh, these sonnets were published in part in English translation as *Through the Eye of the Door: Prison Sonnets* (Aberystwyth: The Cambrian News Ltd, 1948).
31. Nicholas, 'Challenge', *Prison Sonnets*, p. 21. Published as 'Her' in T. E. Nicholas, *Llygad y Drws: Sonedau'r Carchar* (1940), p. 128.
32. Nicholas, 'Through the Window', *Prison Sonnets*, p. 34.
33. Nicholas, 'Through the Window', p. 34.

NOTES

211

34 See, for example, Bateman, Diamond and Schreiber, *Save the Birds*, p. 297.
35 Nicholas, 'The Urge', *Prison Sonnets*, p. 77.
36 Bateman, Diamond and Schreiber, *Save the Birds*, p. 30.
37 Nicholas, 'To a Sparrow', *Prison Sonnets*, p. 91.
38 Jennifer Ackerman, *The Genius of Birds* (2016; rpt. London; Corsair, 2017), p. 228.
39 Kurki, *International Relations in a Relational Universe*, p. 164.
40 Kurki, *International Relations in a Relational Universe*, p. 165.
41 Nicholas, 'Disgust', *Prison Sonnets*, p. 29.
42 Nicholas, 'Disgust', p. 29.
43 Joseph A. Quine, 'Finding Where the Cuckoos Sing: R. S. Thomas and the Poiesis of Birdwatching' (PhD thesis, University of Melbourne, July 2019), p. 6.
44 Quine, 'Finding Where the Cuckoos Sing', p. 15.
45 R. S. Thomas, 'Swifts', *Collected Poems 1945–1990* (1993; rpt. London: Phoenix, 2010), p. 154.
46 R. S. Thomas, 'Bird Book'. R. S. Thomas archive, Bangor University, Wales.
47 Quine, 'Finding Where the Cuckoos Sing', p. 18.
48 Quine, 'Finding Where the Cuckoos Sing', p. 19.
49 Quine, 'Finding Where the Cuckoos Sing', p. 19.
50 Quine, 'Finding Where the Cuckoos Sing', p. 19.
51 Thomas, 'Swifts', *Collected Poems*, p. 154.
52 Milja Kurki, *International Relations in a Relational Universe*, p. 119.
53 Quine, 'Finding Where the Cuckoos Sing', p. 202.
54 Quine, 'Finding Where the Cuckoos Sing', p. 172.
55 Kurki, *International Relations in a Relational Universe*, p. 119.
56 Kurki, *International Relations in a Relational Universe*, p. 119.
57 Quine, 'Finding Where the Cuckoos Sing', p. 172.
58 Thomas, 'Moorland', *Collected Poems*, p. 513.
59 Thomas, 'Moorland', *Collected Poems*, p. 513.
60 'R. S. Thomas in conversation with Molly Price-Owen', *The David Jones Journal: R. S. Thomas Special Issue* (summer/autumn 2001), 93 [93–110].
61 Thomas, *Collected Poems*, p. 513.
62 Waldau, *Animal Studies*, p. 32.
63 Leslie Norris, 'The Mallard', *Sliding: Short Stories* (1971; rpt. London: Dent, 1978), p. 44.
64 Norris, 'The Mallard', p. 44.
65 Yi-Fu Tuan, *Dominance and Affection: The Making of Pets* (New Haven and London: Yale University Press, 1984), p. 4.
66 Norris, 'The Mallard', p. 44.
67 Norris, 'The Mallard', p. 44.
68 Norris, 'The Mallard', pp. 47 and 48.
69 Steven Johnson, 'The Genius of the Tinkerer', *Wall Street Journal* (25 September 2010). Cit. Marc Bekoff and Jessica Pierce, *The Animals' Agenda: Freedom, Compassion, and Coexistence in the Human Ages* (Boston: Beacon Press, 2017), p. 179.
70 Norris, 'The Mallard', p. 49.
71 Leslie Norris, 'Prey', p. 98.

72 Norris, 'Prey', pp. 98–9.
73 Ackerman, *The Genius of Birds*, p. 3.
74 Ackerman, *The Genius of Birds*, pp. 69–70.
75 See, Bateman, Diamond and Schreiber, *Save the Birds*, pp. 298–317.
76 Bateman, Diamond and Schreiber, *Save the Birds*, p. 369.
77 Bateman, Diamond and Schreiber, *Save the Birds*, pp. 369, 368 and 369.
78 Waldau, *Animal Studies*, pp. 93–4.
79 Bateman, Diamond and Schreiber, *Save the Birds*, p. 360.
80 *Cymru'r Plant* (Wrexham: Hughes a'i Fab, 1892–1987).
81 See, for example, John A. Walpole-Bond, *Bird Life in Wild Wales* (1903); George Bolam, *Wild Life in Wales* (1913); T. A. Coward, *Bird Haunts and Nature Memories* (1922); H. A. Gilbert and A. Brook, *Watchings and Wanderings among Birds* (1931); Geoffrey C. S. Ingram and H. Morrey Salmon, *Birds in Britain Today* (1933).
82 Waldau, *Animal Studies*, pp. 34 and 35.
83 Waldau, *Animal Studies*, p. 101.
84 Roger Lovegrove, *The Kite's Tale: The Story of the Red Kite in Wales* (Sandy, Bedfordshire: Royal Society for the Protection of Birds, 1990), p. 2.
85 Waldau, *Animal Studies*, p. 248.
86 Waldau, *Animal Studies*, p. 248.
87 Lovegrove, *The Kite's Tale*, pp. 44 and 89.
88 Lovegrove, *The Kite's Tale*, p. 7.
89 Menna Elfyn, 'Dynwared Adar' (Birdsong), *Murmur* (Highgreen, Northumberland: Bloodaxe Books Ltd, 2012, rpt. 2013), pp. 72–3.
90 Derek Ryan, *Animal Theory: A Critical Introduction* (Edinburgh: Edinburgh University Press, 2015), p. 4.
91 Ryan, *Animal Theory*, p. 4.
92 Ryan, *Animal Theory*, p. 4.
93 Waldau, *Animal Studies*, p. 208.
94 Gillian Clarke, 'Heron at Port Talbot', *Collected Poems* (Manchester: Carcanet Press Ltd, 1997), p. 61.
95 Clarke, 'Heron at Port Talbot', *Collected Poems*, p. 61.
96 Leslie Norris, 'Prey', *Sliding: Short Stories* (1971; rpt. London: Dent, 1978), p. 99.
97 Norris, 'Prey', p. 99.
98 Neil Ansell, *Deep Country: Five Years in the Welsh Hills* (London: Hamish Hamilton, an imprint of Penguin Books, 2011), p. 76.
99 Hilda Murrell, *Nature Diaries, 1961–1983*, ed. Charles Sinker (London: Collins, 1987), p. 70.
100 Ackerman, *The Genius of Birds*, p. 223.
101 Leslie Norris, 'The Waxwings', *Sliding: Short Stories*, p. 6.
102 Norris, 'The Waxwings', pp. 7 and 6.
103 Norris, 'The Waxwings', p. 7.
104 Hilda Murrell, *Nature Diaries*, p. 107.
105 Murrell, *Nature Diaries*, pp. 48–9.
106 Waldau, *Animal Studies*, p. 33.
107 John Downer, *Supersense: Perception in the Animal World* (London: BBC Books), pp. 67–94.

108 D. Parry-Jones, *Welsh Country Characters*, with illustrations by Lynton Lamb (London and New York: B. T. Batsford Ltd, 1952), p. 71.
109 Murrell, *Nature Diaries*, p. 93.
110 Ansell, *Deep Country*, p. 107.
111 Butler, *The Owl House*, p. 77.
112 Downer, *Supersense*, p. 67.
113 Butler, *The Owl House*, p. 55.
114 Clarke, 'Peregrine Falcon', *Collected Poems*, p. 119.
115 Butler, *The Owl House*, p. 55.
116 Butler, *The Owl House*, p. 55.
117 Clarke, 'Peregrine Falcon', p. 119.
118 Quine, 'Finding Where the Cuckoos Sing', p. 171.
119 Kurki, *International Relations in a Relational Universe*, p. 119.
120 See, for example, Quine, 'Finding Where the Cuckoos Sing', p. 167.
121 Quine, 'Finding Where the Cuckoos Sing', p. 168.
122 Jeremy Hooker, 'Hill Country Rhythms', *A View from the Source: Selected Poems* (Manchester: Carcanet New Press, 1982), p. 92 [pp. 92–3]. The poem is also available in Susan Butler (ed.), *Common Ground: Poets in a Welsh Landscape* (Bridgend: Poetry Wales, 1985), p. 113.
123 Waldau, *Animal Studies*, pp. 34 and 35.
124 Hooker, 'Hill Country Rhythms', p. 92.
125 Hooker, 'Hill Country Rhythms', pp. 92–3.
126 Ansell, *Deep Country*, p. 129.
127 Leslie Norris, 'Prey', *Sliding: Short Stories*, p. 101.
128 Jonathan Balcombe, *Second Nature: The Inner Lives of Animals* (Basingstoke: Palgrave Macmillan, 2010), p. 77.
129 Thomas, 'The Place', *Collected Poems*, p. 207.
130 Ryan, *Animal Theory*, p. 34.
131 Thomas, 'The Place', *Collected Poems*, p. 207.
132 Quine, 'Finding Where the Cuckoos Sing', p. 181.
133 Quine, 'Finding Where the Cuckoos Sing', p. 171.
134 Thomas, 'Barn Owl', *Collected Poems*, p. 319.
135 Thomas, 'Barn Owl', p. 319.
136 Thomas, 'Barn Owl', p. 319.
137 Thomas, 'Barn Owl', p. 319.
138 Thomas, 'Barn Owl', p. 319.

7 Domestication and 'Domesecration'

1 See, for example, Yi-Fu Tuan, *Dominance and Affection: The Making of Pets* (New Haven and London: Yale University Press, 1984); Roger A. Caras, *A Perfect Harmony: The Intertwining Lives of Animals and Humans throughout History* (New York: Simon & Schuster, 1996); David A. Nibert, *Animal Oppression and Human Violence: Domesecration, Capitalism, and Global Conflict* (New York: Columbia University Press, 2013); Marc Bekoff and Jessica Pierce, *The Animals' Agenda: Freedom, Compassion and Coexistence in the Human Age* (Boston: Beacon, 2017).

2 Tuan, *Dominance and Affection*, p. 107.
3 Paul Waldau, *Animal Studies: An Introduction* (Oxford: Oxford University Press, 2013), pp. 27–8.
4 Derek Ryan, *Animal Theory: A Critical Introduction* (Edinburgh: Edinburgh University Press, 2015), p. 86.
5 See, for example, Margo DeMello, *Animals and Society: An Introduction to Human–Animal Studies* (2012; rev. New York: Columbia University Press, 2nd edn, 2021); Lori Gruen (ed.), *Critical Terms for Animal Studies* (Chicago and London: The University of Chicago Press, 2018); Lynn Turner, Undine Sellbach and Ron Broglio (eds), *The Edinburgh Companion to Animal Studies* (Edinburgh: Edinburgh University Press, 2018); and Ryan, *Animal Theory*.
6 Gary Francione, *Introduction to Animal Rights: Your Child or the Dog* (Philadelphia: Temple University Press, 2000), p. 169. See, also, Ryan, *Animal Theory*, p. 87.
7 Nibert, *Animal Oppression and Human Violence*, p. 14.
8 Nibert, *Animal Oppression and Human Violence*, pp. 14–15.
9 Nibert, *Animal Oppression and Human Violence*, p. 15.
10 Nibert, *Animal Oppression and Human Violence*, p. 12.
11 Nibert, *Animal Oppression and Human Violence*, p. 12.
12 Tuan, *Dominance and Affection*, p. 107.
13 Tuan, *Dominance and Affection*, p. 107.
14 Ryan, *Animal Theory*, p. 88.
15 Donna Haraway, *The Companion Species Manifesto: Dogs, People, and Significant Otherness* (Chicago: Prickly Paradigm Press, 2003), p. 25. See Ryan, *Animal Theory*, p. 95.
16 Nibert, *Animal Oppression and Human Violence*, pp. 11–12.
17 Lori Marino, 'Captivity', in Lori Gruen (ed.), *Critical Terms for Animal Studies* (Chicago and London: The University of Chicago Press, 2018), p. 101 [pp. 99–111].
18 Tuan, *Dominance and Affection*, p. 5.
19 Ryan, *Animal Theory*, p. 4.
20 Tuan, *Dominance and Affection*, p. 5.
21 Tuan, *Dominance and Affection*, p. 5.
22 Tuan, *Dominance and Affection*, p. 5.
23 Tuan, *Dominance and Affection*, p. 5.
24 Alasdair Cochrane, *Animal Rights Without Liberation: Applied Ethics and Human Obligations* (New York: Columbia University Press, 2012), pp. 129–30.
25 Cochrane, *Animal Rights Without Liberation*, p. 130.
26 Cochrane, *Animal Rights Without Liberation*, p. 130.
27 Cochrane, *Animal Rights Without Liberation*, pp. 130–1.
28 D. Parry-Jones, *Welsh Country Upbringing* (1948; rpt. London: B. T. Batsford Ltd, 1949), p. 42.
29 Parry-Jones, *Welsh Country Upbringing*, p. 43.
30 Parry-Jones, *Welsh Country Upbringing*, p. 42.
31 Mari Jones, 'Tim', *Trwy Lygad y Bugail* (1970; rev. Llansawel: Mudiad Efengylaidd Cymru, Gwasg y Dderwen, 1973), p. 7.
32 Jones, 'Tim', p. 7.

NOTES 215

33 Roland Barthes, *How to Live Together: Novelistic Simulations of Some Everyday Spaces*, trans. Kate Briggs (New York: Columbia University Press, 2013), p. 26.
34 Barthes, *How to Live Together*, p. 26.
35 M. Wynn Thomas, *In the Shadow of the Pulpit: Literature and Nonconformist Wales* (Cardiff: University of Wales Press, 2010), p. 207.
36 Gwyn Jones, 'The Brute Creation', *Collected Stories of Gwyn Jones* (Cardiff: University of Wales Press, 1998), p. 299 [pp. 299–306]. This story was originally published in *The Shepherd's Hey* (1953).
37 Jones, 'The Brute Creation', p. 300.
38 Susan McHugh, *Dog* (London: Reaktion Books, 2004), p. 111.
39 Jones, 'The Brute Creation', p. 301.
40 Jones, 'The Brute Creation', p. 303.
41 Jones, 'The Brute Creation', p. 306.
42 Jones, 'The Brute Creation', p. 306.
43 Gwyn Jones. 'Take Us the Little Foxes', *Collected Stories of Gwyn Jones*, p. 122 [pp. 120–30].
44 Jones, 'Take Us the Little Foxes', p. 121.
45 Jones, 'Take Us the Little Foxes', p. 122.
46 Jones, 'Take Us the Little Foxes', p. 122.
47 Jones, 'Take Us the Little Foxes', p. 122.
48 Virginia Morell, 'Urban foxes may be self-domesticating in our midst', *Science* (2 June 2020). Online. Available at *www.sciencemag.org* (accessed 27 March 2021).
49 Jones, 'Take Us the Little Foxes', p. 122.
50 Jones, 'Take Us the Little Foxes', p. 122.
51 Jones, 'Take Us the Little Foxes', p. 123.
52 McHugh, *Dog*, p. 21.
53 McHugh, *Dog*, pp. 21–2.
54 Jones, 'Take Us the Little Foxes', p. 124.
55 Jones, 'Take Us the Little Foxes', p. 124.
56 Daniel Butler, *The Owl House* (Bridgend: Seren, 2020), pp. 187–8.
57 Jones, 'Take Us the Little Foxes', p. 124.
58 Jones, 'Take Us the Little Foxes', p. 125.
59 Jones, 'Take Us the Little Foxes', p. 125.
60 Derek Ryan, 'Literature', in Lynn Turner, Undine Sellbach and Ron Broglio (eds), *The Edinburgh Companion to Animal Studies* (Edinburgh: Edinburgh University Press, 2018), p. 332 [pp. 321–36].
61 Jones, 'Take Us the Little Foxes', p. 129.
62 Donna Haraway, *Primate Visions: Gender, Race, and Nature in the World of Modern Science* (London and New York: Routledge, 1989), p. 6.
63 Milja Kurki, *International Relations in a Relational Universe* (Oxford: Oxford University Press, 2020), p. 68.
64 See, for example, 'Red fox – People's Trust for Endangered Species'. Online. Available at *https://ptes.org/get-informed/facts-figures/red-fox* (accessed 27 March 2021).
65 Tuan, *Dominance and Affection*, p. 175.

66 Tony Brown, 'Notes', in Tony Brown (ed.), *The Collected Stories of Glyn Jones* (Cardiff: University of Wales Press, 1999), p. 402.
67 Glyn Jones 'The Golden Pony', in *The Collected Stories of Glyn Jones*, p. 340 [pp. 340–53].
68 Jones, 'The Golden Pony', p. 341.
69 Jones, 'The Golden Pony', p. 343.
70 Jones, 'The Golden Pony', p. 344.
71 Jones, 'The Golden Pony', p. 347.
72 Jones, 'The Golden Pony', p. 344.
73 Jones, 'The Golden Pony', p. 348.
74 *The fate of racing greyhounds and working lurchers in Wales: A survey of greyhounds and lurchers entering local authority pounds in Wales* (Cardiff: All Party Group for Animal Welfare, in association with Greyhound Rescue Wales, 2001), p. 7.
75 Leslie Norris, 'The Highland Boy', *Sliding: Short Stories* (1971; rpt. London: Dent, 1978), p. 32.
76 Norris, 'The Highland Boy', p. 34.
77 McHugh, *Dog*, p. 9.
78 McHugh, *Dog*, p. 9.
79 Norris, 'The Highland Boy', p. 40.
80 McHugh, *Dog*, p. 111.
81 Norris, 'The Highland Boy', pp. 32 and 33.
82 Norris, 'The Highland Boy', pp. 35, 36, 38 and 42.
83 Norris, 'The Highland Boy', pp. 34 and 37.
84 Norris, 'The Highland Boy', p. 42.
85 Steven Johnson, 'The Genius of the Tinkers', *Wall Street Journal* (25 September 2010), cit. Marc Bekoff and Jessica Pierce, *The Animals' Agenda*, p. 179.
86 Johnson, 'The Genius of the Tinkers', cit. Bekoff and Pierce, *The Animals' Agenda*, p. 179.

8 The Children's Book Pet

1 Rachel Poliquin, *The Breathless Zoo: Taxidermy and the Cultures of Longing* (Pennsylvania: Pennsylvania State University Press, 2012), p. 185.
2 Poliquin, *The Breathless Zoo*, p. 186.
3 Yi-Fu Tuan, *Dominance and Affection: The Making of Pets* (Hew Haven and London: Yale University Press, 1984), p. 5.
4 Tuan, *Dominance and Affection*, p. 5.
5 M. Wynn Thomas, *In the Shadow of the Pulpit: Literature and Nonconformist Wales* (Cardiff: University of Wales Press, 2010), p. 206.
6 Nel Wyn, 'Preface', *Hywel a'r Gath* (Caernarfon: Cwmni i Wasg Genedlaethol Gymreig, 1899).
7 M. Wynn Thomas, *In the Shadow of the Pulpit*, p. 211.
8 Ian MacLaren (Parch John Watson, MA, DD), *Yr Hen Ddoctor* (Gwrecsam: Hughes A'I Fab, 1905).

NOTES 217

9   E. R. Boyce, 'Tim', *Y Llyfr Gwyrdd*, Cyfres Darllen Difyr (London: Macmillan and Co. Ltd, 1953), p. 31.
10 Enid Blyton, *Llyfrau Natur*, cyfieithwyd gan Daisy Meirion Roberts (London: MacMillan & Co., 1953).
11 Blyton, *Llyfrau Natur*, 'Gair i'r Athro'. The word 'swynol' can be translated as 'charming' but it can also mean 'magical' (or 'fascinating'), which is a better interpretation in the context.
12 Gillian Clarke, 'The Osprey', *The Animal Wall and Other Poems*, illustrated by Karen Pearce (1999; rpt. Landysul: Ponty Poetry, Gomer Press, 2001), p. 35.
13 Clarke, 'The Osprey', p. 35.
14 Clarke, 'The Osprey', p. 35.
15 See, for example, Jennifer Ackerman, *The Genius of Birds* (2016; rpt. London; Corsair, 2017).
16 Bats are protected by the Conservation of Habitats and Species Regulations 2017 and the Wildlife and Countryside Act 1981 (as amended).
17 See, for example, Elin Meek, *Factfile Cymru: Animals in Wales* (Llandysul, Ceredigion: Gomer Press, 2013), p. 32.
18 Sam Dyer, 'The important role bats play in Wales's echo system', Cyfoeth Naturiol Cymru [Natural Resources Wales] (21 April 2021). Online. Available at *www.cyfoethnaturiol.cymru*. Accessed 16 July 2021. See, also, 'Wales Bat Project', Bat Conservation Trust. Online. Available at *www.bats.org.uk* (accessed 16 July 2021).
19 Hilary Llewellyn-Williams, 'Feeding the Bat', *The Book of Shadows* (Bridgend: Seren Books, 1990), p. 11.
20 Llewellyn-Williams, 'Feeding the Bat', p. 11.
21 Llewellyn-Williams, 'Feeding the Bat', p. 11.
22 Llewellyn-Williams, 'Feeding the Bat', p. 11.
23 Llewellyn-Williams, 'Feeding the Bat', p. 11.
24 Llewellyn-Williams, 'Feeding the Bat', p. 12.
25 See, Lori Gruen, 'Empathy', in L. Gruen (ed.), *Critical Terms for Animal Studies* (Chicago and London: University of Chicago Press, 2018), p. 148 [pp. 141–53].
26 Llewellyn-Williams, 'Feeding the Bat', p. 11.
27 Llewellyn-Williams, 'Feeding the Bat', p. 12.
28 Llewellyn-Williams, 'Feeding the Bat', p. 11.
29 Anne Mortimer (stori lluniau) a Matthew Sturgis (stori), *Nadolig Tosca* (Caerdydd: Gwasg y Dref Wen, 1990).
30 Adrian Franklin, *Animals and Modern Cultures: A Sociology of Human–Animal Relations in Modernity* (London: Sage Publications Ltd, 1999), p. 98.
31 Franklin, *Animals and Modern Culture*, p. 98.
32 Gruen, 'Empathy', p. 148.
33 Bethan Mair (addasiad Cymraeg), *Yr Arch Anifeiliaid Bach: Y Gath Fach Fusneslyd* (The Animal Arc: The Small Meddlesome Cat), lluniau gan Andy Ellis (Hengoed: Rily Publications, 2012).
34 Angharad Price, *Rhwng Gwyn a Du: Agweddau ar Rhyddiaith* (Caerdydd: Gwasg Prifysgol Cymru, 2002), p. 81.
35 Price, *Rhwng Gwyn a Du*, p. 81.

9 Conflicting Cosmologies: Three Stories by Gwyn Jones

36 Derek Ryan, *Animal Theory: A Critical Introduction* (Edinburgh: Edinburgh University Press, 2015), p. 86.
37 Clarke, 'Jac the Cat', *The Animal Wall*, p. 37.
38 Clarke, 'Breaking the Horse', *The Animal Wall*, p. 25.
39 Elaine Walker, *Horse* (2008; rpt. London: Reaktion Books, 2013), p. 19.

1 Paul Waldau, *Animal Studies: A Critical Introduction* (Oxford: Oxford University Press, 2013), pp. 34 and 35.
2 Gwyn Jones, 'The Pit', *Collected Stories of Gwyn Jones* (Cardiff: University of Wales Press, 1998), p. 14.
3 Jones, 'The Pit', p. 8.
4 Waldau, *Animal Studies*, p. 243.
5 Karen Sayer, 'The "modern" management of rats: British agricultural science in farm and field during the twentieth century' (Cambridge: Cambridge University Press, 2017). Online. Available at: *www.cambridge.org* (accessed 25 June 2020).
6 Sayer, 'The "modern" management of rats'. Online.
7 Waldau, *Animal Studies*, p. 243.
8 Jonathan Burt, *Rat* (London: Reaktion Books, 2006), p. 15.
9 Jonathan Balcombe, *Second Nature: The Inner Lives of Animals* (Basingstoke: Palgrave Macmillan, 2010), p. 24.
10 Burt, *Rat*, p. 21.
11 See, Burt, *Rat*, pp. 49–88 (on general cultural representations of the rat) and 115–29 (on its cultural association with plague and pollution).
12 See, also, Burt, *Rat*, pp. 12–14.
13 Jones, 'The Pit', p. 24.
14 Jones, 'The Pit', p. 25.
15 Jones, 'The Pit', p. 25.
16 Jones, 'The Pit', p. 26.
17 Jones, 'The Pit', p. 27.
18 Gwyn Jones, 'The Green Island', *Collected Stories of Gwyn Jones*, p. 131.
19 Jones, 'The Green Island', p. 131.
20 Jones, 'The Green Island', p. 131.
21 Jones, 'The Green Island', p. 140.
22 Jones, 'The Green Island', p. 158.
23 Jones, 'The Green Island', p. 144.
24 Jones, 'The Green Island', p. 170.
25 Jones, 'The Green Island', p. 180.
26 Jones, 'The Green Island', p. 180.
27 Jones, 'The Green Island', p. 180.
28 Jones, 'The Green Island', p. 184.
29 Jones, 'The Green Island', p. 184.
30 Jones, 'The Green Island', p. 161.
31 Gwyn Jones, 'Shepherd's Hey', *Collected Stories of Gwyn Jones*, p. 268.
32 Jones, 'Shepherd's Hey', p. 271.

NOTES 219

33 Jones, 'Shepherd's Hey', p. 272.
34 Waldau, *Animal Studies*, p. 35.
35 Jones, 'Shepherd's Hey', p. 278.
36 Jones, 'Shepherd's Hey', p. 281.
37 Jones, 'Shepherd's Hey', p. 283.
38 Jones, 'Shepherd's Hey', p. 283.
39 Jones, 'Shepherd's Hey', p. 283.
40 Jones, 'Shepherd's Hey', pp. 287 and 288.
41 Waldau, *Animal Studies*, p. 33.
42 Jones, 'Shepherd's Hey', p. 288.
43 Jones, 'Shepherd's Hey', pp. 280–1.
44 Jones, 'Shepherd's Hey', p. 288.
45 Jones, 'Shepherd's Hey', p. 288.
46 Derek Ryan, *Animal Theory: A Critical Introduction* (Edinburgh: Edinburgh University Press, 2015), pp. 5 and 142–8.
47 Waldau, *Animal Studies*, p. 209.
48 Jones, 'Shepherd's Hey', p. 298.

10 Entangled Empathies: Gillian Clarke and Keith Bowen

1 Lori Gruen, 'Empathy', in Lori Gruen (ed.), *Critical Terms for Animal Studies* (Chicago and London: The University of Chicago Press, 2018), p. 148 [pp. 141–53].
2 Gruen, 'Empathy', p. 148.
3 Roger Lovegrove, *The Kite's Tale: The Story of the Red Kite in Wales* (Sandy, Bedfordshire: Royal Society for the Protection of Birds, 1990), p. 97.
4 Walter Lippmann, *Public Opinion* (New York: Harcourt, Brace & Co. 1922), p. 81.
5 Philip Armstrong, *Sheep* (2006; rpt. London: Reaktion Books Ltd, 2017), p. 13.
6 Armstrong, *Sheep*, p. 18.
7 Armstrong, *Sheep*, p. 20.
8 Armstrong, *Sheep*, p. 20.
9 C. Bryner Jones (ed.), *Live Stock of the Farm*, vol. iv (London: The Gresham Publishing Company Ltd, n.d.), p. 224 plates. The content of the book suggests that it was published shortly before the First World War.
10 Armstrong, *Sheep*, p. 7.
11 Gillian Clarke, 'One Year', *Zoology* (Manchester: Carcanet Press Ltd, 2017). Keith Bowen, *Snowdon Shepherd: Four Seasons on the Hill Farms of North Wales* (1991; rpt. Llandysul, Ceredigion: Gomer Press, 1997).
12 Bowen, *Snowdon Shepherd*, p. 77.
13 Henry Moore, *Henry Moore's Sheep Sketchbook*, comments by Henry Moore and Kenneth Clark (1998; rpt. London: Thames & Hudson, 2017), end pages.
14 Clark, *Henry Moore's Sheep Sketchbook*, end pages.
15 Clark, *Henry Moore's Sheep Sketchbook*, end pages.
16 Clark, *Henry Moore's Sheep Sketchbook*, end pages.
17 Jones, *Live Stock of the Farm*, pp. 93–4.

[18] Gillian Clarke, 'A Year at Hafon Y Llan', *Zoology*, p. 43.
[19] Gillian Clarke, *Zoology*, p. 115.
[20] Daniel Butler, *The Owl House* (Bridgend: Seren, 2020), p. 16.
[21] Bowen, *Snowdon Shepherd*, p. 50.
[22] Bowen, *Snowdon Shepherd*, p. 50.
[23] Gillian Clarke, 'Black', *Zoology*, p. 52.
[24] Clarke, 'Black', p. 52.
[25] Bowen, *Snowdon Shepherd*, p. 31.
[26] Bowen, *Snowdon Shepherd*, p. 31.
[27] Bowen, 'The first suckle', *Snowdon Shepherd*, p. 33.
[28] Moore, *Henry Moore's Sheep Sketchbook*, end pages.
[29] Gillian Clarke, 'Birth', *Zoology*, p. 55.
[30] Gillian Clarke, 'Last Gather', *Zoology*, p. 45.
[31] Clarke, 'Last Gather', p. 45.
[32] Bowen, *Snowdon Shepherd*, p. 75.
[33] Bowen, *Snowdon Shepherd*, p. 31.
[34] William Welstead, *Writing on Sheep: Ecology, the Animal Turn and Sheep in Poetry* (Manchester: Manchester University Press, 2021), p. 177.
[35] Welstead, *Writing on Sheep*, p. 179.

SELECT BIBLIOGRAPHY

Texts

Ansell, N., *Deep Country: Five Years in the Welsh Hills* (London: Hamish Hamilton, an imprint of Penguin Books, 2011).
Blyton, E., *Llyfrau Natur*, cyfieithwyd gan D. M. Roberts (London: MacMillan & Co., 1953).
Bowen, E., 'The Swan', in *The Penguin Book of Welsh Verse*, trans. A. Conran, in association with J. E. Caerwyn Williams (Harmondsworth: Penguin Books Ltd, 1967).
Bowen K., *Snowdon Shepherd: Four Seasons on the Hill Farms of North Wales* (1991; rpt. Llandysul, Ceredigion: Gomer Press, 1997).
Boyce, E. R., 'Tim', *Y Llyfr Gwyrdd*, Cyfres Darllen Difyr (London: Macmillan and Co. Ltd, 1953). Welsh translation from English.
Bromwich, R. (ed. and trans.), *Selected Poems of Dafydd ap Gwilym: A New Edition* (Harmondsworth: Penguin Books, 1985).
Brown, T. (ed.), *The Collected Stories of Glyn Jones* (Cardiff: University of Wales Press, 1999).
Butler, D., *The Owl House* (Bridgend: Seren, 2020).
Clarke, G., *The Animal Wall and Other Poems*, illustrated by K. Pearce (1999; rpt. Llandysul: Ponty Poetry, Gomer Press, 2001).
Clarke, G., *Collected Poems* (Manchester: Carcanet Press Ltd, 1997).
Clarke, G., *Letting in the Rumour* (Manchester: Fyfield Books, Carcanet Press Ltd, 1989).
Clarke, G., *Making the Beds for the Dead* (Manchester: Carcanet Press Ltd, 2004).

Clarke, G., *Zoology* (Manchester: Carcanet Press Ltd, 2017).
Clarke, G., *Roots Home: Essays and a Journal* (Manchester: Carcanet Press Ltd, 2021).
Conran, A., in association with J. E. Caerwyn Williams, *The Penguin Book of Welsh Verse* (Harmondsworth: Penguin Books Ltd, 1967).
Constantine, M.-A., 'The Elephant at Tregaron', in M.-A. Constantine, *The Breathing* (Aberystwyth: Planet, 2008) [pp. 33–42].
Curtis, T., *War Voices* (Bridgend: Seren Books, 1995).
Cymru'r Plant (Wrexham: Hughes a'i Fab, 1892–1987).
Davies, S. (trans.), *The Mabinogion* (Oxford: Oxford University Press, 2007).
Elfyn, M. and Rowlands, J. (eds), *The Bloodaxe Book of Modern Welsh Poetry: 20th-century Welsh-language poetry in translation* (Tarset, Northumberland: Bloodaxe Books Ltd, 2003).
Griffith, W., *Anturiaethau Cymro yn Affrica* (Swyddfa Cymru: Cwmni y Cyhoeddwyr Gymreig, 1912).
Hooker, J., *A View from the Source: Selected Poems* (Manchester: Carcanet New Press, 1982).
Hughes, T., *Moortown* (London: Faber & Faber, 1979).
Hughes, T. R., *William Jones*, trans. R. Ruck (Aberystwyth: Gwasg Aberystwyth, 1953).
Humphreys, E., *Collected Poems* (Cardiff: University of Wales Press, 1999).
Jenkins, I. (ed.), *The Collected Poems of Idris Davies* (1972; rpt. Llandyssul: Gomerian Press, 1990).
Jones, C. B. (ed.), *Live Stock of the Farm*, vol. iv (London: The Gresham Publishing Company Ltd, c.1912).
Jones, G., *Collected Stories of Gwyn Jones* (Cardiff: University of Wales Press, 1998).
Jones, J. M., Price, W. J. and Thomas, T. M., *Gwewrsi i'r Safonau* (Cardiff and Wrexham: The Educational Publishing Company, n.d.).
Jones, M., *Trwy Lygad y Bugail* (1970; rev. Llansawel: Mudiad Efengylaidd Cymru, Gwasg y Dderwen, 1973).
Law, J., *Meddyg y Fferm* (Edinburgh: Thomas C. Jack, Grange Publishing Works; Bangor: Evan Ingram, 1881).
Llewellyn-Williams, H., *The Tree Calendar* (Bridgend: Poetry Wales Press, 1987).
Llewellyn-Williams, H., *Book of Shadows* (Bridgend: Seren Books, 1990).
Llewellyn-Williams, H., *Animalculture* (Bridgend: Seren Books, 1997).
Llyfr Coginio (Wrexham: Hughes and Son, n.d.).
MacLaren, I. (Parch John Watson, MA, DD), *Yr Hen Ddoctor* (Gwrecsam: Hughes a'i Fab, 1905). Welsh translation from English.

Mair, B. (Addasiad Cymraeg), *Yr Arch Anifeiliaid Bach: Y Gath Fach Fusneslyd*, lluniau gan Andy Ellis (Hengoed: Rily Publications, 2012).

Moore, H., *Henry Moore's Sheep Sketchbook*, comments by H. Moore and K. Clark (1998; rpt. London: Thames & Hudson, 2017).

Mortimer, A. (stori lluniau) a Sturgis, M. (stori), *Nadolig Tosca* (Caerdydd: Gwasg y Dref Wen, 1990). Welsh translation from English.

Murrell, H., *Nature Diaries, 1961–1983*, ed. C. Sinker (London: Collins, 1987).

Nicholas, T. E., *Llygad y Drws: Sonedau'r Carchar* (1940; rpt. Dinbycb: Gwasg Gee, 1941).

Nicholas, T. E., *Prison Sonnets* (Aberystwyth: The Cambrian News Ltd, 1948).

Norris, L., *Sliding: Short Stories* (1971; rpt. London: Dent, 1978).

Parry-Jones, D., *Welsh Country Characters*, with illustrations by L. Lamb (London and New York: B. T. Batsford Ltd, 1952).

Parry-Jones, D., *Welsh Country Upbringing* (1948; rpt. London and New York: B. T. Batsford Ltd, 1949).

Stephens, M. (ed.), *Poetry 1900–2000* (Cardigan: Parthian, Library of Wales, 2016).

Thomas, R. S., *Collected Poems 1945–1990* (1993; rpt. London: Phoenix, 2000).

Thomas, R. S., 'R. S. Thomas in conversation with Molly Price-Owen', *The David Jones Journal: R. S. Thomas Special Issue* (summer/autumn 2001), 93 [93–110].

Williams, D. J., *The Old Farmhouse*, trans. W. Williams (London: George G. Harrap & Co. Ltd, 1961).

Williams, F., *Flotsam* (Bridgend: Poetry Wales Press, 1987).

Wyn, N., *Hywel a'r Gath* (Caernarfon: Cwmni i Wasg Genedlaethol Gymreig, 1899).

Welsh Press

Aberystwyth Observer
Amman Valley Chronicle and East Carmarthen News
Baner ac Amserau
Barry Herald
Cambria Daily Leader
Cambrian, The
Cardiff and Merthyr Guardian, Glamorgan, Monmouth and Brecon Gazette
Chester Courant and Advertiser for North Wales, The

County Observer and Monmouthshire Central Advertiser, Abergavenny and Raglan Herald, Usk and Pontypool Messenger and Chepstow Argus
Denbighshire Free Press
Evening Express
Llangollen Advertiser, Denbighshire, Merionethshire and North Wales Journal
Merthyr Express, The
Pembrokeshire Herald and General Advertiser
Pontypridd Chronicle and Workman's News, The
Rhos Herald, The
Rhyl Record and Advertiser
South Wales Daily News
South Wales Echo
Weekly Mail
Welsh Gazette and West Wales Advertiser

Welsh Media

Jones, J., 'Mandatory CCTV in Welsh slaughterhouses to improve animal welfare', *Nation.Cymru* (6 November 2021). Online. Available at *https://nation.cymru/news/mandatory-cctv-in-welsh-slaughterhouses-to-improve-animal-welfare/* (accessed 6 November 2021).

Lawrence, H., 'Wales lynx escape: Zoo "outraged" over killing of escaped big cat', *Independent* (11 November 2017). Online. Available at *https://www.independent.co.uk/news/uk/home-news/escaped-lynx-killed-borth-zoo-lilleth-humanely-destroyed-ceredigion-wales-a8049401.html* (accessed 18 August 2020).

'Council blames Borth zoo for escaped lynx shooting', BBC Wales (15 November 2017). Online. Available at *https://www.bbc.co.uk/news/uk-wales-mid-wales-41996377* (accessed 18 August 2020).

'Welsh farmers raise concerns over rise in veganism', BBC News (23 October 2017). Online. Available at *https://www.bbc.co.uk/news/uk* (accessed 13 November 2021).

Criticism, Theory and Secondary Works

Ackerman, J., *The Genius of Birds* (2016; rpt. London: Corsair, 2017).
Adams, C. J., *The Sexual Politics of Meat: A Feminist-Vegetarian Critical Theory* (1990; rev. London and New York: Bloomsbury Academic, 2018).
Armstrong, P., *Sheep* (2006; rpt. London: Reaktion Books Ltd, 2017).

Balcombe, J., *Second Nature: The Inner Lives of Animals* (Basingstoke: Palgrave Macmillan, 2010).

Barthes, R., *How to Live Together: Novelistic Simulations of Some Everyday Spaces*, trans. Kate Briggs (New York: Columbia University Press, 2013).

Bateman, R., Diamond, A. W. and Schreiber, R. L., *Save the Birds* (1987; rev. St John's, Newfoundland: Breakwater Books, 1989).

Bekoff, M., *The Emotional Lives of Animals: A Leading Scientist Explores Animal Joy, Sorrow and Empathy and Why They Matter* (Novato, CA: New World Library, 2007).

Bekoff, M., *Minding Animals: Awareness, Emotions and Heart* (Oxford: Oxford University Press, 2002).

Bekoff, M. and Pierce, J., *The Animals' Agenda: Freedom, Compassion and Coexistence in the Human Age* (Boston: Beacon Press, 2017).

Bell, H. I., 'The Twentieth Century', appendix to T. Parry, *A History of Welsh Literature*, trans. I. Bell (Oxford: Clarendon Press, 1955).

Boehrer, B., Hand, M. and Massumi, B., (eds), *Animals, Animality, and Literature* (Cambridge: Cambridge University Press, Cambridge Critical Concepts, 2018).

Boehrer, B. and Hand, M., 'Introduction: Beasts in the Republic of Letters', in B. Boehrer, M. Hand and B. Massumi (eds), *Animals, Animality and Literature* (Cambridge: Cambridge University Press, Cambridge Critical Concepts, 2018).

Boetze, A., 'Art', in L. Turner, U. Sellbach and R. Broglio (eds), *The Edinburgh Companion to Animal Studies* (Edinburgh: Edinburgh University Press, 2018).

Burnett, J., *Plenty and Want* (London and New York: Routledge, 1989).

Burt, J., *Rat* (London: Reaktion Books, 2006).

Butler, S. (ed.), *Common Ground: Poets in a Welsh Landscape* (Bridgend: Poetry Wales, 1985).

Caras, R. A., *A Perfect Harmony: The Intertwining Lives of Animals and Humans throughout History* (New York: Simon & Schuster, 1996).

Cochrane, A., *Animal Rights Without Liberation: Applied Ethics and Human Obligations* (New York: Columbia University Press, 2012).

Cochrane, A., *Sentient Politics: A Theology of Global Inter-species Justice* (Oxford University Press, 2018).

Coetzee, J. M., *The Lives of Animals*, ed. A. Gutmann (Princeton: Princeton University Press).

Collingham, L., *The Hungry Empire: How Britain's Quest for Food Shaped the Modern World* (2017; rpt. London: Vintage, 2018).

Cowie, H., *Exhibiting Animals in Nineteenth-century Britain: Empathy, Education, Entertainment* (Basingstoke: Palgrave Macmillan, 2014).
Dalziel, H., *British Dogs: Their Varieties, History, Characteristics, Breeding, Management and Exhibition* (London: The Bazaar Office, 1979).
Davies, J. A., 'Dylan Thomas and His Welsh Contemporaries', in M. Wynn Thomas (ed.), *Welsh Writing in English* (Cardiff: University of Wales Press, 2003) [pp. 120–64].
Dawkins, M. S., *Why Animals Matter: Animal Consciousness, Animal Welfare, and Human Well-Being* (Oxford: Oxford University Press, 2012).
Deleuze, G. and Parnet, C., 'A Is for Animal', in *Gilles Deleuze from A to Z*, dir. P.-A. Boutane, trans. C. J. Stivale (Cambridge: Semiotext(e)/Foreign Agents at the MIT Press, 2011). Film.
DeMello, M., *Animals and Society: An Introduction to Human–Animal Studies* (2012; rev. New York: Columbia University Press, 2nd edn, 2021).
Derrida, J., *The Animal That Therefore I Am* (New York: Fordham University Press, 2008).
Elfyn, M. (ed.), *Trying the Line: A Volume of Tribute to Gillian Clarke* (Llandysul, Ceredigion: Gomer Press, 1997).
Ferguson, M., *Animal Advocacy and Englishwomen, 1780–1900: Patriots, Nation and Empire* (Ann Arbor: University of Michigan Press, 1998).
Forster, C., 'Family at the heart of organic diversification', *Farmers Guardian*, 25 January 2019, 22–4.
Francione, G., *Introduction to Animal Rights: Your Child or the Dog* (Philadelphia: Temple University Press, 2000).
Franklin, A., *Animals and Modern Cultures: A Sociology of Human–Animal Relations in Modernity* (London: Sage Publications Ltd, 1999).
Geier, T., *Meat Markets: The Cultural History of Bloody London* (Edinburgh: Edinburgh University Press, 2017).
Godfrey-Smith, P., *Other Minds: The Octopus and the Evolution of Intelligent Life* (London: William Collins, 2017).
Grigson, C., *Menagerie: The History of Exotic Animals in England* (Oxford: Oxford University Press, 2016).
Gruen, L., 'Empathy', in L. Gruen (ed.), *Critical Terms for Animal Studies* (Chicago and London: The University of Chicago Press, 2018) [pp. 141–53].
Gruen, L. (ed.), *Critical Terms for Animal Studies* (Chicago and London: The University of Chicago Press, 2018).
Haraway, D., *Primate Visions: Gender, Race, and Nature in the World of Modern Science* (London and New York: Routledge, 1989).

Haraway, D., *The Companion Species Manifesto: Dogs, People, and Significant Otherness* (Chicago: Prickly Paradigm Press, 2003).
Haraway, D., *When Species Meet* (Minneapolis: University of Minnesota Press, 2008).
Haraway, D., *Staying with the Trouble: Making Kin in the Chthulucene* (Durham, NC: Duke University Press, 2016).
Harvey, G., *Animism: Respecting the Living World* (2005; rev. London: C. Hurst & Co., 2017).
Heidegger, M., *The Fundamental Concepts of Metaphysics: World, Finitude, Solitude* (Bloomington and Indianapolis: Indiana University Press, 1995).
Horovitz, A., 'Behavior', in L. Gruen, *Critical Terms for Animal Studies* (Chicago and London: The University of Chicago Press, 2018) [pp. 64–78].
Howells, R., *Farming in Wales* (Llandyssul: Gomerian Press, 1965).
Humphreys, E., *Conversations and Reflections*, ed. M. Wynn Thomas (Cardiff: University of Wales Press, 2002).
Johnes, M., 'Pigeon Racing and Working-Class Culture in Britain, c. 1870–1950', *Cultural and Social History*, 4/3 (2007), 369–71.
King, B. J., *How Animals Grieve* (Chicago and London: University of Chicago Press, 2013).
Kirkpatrick, K. and Faragó, B., *Animals in Irish Literature and Culture* (London and New York: Palgrave, 2015).
Kulchyski, P., 'Bush/Animals', in B. Boehrer, M. Hand and B. Massumi (eds), *Animals, Animality and Literature* (Cambridge: Cambridge University Press, Cambridge Critical Concepts, 2018) [pp. 319–33].
Kurki, M., *International Relations in a Relational Universe* (Oxford: Oxford University Press, 2020).
Lamarre, T., 'Animation and Animism', in B. Boehrer, M. Hand and B. Massumi (eds), *Animals, Animality and Literature* (Cambridge: Cambridge University Press, Cambridge Critical Concepts, 2018) [pp. 284–300].
Lemm, V., 'Friederich Nietzsche on Human Nature: Between Philosophical Anthropology and Animal Studies', in B. Boehrer, M. Hand and B. Massumi (eds), *Animals, Animality and Literature* (Cambridge: Cambridge University Press, 2018) [pp. 197–214].
Lippmann, W., *Public Opinion* (New York: Harcourt, Brace & Co. 1922).
Lloyd-Jones, D. M., 'Rhagair', in M. Jones, *Trwy Lygad y Bugail* (1970; rev. Llansawel: Mudiad Efengylaidd Cymru, Gwasg y Dderwen, 1973).
Lovegrove, R., *The Kite's Tale: The Story of the Red Kite in Wales* (Sandy, Bedfordshire: Royal Society for the Protection of Birds, 1990).

Lowen, J., 'The State of Nature in the UK', *The Countryman* (January 2019), 16–23.
Lundblad, M., '*Opening Up a Dossier: Animals, Animalities, and Living Together with Roland Barthes*', in B. Boehrer, M. Hand and B. Massumi (eds), *Animals, Animality and Literature* (Cambridge: Cambridge University Press, 2018) [pp. 217–30].
Maitland, E., *Anna Kingsford: Her Life, Letters, Diary and Work*, vol. 1 (London: Redway, 1896).
Marino, L., 'Captivity', in L. Gruen (ed.), *Critical Terms for Animal Studies* (Chicago and London: The University of Chicago Press, 2018) [pp. 99–111].
Matheson, C., *Changes in the Fauna of Wales within Historic Times* (Cardiff: National Museum of Wales Press, 1932).
McCance, D., *Critical Animal Studies: An Introduction* (London and New York: Palgrave, 2010).
McCorry, S. and Miller, J., *Literature and Meat Since 1900* (London: Palgrave, 2019).
McHugh, S., *Dog* (London: Reaktion Books, 2004).
McHugh, S. et al., *The Palgrave Handbook of Animals and Literature* (London and New York: Palgrave, 2021).
Merleau-Ponty, M., *The Visible and The Invisible*, trans. A. Lingis (Evanston, IL: Northwestern University Press, 1968).
Metcalf, R. S., *Meat Commerce and the City: The London Food Market, 1800–1855* (London: Pickering & Chatto, 2012).
Miller, J., *Empire and the Animal Body: Violence, Identity and Ecology in Victorian Adventure Fiction* (London: Anthem Press, 2012).
Mitchell, A., *International Intervention in a Secular Age: Re-enchanting Humanity* (Abingdon: Routledge, 2014), p. 10.
Moore-Colyer, R., *Farming in Wales 1936–2011*, ed. T. O'Regan (Talybont, Ceredigion: Y Lolfa, 2011).
Morris, D., *Monkey* (London: Reaktion Books, 2013).
Morris, J., 'Foreword', in K. Bowen, *Snowdon Shepherd: Four Seasons on the Hill Farms of North Wales* (1991; rpt. Landysul: Gomer Press, 1997).
Morse, D., 'Animal Subjectivities: Gendered Literary Representation of Animal Minds in Anna Sewell's *Black Beauty*', in B. Boehrer, M. Hand and B. Massumi, *Animals, Animality and Literature* (Cambridge: Cambridge University Press, Cambridge Critical Concepts, 2018) [pp. 180–96].
Morton, T., *The Ecological Thought* (Boston: Harvard University Press, 2010).

SELECT BIBLIOGRAPHY 229

Nibert, D. A., *Animal Oppression and Human Violence: Domesecration, Capitalism, and Global Conflict* (New York: Columbia University Press, 2013).

Nietzsche, F., *Beyond Good and Evil: Prelude to a Philosophy of the Future*, trans. W. Kaufmann (New York: Vintage Books, 1989).

Peach, L., *The Fiction of Emyr Humphreys: Contemporary Critical Perspectives* (Cardiff: University of Wales Press, 2011).

Peach, L., *Pacifism, Peace and Modern Welsh Writing* (Cardiff: University of Wales Press, 2019).

Poliquin, R., *The Breathless Zoo: Taxidermy and the Cultures of Longing* (Pennsylvania: Pennsylvania State University Press, 2012).

Preece, R., *Coal Mining and the Camera* (Overton: National Coal Mining Museum for England Publications, 1998).

Quine, J. A., 'Finding Where the Cuckoos Sing: R. S. Thomas and the Poiesis of Birdwatching' (PhD thesis, University of Melbourne, July 2019).

Regan, T., *The Case for Animal Rights* (London: Routledge and Kegan Paul, 1983).

Ryan, D., *Animal Theory: A Critical Introduction* (Edinburgh: Edinburgh University Press, 2015).

Safina, C., *Beyond Words: What Animals Think and Feel* (New York: Henry Holt and Company, 2015).

Saunders, D., *A Guide to the Birds of Wales* (London: Constable, 1974).

Sears, P., 'Ecology – a Subversive Subject', *BioScience*, 14/7 (1964), 11–13.

Sheldrick, D., 'The Rearing and Rehabilitation of Orphaned African Elephant Calves in Kenya', in D. L. Forthman, L. F. Kane, D. Hancocks and P. F. Waldau (eds), *An Elephant in the Room: The Science and Well-Being of Elephants in Captivity* (North Grafton, MA: Center for Animals and Public Policy, 2008) [pp. 208–12].

Sinker, C., 'Introduction', *Hilda Murrell's Nature Diaries, 1961–1983*, ed. C. Sinker (London: Collins, 1987).

Smolin, L., *The Life of the Cosmos* (London: Phoenix, 1997).

Smolin, L., *Three Roads to Quantum Gravity* (London: Phoenix, 2000).

Smolin, L., *The Trouble with Physics: The Rise of String Theory, The Fall of Science and What Comes Next* (London: Penguin, 2008).

Smolin, L., *Time Reborn: From the Crisis in Physics to the Future of the Universe* (Boston: Mariner Books, 2014).

Spencer, C., *Vegetarianism: A History* (2016; rpt. London: Grub Street, 2017).

Thomas, B., *Talking with Animals: How to Communicate with Wildlife* (London: W. H. Allen, 1986).
Thomas, M. W., *Internal Difference: Literature in Twentieth-century Wales* (Cardiff: University of Wales Press, 1992).
Thomas, M. W., *In the Shadow of the Pulpit: Literature and Nonconformist Wales* (Cardiff University of Wales Press, 2010).
Thomas, M. W., *Emyr Humphreys* (Cardiff: University of Wales Press, Writers of Wales Series, 2018).
Tuan, Y.-F., *Dominance and Affection: The Making of Pets* (New Haven and London: Yale University Press, 1984).
Turner, L., Sellbach, U. and Broglio, R. (eds), *The Edinburgh Companion to Animal Studies* (Edinburgh: Edinburgh University Press, 2018).
Unger, R. M. and Smolin, L., *Singular Universe and the Reality of Time* (Cambridge: Cambridge University Press, 2015).
Waldau, P., *Animal Studies: An Introduction* (Oxford: Oxford University Press, 2013).
Walker, E., *Horse* (2008; rpt. London: Reaktion Books, 2013).
Welstead, W., *Writing on Sheep: Ecology, the animal turn and sheep in poetry* (Manchester: Manchester University Press, 2021).
Williams, D., *A History of Modern Wales* (1950; London: John Murray, 1969).
Wilson-Rich, N., *The Bee: A Natural History* (Princeton and Oxford: Princeton University Press, 2018).
Wise, S., *Drawing the Line: Science and the Case for Animal Rights* (Cambridge, MA: Perseus Books, 2002).
Wise, S., *Rattling the Cage: Toward Legal Rights for Animals* (Cambridge, MA: Perseus Books, 2000).
Wood, D., 'Homo Sapiens', in L. Turner, U. Sellbach and R. Broglio (eds), *The Edinburgh Companion to Animal Studies* (Edinburgh: Edinburgh University Press, 2018) [pp. 292–306].
Wylie, D., *Elephant* (London: Reaktion Books, 2008).

Index

A
abattoirs 35–9
Aberdare Times, The 45
Aberdaron 112
Abergavenny and Raglan Herald 66
Aberystwyth and Tregaron Bank 180
Aberystwyth Observer, The 74, 78
Ackerman, Jennifer 6, 8, 111, 116, 122,
Adams, Carol J. 30, 37
'adjacent possible' 5, 56, 115–16, 151
  see also Johnson, Steven
Africa 80–1, 83, 87–90, 157
Agamben, Giorgio 2
agriculture 18, 19, 27, 28, 32–3, 42, 45, 46, 48, 51, 54, 56
  agro-ecological practices 33
  arable farming 42
  industry 18, 19, 32, 48–56
  land 27
  mechanisation 32, 33
  mechanised harvesting 42
America 55, 56, 132, 140, 180

Amman Valley Chronicle and East Carmarthen News, The 64
anaesthetics 28
Animal Aid 36, 65
animal, 'animal'
  autonomy 102, 126, 129, 156–60
  behaviours 5, 6, 9, 14, 15, 26, 31, 49, 50, 52, 72, 84, 136–9, 142, 148, 185, 191
  captivity xiii, 9, 18–20, 49, 50, 52, 55, 64, 73, 74, 81–5, 90, 106, 132, 133, 137, 149, 156–7, 160, 161, 190–1: *see also* circuses; travelling menageries; zoos
  changing concepts of xv, 3–5, 9, 12, 16, 16, 51, 62, 67, 77, 84, 90, 103, 116, 117, 126, 164, 190,
  consciousness 9, 17, 30, 69, 167, 185
  in folklore 95, 105–6, 168
  freedom 5, 12, 17, 18–20, 105, 110, 111, 115, 136, 142, 147–8, 151, 156, 162–3

animal, 'animal' (continued)
  herd (and herding) 10, 11, 32, 36, 50, 58, 76, 79
  history and psychology xiii, 9–12, 13, 18, 25, 27–32, 33, 43–4, 45–6, 48, 49, 51, 56, 57, 71, 87, 107, 108, 114, 115, 118–19, 122, 149, 170, 189–90
  human encounters and relations with xiv, xv, 11, 18, 23, 24, 26, 51, 74, 88, 89, 90, 91–100, 102–3, 106–8, 111, 120, 121, 123, 125–7, 133, 136, 145–7, 164, 168, 169, 189: see also benign partnership; generalised imaginary; Williams Parry, R., 'Y Llwynog'; zoological gaze
  as ill-omen 105
  in industrial contexts 120–2, 23, 27, 31, 32–5, 40, 42, 45, 46, 48–56, 63, 64, 66, 120–1, 131, 155, 185: see also domesecration; domestication; Norris, Leslie
  intelligence (other-than-human) and communication xiii, xiv, xv, xvi, 2, 5–7, 8, 9, 12, 14, 16, 22, 72, 73–4, 78, 87, 90, 101, 103, 109, 115, 116–20, 121, 125, 129, 136, 137–8, 143–4, 146, 151, 156, 158, 167, 169, 181, 186–8, 189–90
  as pets 10–11, 19, 69–90 *passim*, 131, 133–4, 153–65 *passim*, 190: see also domestication, protection (incl. literature) 16, 36, 50, 57, 59, 64, 66, 191

  psychological and physical realities 17, 23, 73–4, 171, 174
  psychological trauma 9, 36, 67, 165
  rights and welfare xiii, 12, 16–18, 19, 20, 30, 33, 36, 39, 42, 48, 50, 57, 59, 61, 64, 65, 67, 85, 131, 134, 191, 196n90
  subjugation of xiv, 10, 11, 18, 39, 74, 115, 131, 133, 177, 190: see also domestication
  theory (the 'imaginary' and the 'symbolic') xiii, xiv, xv, 1–2, 4–5, 7–8, 10, 11, 12, 14–15, 17, 19, 23, 34, 35, 48, 51–2, 61, 69, 81, 82, 83, 91, 95, 102, 105, 107, 109, 115, 117, 120, 124, 126, 131, 143, 148, 149, 153, 176, 180, 189, 190: see also Adams, Carol J.; Cochrane, Alasdair; Marino, Lori; Tuan, Yi-Fu; Ryan, Derek; von Uexküll, Jakob
  vocalisations 6
Animal Liberation Front 33
animals
  adder 88
  ant 26, 70, 124
  badger 24, 54, 99: see also animals, burrowing pig; badger baiting
  bat 158–60
  bear 74, 76, 87, 92; see also Madame Batavia
  bee 7, 26, 100, 102, 124: see also wagging dance
  black grouse 34
  Bream 150
  broiler 35–6

INDEX

buck 150
bull 74
bullock 39
burrowing pig 24: *see also* animals, badger
buzzard 107
camel 76, 141
capuchin monkey 71
carrion crow 42
carthorse 75
cat 156, 161, 162–4
cattle (incl. calves) 27, 30, 35–6, 39, 45, 59: *see also* commodity (animal)
chaffinch 105
chimpanzee 17, 87
chough 105
cockatoo 80
cockchafer 102
cockerel 154
cockroach 70
curlew 105, 108–9, 119
deer 15
dog 6, 12, 14, 54–5, 76, 135–9, 141, 145–7, 148, 149, 150, 175, 177,
duck 114–16, 142
elephant 5–6, 17, 20, 74, 76, 80–2, 141: *see also* Constantine, Mary-Ann; Lizzie (Madame Jumbo); Jumbo; Jumbo Junior; Jwmbo
elk 87
flea 77
fox 6, 13, 72, 93–7, 100, 107, 139–44, 154, 189
goat (and scapegoat) 35, 76, 132, 180
golden lion 87

golden plover 34
gorilla 74, 87: *see also* Pongo
Green Woodpecker 124
greenfinch 105
greyhound xiv, 53–5, 148–51
hare 31, 100–1, 171, 209n33
hawk 14, 113, 116, 119, 121, 126–7, 142, 143, 171
hedgehog 141
hens 35
heron 120–1, 125
herring 38
horse (incl. English Shire, foal, Hackney, pit pony, stallion, Welsh Cob) xiv, 9–10, 11, 12, 30, 35, 46, 49, 50–1, 52, 55, 56, 58, 59, 60–1, 62–7, 74–7, 78, 79, 132, 135, 145, 146–8, 155, 164–5, 189, 204n26
jackdaw 168
kangaroo 74, 77
kestrel 116, 122
killer whale 87
kite (and red kite) 24, 105, 118–19, 121
leatherback turtle 87
lion 80
long-tailed tit 124
lynx 79, 85–6
mallard duck 114–15
mammoth 75, 87
marten 127
mouse 40, 123
mole 100–2, 175, 189
monkey 71–4, 76, 77, 80, 81, 143
night adder 89
orangutan 87
owl 128
parrot 77, 154

animals (continued)
  peregrine falcon 125
  pheasant 41
  pig 37, 139,
  pigeon xiv, 51–2, 55, 56
  prawn 38
  puff adder 89
  python 80, 87, 88–9
  rabbit 24, 38, 97–8, 116, 143, 172
  ram 180, 182
  rat 168, 169–70, 171
  raven 122
  reed bunting 124
  reindeer 87
  robin 119, 145, 157,
  rook 105
  scad 38
  seagull 106: see also 'llatai'; Dafydd ap Gwilym
  sedge 102, 107
  serpent 88, 176
  sheep (incl. lambs, ewes, Black Welsh Mountain Sheep, wethers) 12, 27, 32, 35, 36, 42, 47, 58, 60, 97, 132, 136, 137, 139, 168, 173–5, 177, 179–88, 189: see also Armstrong, Philip; Moore, Henry
  sheepdog 75, 135–8, 174
  skylark 106, 108
  snake 72, 88–90, 175–6
  sparrow 105, 110, 111, 150
  spider 26, 70, 172
  squirrel 40, 154
  starling 105, 111, 119
  stoat 92
  stonechat 105
  swift 112–13, 116, 124, 127
  thrush 106, 127
  tiger 162
  treecreeper 123
  turkey 35, 40
  vixen 24
  vole 116
  vulture 150
  waxwing 123
  weasel 24, 42, 97–8, 141
  whale 7
  whitethroat 124
  wolf 6, 87, 139, 141
  woodcock 14
  wren 27
  yellow wagtail 124
anodynes 28
Ansell, Neil xv, 92, 99–100, 122, 124, 127, 129
antacids 28
anthropomorphism 114, 128, 157, 160, 171
antiseptics 28
ap Gwilym, Gwynn xiv, 99
  'The Badger' 99
aquariums 19, 131, 190
Aristotle 78, 124
Armstrong, Philip 12, 180, 181
Arthur (of legend) 99
Athens 190
Atlantic Monthly 56
'autobiographical animal' 4
  see also Derrida, Jacques
automatic feeders 18
avian influenza 46

B
badger baiting 54
Balcombe, Jonathan 8, 128, 169
Baner ac Amserau 28, 64
Bangor-on-Dee 53

INDEX

barley-beef (feed) 33
Barry Herald 70
Barthes, Roland 136
Bateman, Robert 105, 110, 117
BBC Wales 86
Bekoff, Marc 2, 5, 6, 12, 21, 56
Bell, Idris 93, 98
benign partnership 132, 134, 136, 138, 151, 153, 159
  see also Nibert, David A.
biodiversity reports
  'State of Birds in Wales 2018' 34
  'State of Nature 2020' 34
bird flu *see* avian influenza
bird studies 20
birds *see under* animals
Birmingham 44
blitz *see* Second World War
Blyton, Enid 156–7
  'Nature Books' 157
Board of Agriculture 58
Boehrer, Bruce 2, 20
Boer War 43
Boetzkes, Amanda 8, 9
Borth Wild Animal Kingdom 79, 85–6
  see also Lillith (the lynx)
Bosnia 40
Bostock-Wombwell Circus and Menagerie 79–80
BSE (Bovine Spongiform Encephalopathy) 46
Bowen, Euros xv, 107–9, 120
  'The Swan' 107–9
Bowen, Keith 181–3, 184–8
  Snowdon Shepherd: Four Seasons on the Hill Farms of North Wales 181–3, 184–8
Boyce, E. R. 156

The Green Book 156
'Tim' 156
Brad y Llyfrau Gleision 29, 57–8
Branwen (in legend) 111
Brentford 79
Brixton 110
Bromwich, Rachel 106
Brown, Tony 145
Brussels 79
Bryner Jones, C. 59, 182
Buchanan, Brett 2
Burt, Jonathan 169
butcher (trade) 14, 30–1, 36–7, 38–9, 40, 44, 164
Butler, Daniel 14, 97, 109, 124, 125, 142, 143, 183

C
Calvert, Samantha 45
Cambria Daily Leader 59
Cambrian, The 65
Canadian Rockies 92
Cardiff 44, 52–3, 55, 58, 59, 75, 76, 150
  Andrews Hall, Queen Street 76
  City Stadium 55
  County Court 58
  Ely racecourse 52–3
  Meeting House 44
  Sophia Gardens Field 75
Cardiff and Merthyr Guardian, Glamorgan, Monmouth and Brecon Gazette 77
Carmarthen 54
Carmarthen Weekly Reporter, The 45
Carmarthenshire 135, 145
Cartesian thought *see* Descartes, René

Ceredigion 80, 85, 111,
Ceridwen Peris 29
Ceylon 70
Chepstow 53
Chepstow Argus 66
Chernobyl 46
Chester Courant and Advertiser for North Wales 61
Christ (divine and human) 81–2, 108, 135, 136
circuses 19, 67, 69, 71, 74–82, 87, 90, 147, 190
  see also travelling menageries; zoos
Clark, Kenneth 182
Clarke, Gillian xiv, xv, 40, 46, 47–8, 86–7, 100–1, 120, 121, 125–6, 129, 157–8, 159, 160, 163–4, 179, 181–8
  'A Year at Hafod Y Llan' 183–4
  The Animal Wall and Other Poems 163
  'Birth' 186
  'Black' 184–5
  'Breaking the Horse' 164
  'The Company of Bones' 86, 87
  'Cynefin' 183–4
  'February' 184
  'The Field Mouse' 49
  'Heron at Port Talbot' 120, 121
  'Jac the Cat' 163–4
  'Labour' 186
  'Last Gather' 186–7
  Letter from a Far Country 120
  'Making the Beds for the Dead' 47–8
  'Mothering' 185
  'One Year' 181–3, 186, 188
  'The Osprey' 157–8, 159, 160
  'Peregrine Falcon' 125–6
  'The Presence' 100–1
  Root Home 40
  'Scan' 184
  'Silent' 86
  'Stillborn' 185
  'To the Mountain' 187
  'The Wethers Leave the Mountain' 187–8
  Zoology 86
Cochrane, Alasdair 17, 20, 42, 48, 61, 134
Coleridge, Samuel Taylor 112
commodity (animal) 27–8, 33, 35–6, 39, 42, 45, 47, 60, 67, 132, 181
companion animal studies 20
comparative psychology 5
Conran, Anthony 23
Constantine, Mary-Ann 80, 81
  'The Elephant at Tregaron' 80, 82
Cork, County 60
cosmology 188, 190–1
County Observer and Monmouth Central Advertiser, Abergavenny and Raglan Herald, Usk and Pontypool Messenger and Chepstow Argus 66
COVID-19 pandemic 134
Crickhowell 47
cultural taxonomy xiii, xiv, 6, 8, 14, 40, 41, 54, 59, 85, 86, 90, 91, 95, 102, 103, 139, 141, 144, 151, 155, 158, 168, 180, 188
Cwmtillery 50
Cymru 118
Cymru'r Plant 117, 118, 158
cynefin 183, 187

INDEX

D
Dafydd ap Gwilym 23, 106
Darwin debate, the (Oxford) 71
Davies, Idris 109
   'The Curlews of Blaen Rhymni' 109
Deleuze, Gilles 94
DeMello, Margo 4, 5
Denbighshire Free Press 71
Derrida, Jacques 3–4, 85
Descartes, René 2, 124
Diamond, Antony W. 105, 110, 117
dog fighting 54
dog shows 131, 54
domesecration 132–7, 139, 145, 148, 149, 151, 153, 155, 156, 157, 162, 164, 165, 190, *see also* Nibert, David A.
domestication xiii, xiv, xv, 10–12, 19, 20, 25, 32, 35, 73, 79, 83, 85–6, 131–43, 145, 147–9, 151, 153, 154, 156–7, 159, 160–5, 175, 181, 190
Downer, John 4, 6, 8, 124
Downing, Graham 15
Dyfed 111

E
Earle, Jean 31
   'Jugged Hare' 31
ecology xiii, xiv, 8, 10, 20–1, 33–5, 42, 56, 91, 109, 113, 117, 118
ecosystem 15, 34, 102, 114, 158
Edward, Prince of Wales 54, 79
Egypt 53, 71, 148
elephant studies 5, 20
Elfyn, Menna 52, 119
   'Colomennod Cwm' 52
   'Dynwared' 119
emotion xiii, xiv, xv, 2, 5–6, 12, 16, 22, 44, 52, 63, 66–7, 73, 77, 90, 93, 95, 98, 103, 124, 129, 138, 146, 161, 165, 170, 185, 186, 189
English Romanticism 112–13
environmentalism 5, 7, 8, 20–2, 33–4, 46, 117, 118, 125, 183, 191, 192
   see also Butler, Daniel
ethology 5, 73, 82, 84, 98, 143
euthanasia 13 4, 148
Evans, Reverend Dafydd 26, 124
Evening Express 44, 76, 77, 79
Evening Press 79
exoticism 69, 70, 71, 74–6, 81, 82–4, 86–8, 90, 141, 158, 190

F
Fabian Society 44
falconry 14, 97, 142
   see also Butler, Daniel
Farming, the Environment and the Welsh Uplands 33–4
farms and farming xiv, xv, 12, 16, 18, 24, 25, 27–30, 32–5, 37, 39, 40, 42, 45–8, 56, 58–63, 75, 96, 118, 126, 135, 137–8, 145, 173, 174, 177, 179, 180, 181–8, 192
Ffos Las Racecourse, Kidwelly 53
First World War 37, 41, 43, 44, 46, 59, 64, 155, 182
'flesh eschewers' *see* vegetarianism
flight animal 10
Flintshire Observer Mining Journal and General Advertiser 43
Fly's Magazine 77
foot and mouth disease 46–7

fowl plague 46
  see also avian influenza
France (and French provinces) 63, 80
Francione, Gary 131
Franklin, Adrian 84, 161
Frenni Fawr (Great Frenni) 111
Fudge, Erica 11

G
Genedl Gymreig, Y 28
Germany 39, 40, 47, 63, 111
  National Socialism 47
  see also Hitler, Adolf
Ginnett's Circus 74, 75
Greece 4, 53, 148, 181
green agenda 33, 120
greyhound, ancestry as a hunting dog 53, 148
Greyhound Board of Great Britain 53
greyhound coursing and racing xiv, 53, 54, 55, 150–1
Griffith, William 87–90
  Anturiaethau Cymro yn Affrica 87–90
Griffiths, Lesley 19
Gruen, Lori 8, 16, 179
Gwersi i'r Safonau 37–8
Gymraes, Y 29

H
Hand, Molly 2, 20
Haraway, Donna 4, 5, 40, 133, 144
Heidegger, Martin 124
heron-roads 121
Hindu religion *see* monkey god
Hitler, Adolf 58
  Mein Kampf 58, 59

Hogarth, William 30
  The Four Stages of Cruelty 30
Hooker, Jeremy 108–9, 126–7, 129
  'Curlew' 108–9
  'Hill Country Rhythms' 126–7
Hope Rescue, Pontyclun 55
Hopi culture 180
Horowitz, Alexandra 8
House of Commons 64
Howells, Roscoe 33
Hughes, T. Rowland 72–3, 143
  William Jones 72–3
Hughes, Ted 96
  'The Thought-Fox' 96
human exceptionalism xiii, xiv, 2, 4, 20, 21, 31, 35, 41, 42, 46, 48, 54, 56, 57, 60, 67, 77, 83, 86, 90, 91, 109–10, 112, 114, 117, 120, 129, 132, 140, 141, 151, 167, 168, 173, 176, 177, 188, 189
humane destruction 85, 204n26
humanism xiii, 20–2
Humphreys, Emyr xiv, 39–1
  'Bullocks' 39
  'Dream for a Soldier' 41
  'Turkeys in Wales' 40–1
hunt saboteurs 33
hunting xiv, 6, 12–16, 35, 48, 54, 80, 86, 117, 125, 127, 132, 144, 148, 190
husbandry 18, 28, 30, 31, 32, 58, 61, 174
Hutchinson, Isobel 65

I
India 70
Iraq 181

INDEX

Irigaray, Luce 69
Ivy Bush *see* Tregaron

J

Jack the Ripper 30
Jackson, Robert 84
Jenkins, J. Geraint 27, 32
Johnes, Martin 51–2
Johnson, Steven 56, 115–16, 151
Jones, Alice Gray *see* Ceridwen Peris
Jones, Cynan xiv, 38
   Everything I Found on the Beach 38
Jones, Glyn xv, 145
   'The Golden Pony' 145–8
Jones, Gwyn xv, 28, 72, 95, 136–44, 167–7, 185
   'The Brute Creation' 136–9
   'The Green Island' 28, 170–3
   'The Pit' 167–70
   'Shepherd's Hey' 173–7, 185
   'Take Us the Little Foxes' 72–3, 95, 139–44
Jones, Jane 36
Jones, Mari xv, 25, 107, 135, 136, 137, 138
   'Y Boda' 107
   'Tim' 137, 138
   Trwy Lygad y Bugail 25
Judaeo-Christian tradition, figures in
   Abel 180
   Abraham 180
   Adam 180
   Ashtaroth, maiden of 175
   Baal, daughter of 175
   Eve 180
   Garden of Eden 88, 176
      serpent 88, 176
   Isaac 180
   Israelites 180
   Lillith 86
   Passover 180
   see also Christ (divine and human)
Jumbo (the African bull elephant) 81
Jumbo Junior (the baby elephant) 76
Jwmbi (the elephant in Welsh literature) 81
   see also Lizzie (Madame Jumbo)

K

Kant, Immanuel 124
Kennel Club, The 54
Kingsford, Anna 44
Kulchyski, Peter 40
Kurki, Milja xiii, 1–2, 5, 8, 21, 35, 38–40, 91, 98, 109, 111, 113, 126, 144

L

Lacan, Jacques 6, 124
lambing 186
Lampeter 63
Lapland 157
Latour, Bruno 5
Law, James 28–30
   Llyfr Coginio 28–30
   Meddyg y Fferm 28–9
Laws of Hywel Dda 53, 62, 148
League Against Cruel Sports, The 55
leather 27
Leeworthy, Daryl 55

legislation and policy
　Agriculture Act (UK, 1957) 32
　Agri-Environmental Regulation (EU, 1992) 33
　Animal Welfare Plan for Wales (WG, 2021) 36
　Betting and Lotteries Act (UK, 1934) 55
　Common Agricultural Policy (EU, 2003) 33
　Foreign Animals Order (UK, 1910) 59
　Game Laws (UK, 1840) 118
　The Pit Ponies Charter (1949 and 1956) 64, 204n26
　Wild Animals and Circus (Wales) Act (WG, 2020)
　Wildlife and Countryside Act (UK, 1981) 33, 120
Levinas, Emmanuel 124
Lillth (the lynx) 86
Lippmann, Walter 179
Lizzie (Madame Jumbo) 81
Llangollen Advertiser, Denbighshire Merionethshire and North Wales Journal 78
Llansawel 80, 81
Llanybyther 63
'llatai' (messenger and symbol of purity) 106, 110, 119, 129
Llewellyn-Williams, Hilary xiv, 100, 101, 102–3, 158–60
　'The Bee-Flight' 100
　'Feeding the Bat' 102–3, 158–60
　'Mole' 100, 101
Lloyd-Jones, D. M. 107
Llŷn peninsula 112
Llywelyn Goch ap Meurig Hen 23

London 45, 60, 64, 74, 76, 81, 83, 155
　Cart Horse Parade 74
　Covent Garden Fancy Dress Ball 76
　Crystal Palace 77
　Lambeth Police Court 77
　Lyceum Theatre 77
　Stock Exchange 76
　Zoological Gardens 83
Lord George Ginnett's Circus *see* Ginnett's Circus
Lord George Sanger's Circus *see* Sanger's Circus
Lovegrove, Roger 24, 25, 118–19, 121, 179
The Kite's Tale 118–19

M
Mabinogi 106, 111, 145, 146
MacLaren, Ian *see* Watson, Reverend John
Madame Batavia (the Malay bear) 76
Madame Jumbo *see* Lizzie
magic lantern shows 74, 83
Manchester 44
marine parks 19
marine studies 20
Marino, Lori 19–20
Marx, Karl 21
McHugh, Susan 6, 12, 138, 141
meat-eating 30, 42–4
　see also vegetarianism
Merleau-Ponty, Maurice 93
Merthyr 43, 53
Merthyr Express, The 65, 77
'Middle Passage' 81
Mitchell, Audra 1

INDEX

mole hills 101
monkey god 71
Moore, Henry 181–2, 186
   Sheep Sketchbook 181–2, 186
Moore-Colyer, Richard 28, 32, 33
Morris, Desmond 71–2, 73
Morse, Deborah 30
Mortimer, Anne 160, 161
Morton, Timothy 21
Murrell, Hilda xv, 122, 123–4, 125
Mynydd Bach 109
myrmecology 70
myrmecophobia 70

N
Nadolig Tosca 160–2
   Tosca's Christmas 160
   see also Sturgis, Matthew; Mortimer, Anne
NCB (National Coal Board) 49,
NFU (National Farmers' Union) 42, 45
Nature 117–18
Navajo culture 180
'New World' 81
New Zealand 180, 181
Newton, Isaac 21, 31, 83, 92, 94, 98
Nibert, David A. 16, 33, 35, 132–4, 153
Nicholas, T. E. 110–11, 112
   'Disgust' 111
   Llygad y Drws 110
   'Midnight' 111
   'Through the Window' 110
   'To a Sparrow' 110–11
   'The Urge' 110

Nonconformity 25–7, 29, 31, 52, 57–8, 88, 96, 99, 106–7, 108, 129, 135–6, 137, 139, 151, 154–5, 170, 198
Norris, Leslie xv, 112, 114–16, 119, 120, 121, 123, 127, 129, 148–51
   'The Highland Boy' 148–51
   'The Mallard' 114–15
   'Prey' 116, 121, 127
   'The Waxwings' 123

O
organ-grinders 71, 72, 73
organic farming 33, 34
'Other', the xiv, 58, 69, 90, 93, 106, 190

P
Paris 82
   Ménagerie du Jardin des Plantes 82
Parry-Jones, D. 23, 25, 26, 63, 67, 124, 135
   Welsh Country Upbringing 63
Pembrokeshire Herald and General Advertiser 59
performing animals 75–8
   see also Jumbo Junior; Lizzie; Madame Batavia
pesticides 18
Pierce, Jessica 2, 5, 6, 12, 21, 56
pig cemetery *see* vegetarianism
pigeon keeping (and pigeon fanciers) xiv, 51–2, 55, 56
   see also Johnes, Martin
Pit Ponies Protection Society 50
Player's cigarettes 180
Poliquin, Rachel 71, 83, 88, 153

Pondoland 70
Pongo (the gorilla) 74
Pontnewynydd 53
Pontypridd 74
Pontypridd Chronicle and Workman's News, The 74
Powell-Duffryn (mining company) 65
predatorship 6, 12–16, 83, 89, 93, 97, 99, 107, 109, 125–6, 127, 153, 180
Preece, Rosemary 49
Prestatyn Weekly 44
Price, Angharad 163
primatology 20
psychoanalysis 6, 10–11, 13, 15, 19, 81, 171, 190
psychobiology 179, 181, 184–8
psychogeography 23, 25

Q
Quine, Joseph A. 112–13, 126, 128

R
Radnorshire 58
Rebecca Riots 135
Regan, Tom 17
Rewilding 192
Rhos Herald, The 65
Roberts, Daisy Meirion 57
    'Y Robin Cyfeillgar' 57
    see also Blyton, Enid
Rome 53, 62, 75, 148, 190
    Roman classification of dogs 148
Rovelli, Carlo xiii, 1
Royal Commission on Mines, The 65
Royal Italian Circus 76, 78

Royal Show 51
RSPB (Royal Society for the Protection of Birds) 105
RSPCA (Royal Society for the Prevention of Cruelty to Animals) 49, 50, 59, 62, 63, 65, 74, 77, 134, 138
    'Pit Ponies and Colliery Horses: The Facts' (pamphlet) 50
    'The Sufferings of Pit Ponies' (pamphlet) 50
Russia 59
Ryan, Agnes 44
Ryan, Derek 2, 3, 5, 6, 7, 9, 10, 11, 18, 23, 35, 57, 69, 73, 81, 85, 91, 120, 128, 131, 133, 143, 153, 163, 176

S
Sanger's Circus 75
Sayer, Karen 169
Schreiber 105, 110, 117
Sears, Paul 20
Second World War 32, 41, 55, 110, 114, 155, 156, 157, 179
Senedd, The 55, 74
Sewell, Anna 30, 62
    Black Beauty 30, 62
sheepdog trials 75, 136–8
Sheldrick, Dame Daphne 5–6, 82
Shelley, Percy Bysshe 108
    'To a Skylark' 108
Shoah (Holocaust) 39–40, 47
Shropshire 122
simulacra 10–11, 15, 81
slaughter (and methods of) xiv, 30–1, 33, 35–42, 44, 45, 46–8, 56, 58, 60, 65, 81, 164, 187
    captive bolt 36

INDEX 243

electric head stunning 36
gas stunned 36
high concentration CO_2 36
non-stun halal methods 36
see also butcher (trade)
Smolin, Lee xiii, 1, 2, 5, 18
Soudan (Sudan) 76
South Wales Daily News 44, 58, 75, 78
South Wales Echo 44, 60
SPCA see RSPCA
speciesism 21, 31, 48, 117, 126, 167, 176, 189
Spencer, Colin 46
sport, gambling and leisure pursuits xiv, 52–5, 138, 148, 150
Srebrenica 40
Sturgis, Matthew 160
Sully Coursing Meeting (incl. the Cog Stakes and Hayes Stakes) 53
Swansea (museum) 81
Sword of Damocles 39

T
Talbot Arms see Tregaron
theology (incl. of birdwatching) 22, 112–14
Theresa (the musical pony) 76
Thomas, R. S. xv, 31, 112–14, 115, 116, 119, 120, 126, 127, 128–9, 137
  'Barn Owl' 128–9
  'Bird Book' 112
  'Moorland' 113
  'The Place' 128
  'Swifts' 112–13
Thomas, Bill 6

Thomas, M. Wynn 25–6, 31, 58, 136, 154
Thompson, Ceri 49–51, 63
Tigger 92
Tosca's Christmas see Nadolig Tosca
travelling menageries 67, 71, 79–82, 83
  see also Bostock-Wombwells
Tregaron 80–2
  see also Aberystwyth and Tregaron Bank
Trwy Lygad y Bugail 25
Tuan, Yi-Fu 10, 11, 13, 14, 15, 19, 69, 72, 83, 106, 115, 131, 132, 133–4, 144, 153

U
Umwelt (worldview) 7, 8, 22, 87, 89, 94, 103, 186, 191, 192
Unger, Roberto Mangabeira xiii, 1
universe (relational and interconnected) xiii, xiv, 1–5, 7–9, 11, 13, 15, 17–21, 31, 35, 38, 42, 44, 47–8, 56, 77, 93–5, 98, 100, 101, 102, 103, 109, 111, 113, 114, 121, 126, 128, 144, 154, 158, 168, 170, 175, 179, 183, 191, 192
University of Wales Trinity Saint David 80

V
vaccinations 18, 47
Vegan Society 42, 44, 45
Vegetarian Federal Union 45
  see also Wade, G. C.
vegetarianism 35, 37, 42–6, 88
vermin 96, 141

veterinary medicine 18, 19, 28, 29, 30, 31, 163
von Frisch, Karl 6
von Uexküll, Jakob 2, 8

W

Wade, G. C. 45
wagging dance (bees) 7
Waldau, Paul 3, 5, 9, 10, 16, 17, 18, 20, 21, 31, 34, 35, 57, 71, 91, 100, 105, 107, 114, 117, 118, 120, 126, 131, 167, 168, 169, 174, 176
Walker, Elaine 9–12, 65, 164
Warner, Constance 59–60
Washburn, S. L. 13
Watson, Reverend John 155
   A Doctor of the Old Style 155
   Yr Hen Ddoctor 155
Weekly Mail 58, 59, 60, 70
Welsh Gazette and West Wales Advertiser 70
Welsh Grand National 52, 53
Welsh Kennel Club, The 54
Welsh Mountain Zoo *see* Wales, National Zoo
Welsh Pony and Cob Society 58–9
Welsh Zoological Society 84
Welstead, William 188
Western Mail, The 43

Wilde, Oscar 110
   'Ballad of Reading Gaol' 110
Williams Parry, R. xiv, 93–6, 97–8, 100, 120, 136, 137
   'Gwenci' 97 – 8
   'Y Llwynog' 98, 100–1, 120, 136, 147
Williams, D. J. 14
Williams, David 32
Williams, Elaine 62
Williams, Frances xiv, 36, 38
   'At the Butchers' 36, 38
Wilson-Rich, Noah 7, 102
Woman's Journal 44
Women's Peace Conventions 44
Wyddfa, Yr xv, 181–3
Wyn, Nel 154
   Hywel a'r Garth 154

Y

Year of the Sheep 180

Z

zoos 19–20, 69, 71, 72, 79, 80, 81, 82–7, 90, 96, 131, 133, 162, 190
zoological gardens 19, 82–6, 131
zoological gaze 84, 85, 90, 190
zoological museums 86–7, 190
see also animal, captivity; circuses; travelling menageries